Gypsy Boy on the Run

MIKEY WALSH

Gypsy Boy on the Run

My Escape from a Life Among the Romany Gypsies

Thomas Dunne Books
St. Martin's Press ✷ New York

Publisher's Note

Mikey Walsh is a pseudonym. All names and other identifying details have been changed to protect the privacy of Mikey's family. Some characters are not based on any one person but are composite characters.

THOMAS DUNNE BOOKS.
An imprint of St. Martin's Press.

GYPSY BOY ON THE RUN. Copyright © 2011 by Mikey Walsh. All rights reserved. Printed in the United States of America. For information, address St. Martin's Press, 175 Fifth Avenue, New York, N.Y. 10010.

www.thomasdunnebooks.com
www.stmartins.com

ISBN 978-1-250-02187-8 (hardcover)
ISBN 978-1-250-02188-5 (e-book)

First published in Great Britain by Hodder & Stoughton, an Hachette UK company

First U.S. Edition: March 2013

10 9 8 7 6 5 4 3 2 1

For my Dad . . . I love you very much

Contents

Acknowledgements

I would like to thank the following people for making this book possible:

Caro Handley; once again you have been here, right by my side, guiding me through and making sure I get this all down right. Bless you. To Stephanie Thwaites; thank you so much for your guidance, support and helping me through these final stages with coffee & chocolate eggs. Fenella Bates . . . It's been a joy and a pleasure to know you, and to have us work together once again on this final part of the story. You're incredible. To Catherine Saunders and Ciara Foley for being there on standby, ready to listen to my moans and groans. Emma Knight, thank you so much for being there to hold my hand.

To my wonderful group of friends, old and new, for your love, your support, for picking up the phone at ridiculous times, for being there with a friendly ear, for taking me for coffees, cocktails, or whatever it was I needed to drag me out of the dark. I cannot thank you enough. To Dee, for the wine, fags, and such incredible belief in me . . . how long have you been listening to this story now? Jesus Christ! Xx. To Alan, Kerry and Joan for your love, your friendship and being such a wonderful part of my life. I love you very much. To the extraordinary Harty's – Olive, Hamish, Annabelle and Stephen.

Bless you! To the lovely Joanie, and her wonderful Jenny.

To my Ball and Chain. I wish you so much love. No matter where you go, you'll always be my family. To my amazing family; my Aunts, Uncles, Grandparents, Cousins and friends from back home that have been so wonderfully supportive of me, not only from my book but also throughout my whole life. I love all very much. I miss you all dreadfully. To my sister; you are the most incredible, strong, supportive and beautiful person I could ever have wished for in my life. My best friend and my partner in crime. I love you always. To the boys; we may be all grown up now, but we'll still be quoting 'Robin Hood Daffy' to each other when we're 60! I love you very much.

YOINKS . . . and AWAY!

Mum . . . for your strength, wisdom, support and love. I see myself in you, more and more every day. Dad . . . I just love you . . . so very much. For all that you have done for me these last years . . . you are incredible.

To all the wonderful readers of *Gypsy Boy* that have shown such incredible support in my journey to where I am today. Your letters, quotes, comments and 'Tweets' mean the absolute world to me. Bless you. To my extraordinary and wonderful culture. I am so very proud to call myself a Gypsy man. To Leigh, how I wish so much that you could be here with me. I miss you. I love you very much. For Kate Bush, for Skeletor, for Michael Jackson, for Sloth and Chunk, for Dorothy Gale . . .

And last of all, for you, the reader of this book . . . I wrote this just for you.

I

Escape

The clouds burst and rain began to hammer against the windscreen as we hit the motorway.

Caleb's face was a mask of concentration as he gripped the steering wheel, pushing his little orange car to slice through the curtains of water at speeds it had never reached before.

Panic gripped me as I looked over my shoulder for the hundredth time.

The road was clear. But for how long?

Caleb reached for my hand. 'We'll be long gone when they find you're missing. I've got us a place to live, a long way from anyone who knows you. We'll be together.'

I tried to smile. 'Yeah, I know. I've been dreaming of this day for so long.'

And I had. I was going to be free, and I would be with Caleb. It was everything I wanted. So why was my heart so heavy with loss?

A tidal wave was falling from the sky. Could the combination of my father's anger and my mother's sadness have caused this rip in the heavens? They would have found my letter by now. I felt the crack of my mother's heart as I pictured her reading it. I ached for her, and for what I was leaving behind. My family, my home. But they would be better off without me. All I had ever brought them was shame.

I looked over at Caleb. I couldn't let him know what I was feeling. I was scared that he might try to convince me to change my mind and turn back. And I didn't want to do that.

I glanced behind us again and watched, heart thudding, as a truck in the distance came closer. For a terrible moment I thought . . .

It wasn't his. I almost fainted with relief. But I knew it was just a matter of time. He would come looking for me. And when he did, I had to be somewhere he could never, ever find me.

I was fifteen years old and I was running away from everything I had ever known. I had grown up in the closed and secretive world of Romany gypsies, part of a culture and a way of life that had existed for centuries, alongside but never part of the rest of the world. We Romanies were proud, fierce, independent people and we held to our ways and customs despite the increasing encroachment of 'normal' society and the hostility of non-Romanies towards us.

My family lived a travelling life, moving from town to town, settling for weeks or months, as long as my father could find work locally, before moving on. Friends and family moved with us in a great convoy of trucks and trailers that wound its way from one place to the next. It was getting harder to find places to stop, free from prejudice and attack, out of the way enough to preserve our privacy and give us space to be together and live the way we had always lived. When we found a good site we would stay for as long as we could, but there always came a time when we had to move on – either because we were hounded out, or when our restless spirit drove us back to the open road.

I was my parents' first son. My father Frank and mother Bettie already had a daughter, my sister Frankie, born almost two years earlier. Soon after she arrived, my mother was diagnosed with a heart murmur and told that if she had another child it could be fatal. My father, thwarted in his hope of a son to take his name, gave it to my sister and tried to accept the hand that fate had dealt him. But my mother knew how much he longed for a son and put aside fears for her health to give her husband the one thing that would make him happier than anything else.

I was born, like so many Romany babies, in the Royal Berkshire hospital. My granny Ivy, a four-foot midget of a woman who, despite her tiny stature, had a temper that cowed grown men, had given birth to her four children there. She and my grandfather, Old Noah, were Gypsy elders whose status was akin to royalty, and as word spread of the excellent treatment she had received, Gypsy women from one end of the land to the other had flocked there to have their babies.

When I arrived, with the whole family present as was the custom, I was apparently so enormous that there was a collective gasp of disbelief. How my mother not only survived but went on to have three more children, I have no idea. It was Granny Ivy, cackling through her mouthful of gold teeth, who declared me to be 'a little pig boy'.

After that the story became part of our family folklore, and as a child I endured endless hours listening to Gypsy women laugh and exclaim over the day Bettie Walsh gave birth to a pig.

As for my father, he was delighted with his bruiser of a son and as he placed a chain with a tiny pair of gold boxing gloves on it around my infant neck, my size only served to fuel his hope that I would be a fine specimen of Gypsy manhood and a prizefighter to make him proud.

My heritage was a noble one. My parents were both born into well-known and highly respected Gypsy families. My mother was the second eldest of six children. Her parents, Old Alfie and Granny Bettie, lived on their own piece of land in a couple of trailers and a clapped-out rainbow-coloured double-decker bus they had bought the kids one Christmas. The whole family were dark-skinned and dark-haired, with Granny Bettie's hefty build – apart from my mother, who emerged pale-skinned and flame-haired and was, as a result, something of an embarrassment to her family. They couldn't understand where this strange-looking creature had come from. Some people even believed she had been cursed, but my mother was an independent spirit who didn't care what people thought and she grew up to be a svelte beauty who turned heads wherever she went.

My mother was close friends with my father's twin sister, Prissy. They met when they were all ten years old, and my mother always said that she fell in love with my father then and there. He fell for her too, but it was several years before he found the courage to ask her out, because when he wasn't talking with his fists, he was painfully tongue-tied and shy. He demonstrated his love by beating up any boy who came near her, but never said a word to her.

Eventually, it was my mother who broke this impasse, flouting Gypsy convention in the process, by marching up to him and demanding that he ask her out or else fuck off and leave her alone. He wisely chose to ask her out and a year or so later, when they were both eighteen, they married. My mother wore a Mary Poppins-style outfit with a parasol and a hat adorned with candy-coloured ribbons, but my father – much to my mother's disgust – was in the grubby old trousers and cardigan he had been wearing the previous day. His one concession to the event was to stick a rose in his breast pocket.

Despite the disappointing lack of effort for his nuptials, my father adored his pretty, red-haired bride, and she adored him. He loved her because she was different from most Gypsy women, not only in her looks but in temperament. She was calm, quiet and self-contained, preferring her own company to a group of gossiping girls. And she loved him for the sensitivity she saw beneath his rough exterior, and because she understood how tough it was for him, desperate to prove himself and always in the shadow of his older, better-looking and more successful brother.

After the wedding they moved into their own trailer, which my mother, like all Gypsy women, kept neat as a pin and sparkling clean. This was the late seventies, so the decor was wall-to-wall brown with splashes of orange in the curtains and bedding and numerous gilt-edged mirrors on the walls.

A year after the wedding Frankie came along and two years after that, in 1980, I arrived. My mother always said I didn't make a sound for the first six months of my life. She and my father were convinced I was a mute until the day she brought home a huge crab – her favourite weekly food treat – and put it on the floor in front of me. I was fascinated, and as I prodded and rolled this odd creature about, I began to gurgle and squeal with delight.

From as far back as I can remember I adored Frankie. With her near-black eyes and thick, curly dark hair, she was fearless, noisy and brave and I followed her around, worshipping her every move. She had our father's temperament and was a natural tomboy. As is the Gypsy custom, she was always dressed like a doll, in little dresses with diamond earrings and ringlets in her hair. She hated it. She would have been happier in the dungarees that I had to wear, but the rules dictate that Gypsy boys and girls live in different worlds. The girls follow their mothers, learning to be homemakers, while the boys are trained very early in the ways of the men, working and providing for their family.

But despite the different paths that we were on, Frankie and I were incredibly close. We played together for hours: dressing up, 'cooking' with mud and Play-Doh and creating imaginary shops in which we bought and sold Frankie's army of Cabbage Patch dolls.

Frankie was always in charge. Her favourite game was dressing me up as Aunt Sally from *Worzel Gummidge*. Neither of us could pronounce Sally, so we called her Aunt Sadly. I would put on one of Frankie's nightgowns and she would make us both up with lurid eye shadows she stole from Granny Bettie. Unfortunately, our father walked in one day and found me in my Aunt Sadly costume and that was the end of that. He was livid and banned me from ever dressing in girls' clothes again.

While my mother kept house, looked after us and visited her parents and her sisters, my father went out to work with the other men. He did a bit of this and that, collecting scrap metal, laying tarmac drives and doing odd jobs like cleaning gutters or fixing roofs. He would go from door to door offering his services, always hoping to strike lucky and find a 'grunter' – an old person who could be charged a lot of money for some trifling job. He would convince them that their roof was falling apart, or their drive needed resurfacing, and then fleece them of as much as he possibly could. He never felt guilty about this because he considered them to be fair game. My father would sometimes take me out to work with him, and I remember seeing elderly men and women crying and pleading with him, as he demanded an exorbitant payment for whatever it was he had 'fixed'. He was a brilliant conman with a golden tongue, but not a skilled workman; cutting corners was his speciality and the 'new' drives he laid were liable to dissolve into tarry puddles with the next shower of rain. But by then he would be long gone.

When he wasn't working, his favourite pastime was training me to be a fighter. Ours was a family of fighting men, and by the time I was four years old he was preparing me to follow in the renowned footsteps of generations of Walsh men.

Bare-knuckle fighting is a Gypsy tradition: in each country where there is a Romany community, there is an unofficial fighting crown that every Gypsy man worth his salt dreams of winning. My great-grandfather Mikey had won it – beating a host of other men to do so – and it had been in our family ever since.

During the Second World War, Mikey, broke and homeless, had moved to England from Eastern Europe, changing his name from Walowski to Walsh along the way. That war almost finished off the Gypsies, who were hated and persecuted by the Nazis. Over 200,000 died, many of them in concentration camps, and after the war many people believed that the Gypsies had been wiped out. But there were those who had survived and who went on to rebuild their communities, including my great-grandfather. He and his wife Ada arrived with five children, and scraped a living any way they could. Ada sold trinkets and charms and Mikey fought his way to prosperity – literally – by putting up his fists for anyone who would pay a few pounds, earning himself a reputation as a champion, and enough money to buy a piece of land to establish a camp for Gypsies.

The crown had passed to Mikey's son Noah, my grandfather. He brought up his own boys – Tory; my father, Frank, and the youngest brother, Joseph – to fight each other and everyone around them. 'Hit 'em so they'll never get back up. One. Good. Hit. Put out your man like a candle,' Noah would repeat. The Walsh boys were always looking for the next fight, picking on anyone who so much as looked at them the wrong way, and as a result they were feared by every other Gypsy man.

My father was a good fighter and he longed for the title, but it went to his older brother Tory, their father's favourite.

After that my father pinned his hopes on his own first son. By the time I was four he was 'training' me on a daily basis. I would stand in front of him, arms in the air, as he landed punches – modest at first, but increasingly hard – on my ribs. The idea was that I would learn how to take at least ten levels of punches without crying, weaving, bobbing or dodging. And I tried, so hard. But the punches hurt so much that after the first few I would be in tears and doubled over in agony, at which point my father would continue punching me – with real punches – while berating me for my cowardice.

As the training was stepped up I spent my days waiting, terrified, for the moment when he would turn to me and say, 'Ready, Mikey?' I was supposed to nod cheerfully and run to get my miniature boxing gloves on. Instead I screamed, kicked, sobbed and begged him not to make me fight – all to no avail. Every day he set out to train me, and every day I failed him. He even made me fight Frankie, in an attempt to humiliate me into succeeding. But Frankie beat me every time.

My mother would often step in to try to protect me. She took many beatings herself as he turned on her, furious at her intervention, throwing her across the room and on occasion even knocking her unconscious. She fought him bravely, and though she never won, she continued to intervene when she felt I had taken enough of a pounding. She never complained when he hurt her, and she never seemed to hold it against him either. She would get up and carry on, without a word, and the affection they had for one another appeared undimmed. He always kissed her when he came home, and in the evenings he would often take her on his lap, calling her his girl.

When I was six my mother gave birth to another son. Unlike me and Frankie, both of us olive-skinned and dark-haired, the new baby, Henry-Joe, took after our mother: pale-skinned with flaming-red hair. From the start my mother seemed determined to keep my father and his fighting family away from this child. She guarded him like a tigress and my father was forced to admit defeat, leaving his second son to my mother and her family. He carried on doing his best to shape me into the fighter I would never be, but feeling twice betrayed by sons who were incapable of carrying on his line, his ferocity seemed to increase in direct proportion to his disappointment.

As I grew older he forced me to fight other, mostly bigger, sometimes much bigger, boys. My uncle Tory owned a boxing club and I would be taken along there and put into the ring with some ugly great brute of a boy. I always lost and came home bruised and battered, with a bloody nose, only to face my father's scorn and derision. I was the world's most hopeless fighter. Every place we moved to would see me bullied and mocked for being such a poor comparison to my father. I was nothing but a disappointment to him. 'I've made you timid,' he'd say. 'Let you spend too much time around women.'

I worshipped my father and his shame and disappointment in me crushed my heart like a rock. I wanted so badly to please him, to see his face light up as it did when he saw Frankie. She could do no wrong in his eyes.

It wasn't until my youngest brother, Jimmy, was born,

when I was eight, that my father finally got the heir he longed for. I knew, peering into Jimmy's cot, that this would be the son to make my father proud. His black eyes were just like my father's and none of us doubted that he would grow up to be a fighter.

While I burned with longing to be what my father wanted me to be and loved and hated him by turns, my relationship with my mother was far simpler. Although she could be distant and was never physically affectionate – cuddles and kisses for boys were considered 'mollycoddling' and were frowned upon – when I was small she was the centre of my world. Any time my father was out, or away working for weeks at a time as he sometimes was, my mother, Frankie and I would have fun and my mother would indulge her passion for music. She had an old stack music system and she would put on records while we all sang along, belting out hits by Michael Jackson or our mother's favourite, Barbra Streisand. Frankie and I spent many happy hours perfecting our zombie impersonations to 'Thriller' and singing along to Donna Summer and Barbra's 'Enough is Enough'.

We also spent many joyous hours watching re-runs of every movie Disney ever produced while scoffing cakes, toffee popcorn and the bowls of Angel Delight our mother would whip up on an almost daily basis. Our favourite film of all was *The Wizard of Oz*. For weeks at a time Frankie and I watched it every day before running outside to re-enact the best scenes. Frankie would always be the wicked witch, and I would be her faithful flying monkey.

My mother never said she loved me. No Gypsy ever

said such things, especially to a boy. But I knew, from the way she looked at me and from the courage with which she fought to defend and protect me, that she did.

2

Awakening

I was not like other boys. It was as if I had completely missed out on any masculine inheritance that my father had to give. At every gathering, boys of my own age had begun to go out of their way to make digs at Frank Walsh's effeminate and ridiculous son. And why wouldn't they? I was an easy target for any red-blooded travelling boy who wanted to assert himself and impress a crowd.

I hated myself for my failings. It wasn't that I was puny or slight. I was tall, and the relentless training in my uncle's gym had made me muscular and strong. And yet I couldn't fight. I lacked the speed, the technique – and the will. I just couldn't see the point of thrashing the stuffing out of some other boy, just for the sake of a misguided sense of 'honour'. This attitude went against everything my father lived by, so I never spoke of it. But he knew.

I was a source of disappointment to all the men in my family, none more than my bear of a grandfather, who watched my first fight in the ring at Tory's club. He turned to my father and said, 'He's a waste of time, that one. He's not right, not right at all. He's no Romany man, that's for sure. He's going to be the one to let the line down, Frank, I can see it now.' At these words my father had walked away, his head bowed in shame.

I thought my lack of fighting ability was the worst of my problems. But by the age of ten I was painfully aware that there was something else deeply wrong with me.

For years my father had been calling me gay; it was the worst form of insult there was for a Gypsy man. Every time I lost a fight or ran crying from my father's punches, he would call me a poof and every other derogatory homo put-down he could think of. I learned very young that to be gay was a terrible thing, a shocking thing, and something that could never, ever be true of a red-blooded Gypsy man. Gypsy men oozed testosterone and masculinity; they fought, drank, argued over women and produced sons. They were most definitely, irrevocably, not gay.

Except that I was.

It's hard to recall the moment I realised I was attracted to men and not women. I grew up knowing it, but of course I tried desperately hard to ignore it and be the he-man my father wanted. To be gay would not just be a problem, it would be a disaster. I knew that if my father ever suspected for a moment that his endless insults were true, he would disown me and drive me away. His shame would be bottomless. So I tried to pretend that it just wasn't true. But the closer I came to puberty, that pretence was harder to maintain.

Puberty comes young to Gypsies. Twelve is officially the age when childhood ends and you are expected, as a Gypsy boy, to go out to work. The brief time I spent in school ended when I was ten, and by twelve I was going out to work with my father six days a week, helping him lay drives and 'fix' roofs and gutters. I was also shaving, driving and drinking.

I was spectacularly bad at most of these activities. I lacked my father's gift of the gab so I was hopeless at persuading householders to 'employ' me on their odd jobs. I had to hang back, shovelling tarmac and carting barrels of it around various drives, while my father laughed and smiled and talked his way into the work.

Most Gypsy boys had their own vans by the age of thirteen. I didn't and it didn't look like I was in any position to get one. I was earning ten pounds a day if I was lucky, but it was probably just as well that I couldn't buy myself a van. After my father had obtained a provisional driver's licence for me by lying about my age (you didn't have to prove age in those days), I had rolled a pickup on its side and written off a new Ford Escort within days of first getting behind a wheel, so I certainly wasn't in the running for the underage driver of the year award.

By the time I turned thirteen I was a fearful and lonely boy. My father had grown so ashamed of me he found it difficult to look me in the face. And I couldn't blame him. Not only was I incapable of fulfilling even one task that he gave me, but my feelings towards men would not go away, and I knew by then that I could do nothing to change them.

I tried so hard to pretend that I was like the other Gypsy boys. I went with them to bars, knocked back beer, did my best to swagger and boast and pretend I wanted to have sex with girls. Gypsy boys will often look for Gorgia girls to have sex with because Gypsy women are untouchable until they are married. When I was thirteen a couple of other lads boasted that they'd found two girls who would have sex with us. I went along with it, sweating and terrified, and only managed to escape the girl – a walrus in a miniskirt nicknamed Gobbler – by pretending I needed to find a condom.

I hated who I was. I wanted to fancy women. I felt trapped and frightened and saw no way out, no future except to be mocked and derided by my own kind. My mother and Frankie had given me refuge, of sorts, as a young boy. But as I got older I was expected to keep the company of men. The days when I could sing karaoke-style to me Mum's Michael Jackson tapes, play imaginary games with Frankie or lose myself in a Disney film were gone. And while my mother still shot me sympathetic looks and did her best to patch me up and offer comfort when I got beaten up, a huge rift had wedged itself between me and Frankie.

It started when Frankie began joining in with my father's insults, calling me a poof and laughing at me. I could just about live with that.

But then she began calling me 'Joseph'.

Joseph was my father's youngest brother. An oversized morbid and moody man who was the butt of many jokes. To be likened to him would be bad enough for any Gypsy boy. But there was something Frankie didn't know – no one did. Joseph had been sexually abusing me since I was seven years old.

Joseph would have been an outcast if he hadn't been the youngest of the Walsh brothers. Because his older brothers were renowned fighters, he was safe. It didn't mean anyone liked him, but they didn't dare pick on him.

Joseph worked with Tory and Old Noah in the family builder's yard. Tory was well off, with a big house known as Tory Manor and the boxing club as well as his share of the yard. Joseph lived with Tory while Old Noah and Ivy lived in an enormous pink trailer in a field behind the house. Old Noah and Tory had bought the house together, the idea being that they would all live in it. But after three days Old Noah and Ivy had been so miserable that they refused to stay in the house a moment longer. They left it to Tory, his wife Maudie, their bruisers of sons Young Tory and Young Noah and their twin daughters, Patti and Violet, and moved back into a home on wheels, where they were blissfully happy. Old Noah kept his Rolls Royce parked on a hard stand next to the trailer, and spent his spare time organising Friday night cock fights and endless family 'get togethers' which we all had to attend, piling into the pink trailer for Granny Ivy's 'ninety per cent turnip' Sunday roasts.

When I was seven my father took me to work in the builder's yard in yet another failed attempt to 'make a man of me'. He wanted to see if his father and older brother could knock me into shape. The idea was that I would spend a week with them, working in the yard and living in Tory Manor. The day my father left me, I was filled with dread. Young Tory and Young Noah already worked there, both of them men before they were thirteen. I eyed them as they hauled bricks and mortar about the yard, both tall, strong and rugged, just as Gypsy men should be. I knew I was nothing like them, and never would be.

On my first day Tory left me in the yard with Joseph while he went out in the lorry with his boys. And at first

I was grateful. Joseph had been kinder to me than most of the men. He seemed more understanding, rubbing my back and winking at me when no one was looking. But that day he took me into the office, stripped me, and abused my body repeatedly. Afterwards he told me that if I ever breathed a word, he would tell my father I had misbehaved. We both knew that would result in a beating.

When my father arrived to collect me, Joseph told him, much to my father's surprise, that I had worked hard and done well.

That was the deal. From then on I had to spend a day a week at the builder's yard. And every week, while the others went out collecting pallets of building material in the truck, Joseph abused me. The things he did to me often left me unable to swallow or sit or even breathe without pain. But he behaved as though we were both enjoying it, chuckling and chatting to me, while I lay, mute and numb, praying for deliverance.

It never came. While the family left my 'training' to Joseph, he was able to do as he wished with me, and it carried on for years. There was one time when I did try to tell my father what was happening, but he beat me for lying. And after that I knew there was no possibility of salvation, I would simply have to endure the abuse. I kept silent.

Frankie knew none of this. Her calling me Joseph cut me to the quick. When she did it once too often I smashed her music centre. After which she shouted to the whole campsite that I was a poof. I couldn't forgive her.

I finally escaped Joseph when I was eleven and my family left the camp in Warren Woods, close to Tory

Manor, where we had been living for the past five years. The place was being taken over by Irish Travellers and the mutual dislike between the two travelling peoples drove us back to the road. We found our next home in a camp in Newark. It was there that my mother gave birth to her last child, a dark-eyed little girl named Minnie. We all adored her, but I didn't spend much time with her as by then I was going out to work with my father and was expected to go out drinking with the other boys in the evenings.

We used to go to the local Dyna Bowl, a bar and bowling alley complex that, unlike many venues around the town, welcomed Gypsies. As word spread that this was a cushti (good) place, Gypsies from far and wide began to gather there to hang out and blow their wages on drink and cigarettes.

It was there, when I was thirteen and bitterly unhappy, that I met Caleb.

He worked behind the bar and I had noticed him before. Irish, and with his dark hair, bright blue eyes and heavily tattooed arms he was hard to miss. But it wasn't done to have a conversation with a Gorgia, so I never got beyond 'Pint of bitter please' when I went up to the bar, until the night when the rest of our crowd decided to go to the cinema. I didn't fancy the film they were seeing, so I stayed behind at the Dyna Bowl, planning to have a last drink and then hitch a lift back to the campsite.

Caleb was behind the bar that night and as I sat on a bar stool nursing a pint, we chatted. He told me he was twenty-five and had left the Army two years earlier. I told him I was nineteen. You had to be eighteen to be served in the bar, and I added a year for luck. Caleb didn't question it – why would he? I drove, drank, smoked and worked full-time, so he assumed that I was much older than my true age.

That first evening we chatted for twenty minutes before he said he was finishing his shift and going off to meet friends. He asked if I'd like to come along, but although I wanted to, I said no. I'd already risked a beating at the hands of my father and his friends, just by talking to him.

I saw Caleb many times after that and he was always friendly, but I never did more than say hello; my companions were always waiting for their drinks at the table behind me.

Then a new trio of Gypsy boys arrived at the Dyna Bowl. I loathed them from the moment they swaggered into the place, hair greased and muscles bulging, looking about for entertainment. They moved in on the girls – Frankie and a couple of other girls we were friendly with. While their heads were being turned by the newcomers' smooth talk, the other boys and I spat with fury in the background. These new boys became a fixture; my sister started dating one of them, Wisdom, and some of our gang of boys joined them.

One evening a bunch of them decided it would be a bit of sport to take me down. I was heading back into the bar after going outside for a smoke when they set on me. I managed to punch one of them in the face with a satisfying thwack to his nose before several of his mates jumped on me, battering me to the ground.

It was Caleb, along with two security staff, who rescued

me. He took me up to the staff toilet, where he got out a first-aid kit and dressed the three gaping cuts on my face. The moment I saw them I knew I'd be in trouble with my father for getting beaten up. By the time my face was patched up, the others had all left. Caleb repeated his invitation to go for a drink, and I explained that it was impossible.

'Don't tell them,' he grinned. 'I've just finished my shift. Come for a drink and then I'll drop you back at the site.'

I decided to take a chance.

Caleb took me to a little country pub where I sat in a quiet corner while he got the drinks, and then we talked.

I was bowled over by him. He seemed such a happy, straightforward person. He told me about being in the Army, about his family, who all lived in Newark, about his friends, his taste in music and his hope that one day he would be a manager at Dyna Bowl. He was warm, funny and interesting. Every now and then I remembered that I was sitting in a Gorgia pub, talking to a Gorgia man. But I was far enough from the site to be fairly certain that no one would see me.

Gypsy boys tend to talk only about money, fighting and girls, so it was a new experience for me, hearing about someone's life, and telling them about mine. That night I told him so much – once I started talking, I couldn't seem to stop. I left out only three things: Joseph, my age and being gay.

That night Caleb dropped me back. I asked him to stop some distance from the campsite, so that I wouldn't

be seen. Caleb invited me out the next night, with some
mates of his. He told me he thought they would like me.
I found it hard to imagine such a thing. But I agreed to
go, asking him to pick me up at a safe hour, when my
father and the other men and boys would have left the
site for the pubs.

That was the beginning. I met Caleb's friends – a group
of men and girls who all welcomed me and laughed and
talked together. It was all so new for me; no pressure to
fight or boast or talk about money. I saw a glimpse into
another world, and I wanted to be part of it.

After that I met Caleb most nights. My father thought
I was out with the other teenagers from the camp, and
they thought I was out with another group. I would meet
Caleb in the car park of a local retirement home, and
we'd go out for a drink or meet his friends or just go
for a walk. He even took me home to meet his mother,
who welcomed me warmly as a friend of his.

For many months we were simply friends. We talked
about our lives and Caleb mentioned girls he'd dated in
the past, but neither of us ever talked about us or what
was happening between us. It felt too big, too new. I
knew that I loved him but I didn't know how he felt
about me.

We spent my fourteenth birthday together, and I felt
bad every time he toasted me being twenty. That night,
walking through the quiet back streets, Caleb told me
he loved me. I joked with him. 'You say that all the time
to your friends,' I teased. But he turned to me and said,
'Mikey, I've loved you since I first saw you.' I told him
I loved him too, and we threw our arms round one

another. I sobbed and he teased me and called me a big softy.

It was a life-changing moment. I had come to believe I would always be alone. I thought I was unlovable. And I was certain I would never, ever be able to tell anyone I was gay. Now here was this beautiful, warm and lovely man, telling me he loved me and holding me in his big tattooed arms.

That night, when I slipped back into camp at three in the morning, I discovered that I hadn't been the only one sneaking out. Frankie had a 10 p.m. curfew but she was slipping out to meet Wisdom after everyone was in bed. She arrived back at our shared trailer just as I did, and she giggled as she told me that Wisdom waited for her every night. I feared for her, because if anyone ever found out what she was up to she would be considered a slut and would never be able to marry. Gypsy girls live by a strict code: no boyfriends, no being alone with a man and most definitely no sex before marriage. Frankie had broken at least two of these rules. I warned her to be careful.

'What about you, then,' she retorted. 'You're off all the time with that Caleb. Don't let Dad find out you have Gorgia friends.'

I breathed a sigh of relief; she thought we were just friends.

We made a mutual pact not to tell on one another. We both had too much to lose.

3

The Plan

In those first months after I started seeing Caleb behind my family's back, I would lie in bed at night, praying that the feelings I was having would leave me and I would wake up cured by the forgiving hand of some god who might take pity on me.

I was in a terrible situation. I could give up Caleb and try once again to be a Gypsy man – and without doubt fail miserably. Or I could carry on seeing him and hope that somehow, by some miracle, we would find a way to be together.

By the time Frankie's sixteenth birthday arrived, I was feeling so desperate that I tried to kill myself. After the rest of the camp had headed off to the place where her party was being held I downed two bottles of vodka and the contents of my mother's medicine box. The pressure of my secret relationship with Caleb and the constant barrage of insults and threats I was getting from many of the people around me, as well as my father's threats and beatings, had escalated to a level that I could no longer cope with. The last thing I remembered was standing up to go and use the toilet block. I woke several hours later in a blank white room with my sister and mother, still in their party dresses, by my side. Frankie and a friend had come back to the camp to see where I

was and had found me on the floor of our trailer, almost
blue and out cold.

My mother was distraught, and my father was angry.
'What the fuck did you do that for?' was all he ever
said. For once I felt he was right.

To try to commit suicide was the most foolish and
selfish of things I had done to escape my own self-
loathing. I regretted putting my family through it, and
I was relieved to be given the chance to come back. I
promised myself then that I would not do it again.

But my fifteenth birthday came and went, and I was
no closer to a solution. Caleb and I still met most nights.
He would park in our meeting place and wait, in the
hope that I could get away. Sometimes I couldn't – I had
to be careful. But most nights, with Frankie covering for
me, I managed it.

Caleb would drive us to the other side of the city,
where we'd sit in a pub and talk over a drink, or walk
through the streets, holding hands for a moment if there
was no one about. The only times when we could be
alone together were in his car. He would park in an
out-of-the-way place and we'd sit in the dark for hours
and talk about our hopes and dreams of a life together.
Caleb said that he had never been attracted to a man
before. I told him he must have been in denial, but he
swore it was just me that made him change – I was
special, and he couldn't help falling in love with me.

Caleb brought out in me attributes that I didn't know
I had. He accepted me for who I was. He liked me, he
wanted to hear what I had to say, he thought I was funny
and interesting. And he thought I was beautiful. When

I was in my bunk, back in the trailer, I would lie for hours remembering the things he had said, and the way he made me feel.

Then Frankie and I got caught. We had been covering for one another – telling our parents, if they asked, that we had been together. But one night they checked up on us, and found neither of us was in our trailer. When we came in, one after the other, they were waiting for us. Amid the shouting and accusations, Frankie, in the hope of deflecting their anger away from herself, told them that I was hanging about with a gay Gorgia man. I swore he was not gay, but my father beat me until he could beat no more.

A couple of days later we upped sticks and left. Our parents had decided to remove both of us from whatever evil influences were keeping us out at night. We moved to a camp in Chertsey and it was several days before I managed to get to a pay phone and let Caleb know. He had been waiting for me each night, worried sick that something had happened.

I sobbed down the phone. 'I don't know when I will be able to see you again.'

'I'll wait,' he promised. 'We'll find a way.'

Meanwhile, Wisdom tracked Frankie down and within weeks she was once again sneaking out to meet him at night. I was glad for her: it was what she wanted.

I managed to ring Caleb again and he offered to come and see me, but I didn't dare let him. If my father heard he was anywhere near the camp he would go after him.

I felt bereft. But all I could do was wait, and hope.

My father took me to work with him and made me

stay in the trailer the rest of the time. I spent my evenings helping my mother with Minnie and the boys, and then chatting to her once they were all in bed. We would go through her CDs and talk, and she would reminisce about the past. To the sounds of her favourite Barbra Streisand songs she would tease me about childhood things.

'Do you remember how my dad used to tell you and Frankie ghost stories? Had you shitting yourself,' she laughed.

Granddad Alfie had been bedridden, with multiple sclerosis, when I was little. He died when I was six, but I remembered him so well. My mother had adored her father and she would often take me and Frankie over to see him and Granny Bettie. My father never came, as he and Bettie hated the sight of one another.

'Me Granddad would make me light his pipe for him,' I said, smiling at the memory. 'I used to sit on his bed and light it and then hold it to his mouth. I had to keep a pint of lemon squash ready, because trying to keep it alight for him made me choke. He taught me how to blow smoke rings. And some of his choicest swear words.'

'Those were good times.' My mother looked wistful. 'D'you remember how he promised to come back and haunt Bettie when she scoffed at his ghost stories? He said he'd come back and when she least expected it, he was going to kick her right up the arse! She swears he did, too. Says he hasn't given her a minute's peace.'

We both laughed. I felt closer to her than I had for a long time, and despite missing Caleb so much, it was a special time. On evenings like this we would sit up together until we heard the men coming back from the pub, when I would slip out to my own trailer before my father got in.

After two months my father decided to take us back to Newark. Work was scarce in Chertsey and he had always felt Newark was lucky for him. My mother convinced him that Frankie and I had learned our lesson, and so we packed up and headed back, and with every mile my excitement mounted.

Back in Newark, I longed to see Caleb, but my father insisted I was still under trailer arrest. He barely ever spoke to me – he was full of rage and I knew that at some point it would erupt. When it did, a week or so after our return, I was shovelling grit. My father decided I was being too slow, so he grabbed the shovel and hit me over the head with it. I fell, and he hit me again and again, until I was covered in blood. When we got back to the site my mother screamed at the sight of me, and then raged at my father, who turned his fury on her, dragging her into the trailer and sending the younger children out to play.

Standing outside, bloody and battered, listening to the sickening sound of my mother being beaten, I knew that I had to find a way to leave. If I didn't, I felt quite certain that he would kill me and I would continue to be the cause of my mother's sufferings.

I ran out of the campsite and down the lane to the car park of the retirement home, where to my joy I saw Caleb's little orange car. He was waiting, just in case I was able to get away. We wept with joy at seeing one another again. It had been almost three months.

Caleb was horrified at the sight of my bloody face.

He drove to a quiet spot where he tried gently to clean me up, while I began, hesitantly, to tell him the things I had never told him before, about my father, about Joseph. He was totally shocked.

We sat in silence for a moment. Then I looked at him and took a deep breath.

'There's something else,' I said. 'I'm fifteen.'

His face went white. 'What? Fifteen?'

I nodded.

'I had no idea. That means you were thirteen when we met?'

'Yes.'

'I thought you were a man. You looked like a man. I wouldn't have asked you out, gone near you, if I had known.'

'That's why I didn't tell you.'

He was silent for several minutes. Eventually he said, 'It makes sense of a few things. I couldn't understand why your father still had such a hold over you.'

'He will have a hold over me as long as I stay here.'

'I'll take you away then.' Caleb's voice had a defiant note to it. 'You'll be sixteen soon, then it's up to you whether you stay or go.'

Caleb told me that he'd been offered a job as manager of a branch of Dyna Bowl in Liverpool and if he took the job, I could join him there. He said we should wait for two months, so that no one would connect his leaving with my disappearance.

'We can start a new life together,' he said. 'Away from everything. Just us.'

As Caleb spelled out the details of his plan, I felt such

mixed emotions. Joy that he wanted to be with me, and for us to make a life together. Sadness at the thought of leaving my family. And fear. Would my father somehow find a way to stop me?

We planned to spend one last day together, before he left. We wouldn't see one another for a couple of months, and emboldened by this, I sneaked out of camp during the day. We spent a few precious hours together and Caleb gave me a picture of a blond girl that he had cut out of an old photograph. He said that when the time came to leave, I should put it in a letter and explain that I had run away with her and would never return. 'It'll help throw them off the scent,' he said. I hoped he was right.

I shoved the picture into my pocket as Caleb explained his plan and gave me the date and the time when he would be returning to Newark to collect me. Afterwards we went to celebrate with a pint of Guinness and a packet of pork scratchings at a little country pub.

The thought of leaving my life, my family and my home, never to come back, was almost too unbearable to take in. But I knew I had no choice. My father's last beating had shown me that. And I couldn't live without Caleb. Even knowing that I would have to wait two months to see him again put a fist through my stomach.

When he dropped me back at our secret spot near the camp, my father was waiting. After he had spent a couple of hours whistling and calling for me, a girl from the camp had told him that I had been sneaking off with the Gorgia man again. As I got out of Caleb's car, my father sped off after him in his van.

My mother grabbed me by the arm. 'What have you done?' she shouted. 'And like a fool, I'm the last one to know!'

As I made my way back up to the camp and through to our trailer, just about everyone I passed threw some kind of abuse at me for trying to get in with a Gorgia man.

There was no hiding now.

I stood with my mother as my father's van skidded back onto the camp. Every family around the site seemed to be doing some kind of outside chore so that they could get a good view of the action that was about to commence.

As my father bounded towards me, I knew from his furious expression that he had failed to find Caleb. I felt so relieved that I hardly cared what he did to me. 'He got away, he got away,' I cried as he marched over and punched me hard and square in the face. I fell to the ground like a crumpled puppet. As the blood ran down my face and chest, he grabbed me by the neck of my shirt and dragged me into the trailer. He threw me onto my bunk.

'You stay here boy, don't you take one step from that trailer door,' he snarled. 'That's the last time you ever meet that Gorgia. You ain't leaving this trailer till I say so. I don't want you seeing or speaking to anyone, you've brought me nothing but shame and disgrace.'

He went out, slamming the trailer door behind him, leaving me lying on my bunk, blood mingling with the tears on my face.

From then on the only time I was allowed to leave the trailer was to go to work with my father, or to use the toilet block, just ten feet away. He thought it would be like torture for me, but I didn't care. I didn't want to go anywhere, unless it was with Caleb, and he had left town to build our new life.

I lasted for just over a month. The days and nights seemed endless as I kept my head down, worked hard and spent the evenings in my trailer or with my mother. My father's wrath appeared to be bottomless.

The day I decided I could take no more, he had snarled and cursed at me from morning till night. By the time I was unloading the last of the tarmac from the lorry, my hands felt like sandpaper and my bones ached beneath my oversized overalls. We had come home, yet again, with the same ton of tarmac we had collected from the quarry that morning. Not one job done all day, not one person willing to take the offer of a new drive, even at a knockdown price.

I stared at the ever-growing pile of useless tarmac. It was becoming more obvious all the time that the days of us travellers knocking on people's doors for work were coming to an end. The work was drying up, as was our lifestyle. The world was changing fast. And everyone was feeling the pinch. It would only be a matter of time before a huge chunk of the travelling community would be forced to conform to a 'normal' way of life.

I knew I wouldn't be around to see it.

I slid the heavy shovel back into its sheath for another day and wiped my palms across my overalls. I could hear the cries of the children playing in the camp. I searched my pockets and pulled out my cigarettes. I was now smoking twenty Benson & Hedges a day. I climbed the cab and sat on the roof of the lorry. I shook the grains of tarmac from my hair, lit a cigarette and looked up into the sky. The clouds clotted into clumps of pink and amber and the evening breeze stroked my face.

I missed Caleb so much it hurt.

As I sat on the roof of the lorry, smoking and watching the sunset, I could hear my father whistling in the distance. It was my curfew time. I'd have to climb down, return the lorry to the car park and be back at camp before he headed off to the pub with the rest of the men.

An hour later, when my father and the others had gone, I slipped from the trailer. My mother opened the door of her trailer, next door to mine and Frankie's. Behind her I could hear Henry-Joe and Jimmy screaming at each other over whose turn it was next on the Sega Megadrive and the wailing of my baby sister Minnie.

'Where are you off to?' my mother said, pushing a clip into her flame-red hair.

'I left a shovel up in the back field.'

She fluffed her tresses. 'Then you'd better go get it, eh? I'm just gonna put these kids to bed, so get yourself washed and I'll make you a coffee.'

'All right, Mum.'

As I turned to run from the plot, she called out, 'Hey.'

'Yeah?'

She paused. 'Don't be long.'

As I darted up through the camp towards the back field, I heard my aunt Minnie, me Mum's sister, calling out, 'Run, Forrest, run!' before laughing herself into a coughing fit. I turned back and blew her a kiss, which she caught, inhaled and blew out in smoke rings.

Aunt Minnie had the looks and mannerisms of Cruella de Vil, and had scared the crap out of me when I was a child. She was a chain-smoking kleptomaniac, wore a battered old floor-length mink coat and red stilettos and had taken me and Frankie on shoplifting expeditions when we were little. She and me Mum's other sister, Sadie, and their families travelled with us from place to place and all of them were so caring, old-fashioned and, in Minnie's case, wonderfully funny. These days she always seemed to be around to make me laugh.

I could never repay my aunts for their kindnesses to me. Without ever having to say a thing, I knew they had an understanding of what it was like to be part of the Walsh family, and the burden that came with the name. I loved them dearly. Aunt Minnie for her constant love, attention, cigarettes and the glass of brandy that came with everything, and Aunt Sadie for her kind words, advice and exquisite sarcasm. I would miss them.

Still laughing at Minnie, I ran up into the field and across three more, towards the little phone box in the nearest village. It was in darkness, apart from the faint light that shone from inside the red phone box. I stepped inside. It stank of piss and there was not an inch that didn't have one of the camp kids' names either carved with a knife or daubed in different shades of nail varnish.

I dialled, and the sound of his voice made my heart leap.

'I can't stand it any longer,' he said.

'Me neither. I miss you so much,' I replied.

He asked if I would be ready if he came for me the next afternoon.

I almost jumped for joy. 'Yes,' I answered.

As I walked back through the camp, I didn't stop to think that this would be the last night I'd ever see it. I wiped my feet and climbed the step into my mother's trailer. Baby Minnie and the boys were sound asleep. I sat by the boys' bed that pulled out from beneath the couch as my mother boiled the kettle.

Earlier I had watched as my father put seven-year-old Jimmy through his 'training'. Déjà vu had set in as I watched him make Jimmy raise his arms over his head and take the sequence of punches. As they got harder, Jimmy began to cry, and was rewarded by another angry punch from our father.

'Leave him alone,' I yelled.

My father turned to throw a punch at me, while my mother raced over.

'I swear to God, Frank, if you touch that child again I'll call the Gavvers (police) and have you put away.'

As the argument raged, I grabbed Jimmy and Henry-Joe and led them away. I walked with them to the back field.

Jimmy's tears hadn't lasted long. He was keen to get back there, and 'put himself right' by having another go at the training with our father. He was a brave little kid. He ran back off into the camp as Henry-Joe and I sat on the edge of a lorry.

Henry-Joe understood the obsession with our family and fighting and we both knew that our father's hopes were firmly fixed on Jimmy. As we sat together, Henry-Joe talked about the worry of knowing that his own fight would be to protect Jimmy. Hearing that crushed me, as did the knowledge that I was about to add to his burdens. I told him I was leaving. He was only nine years old, and I knew it wasn't fair to ask him to keep the secret, but I needed to tell someone in the family.

There was something else I needed to tell him. Without going into any detail, I warned him that he and Jimmy should never be alone with Uncle Joseph.

Henry-Joe sat on the edge of the lorry, his feet dangling over the edge. The wind tugged through his wiry red hair as he rocked back and forth, looking down at his unlaced boots. 'I'll remember,' he said as he looked up at me. I reached down and grabbed him, holding him as tight as I could.

'Your big brother loves you. Tell Jimmy, and Minnie too.'

We had walked back to camp together, my heart aching at the thought of leaving them.

Now the boys were sleeping like babes. As I sat beside their bed, I pulled the blanket up more tightly around them.

My mother carried the coffees out under the awning. With the heat on full, the area under the awning attached to the trailer – my mother's pride and joy – was warmer than the trailer itself, although the smell of heated plastic was almost overwhelming. I sat on one of the large revolving chairs, throwing a bright furry pink cushion to my mother who sat herself on the floor in front of the mirror. She took a sip from her coffee, not turning from her own reflection but looking back at me as she applied her face cream.

'When I was a little girl, I never used to speak to a single soul, did you know that?'

'No,' I replied.

'It's true,' she said as she rubbed the cream into her cheekbones. 'I never spoke to anyone. I wasn't shy – don't get me wrong. I just felt like I didn't have anything to say. I'd spend most days in the back field, singing to the horses. I swear people must have thought I was touched. And with this red hair and white face, I've spent my life with people either thinking I'm a Gorgia, or a witch. But I don't care. If anything, it's given me some peace. This is who I am. And I was given all of this stuff for a reason.'

She laughed, and then subsided into a thoughtful stillness. She turned from the mirror, giving me a look that went right into my soul, her dark eyes glistening in the dim light.

'We don't look it, but me and you, we're the same. I see me in you, more and more every day. I know you're unhappy, Mikey, but things will get better, I promise you they will. You wouldn't be my boy if you were like every other one of those fools out there. People are scared of what they can't understand. One day, you'll find *your* way. And I hope you leave all these behind. Be proud of being different, Mikey. Don't let the jealousy of this lot ever crush that special person that I see in you.'

In that moment it hit me. The next morning I would be leaving, never to return. I might never see her again. I kissed her cheek as I said goodnight.

'Get away with you,' she laughed, brushing me off. But I could see she was pleased.

Back in my trailer I barely slept. I sat writing the letter I would leave them. In large scrawled capital letters, every word misspelled, I said that I was sorry and that after everything that had happened I couldn't stay any longer, for it would only make things worse for everyone. I would be going far away, I had found a girlfriend who I was going to be very happy with and I was not coming back. Last of all, I said that I loved them all very much and that once I was settled, I would contact them again.

4

Free

The next morning my mother wasn't there. As I stared at the empty space where the van was usually parked, my father said she had gone to my grandmother's for the day with the baby and the boys. After our granddad Alfie's death a few months earlier, Granny Bettie had settled into a bungalow half an hour's drive away and our mother liked to go over and see her.

It was the greatest of tests. I had hoped I would see her one last time. Now Caleb was on his way, and I had to choose. I felt overwhelmed by sadness and loss. 'Forgive me,' I whispered.

It was a Sunday, so my father wasn't working. He ordered me to stay in the trailer and went to the pub with some of the other men.

Frankie was nowhere to be seen. Days earlier she had come into our trailer, late at night, grinning, and announced that she had secretly married Wisdom in a register office. 'He's the one, Mikey,' she said. 'We didn't want to wait.'

I had imagined a big wedding for her, with the whole family and everyone we knew there, and Frankie in the middle, showing off in a gorgeous dress. I felt sad. She could only ever have one wedding, and this had been it. I just hoped that she and Wisdom would make a go of it. He was a thug, but she loved him. 'Congratulations,' I said. 'When are you going to tell me Mum and Dad?'

'I'll find the right moment,' she said. I hoped she would.

Now there was nothing left to do except go. I slipped out of the trailer, collected the bag of clothes I had hidden earlier and ran to the place where Caleb had said he would wait.

He was there. I pulled open the car door and jumped in.

He turned to me, with a smile, and revved the engine.

My heart was in my mouth as we hit the road and the rain fell in a deluge. But as the miles flew by and there was no sign of my father chasing us, I relaxed, just a little. Eventually I curled up in the passenger seat and tried to doze. I thought of my father and his anger, of Frankie and her miserable husband, and of Henry-Joe and Jimmy. What would become of my little boys? I feared that one day my brothers would grow to hate me for deserting them. And I couldn't blame them. As for baby Minnie – she was so small that I wondered if she would even remember me.

Most of all I thought of my mother. She would soon be home from Old Bettie's . . .

It was years before I heard what happened that night when she was told that I'd gone. She leaped from the car and ran into the trailer I shared with Frankie, opening every one of my empty cupboards, before discovering the letter I had left. As she read it, she gasped with shock and fell to the floor, in floods of tears. When my father came in, she leaped up, kicking, punching and screaming at him, with everything that she had. He walked from the trailer, slamming the door behind him, and she collapsed back on the floor, stricken with grief. I knew nothing of that, thank God. My heart was near enough to breaking as it was.

I must have fallen asleep because I woke to the repetitive strobes of street lamps and headlights. The storm was over, darkness had fallen, and we were in Liverpool. I stretched, yawned and slicked my fingers through my hair, then rubbed the excess grease across the chest of my jumper.

'We're just a couple of miles away now,' Caleb smiled.

I pulled the crumpled gold box from my pocket, cracked open a window and lit a cigarette. I huddled back against the seat, feeling the little zap of breeze through my hair as I watched my cigarette smoke being sucked from the window and out of existence.

Minutes later we turned into a street lined on both sides with terraced houses. Caleb pulled into the drive of one of them and turned to me. 'This is it! Our new home.'

The lights from the car shone upon a dull green garage door, welded shut by vines.

He pulled the handbrake on, clicked off the lights and switched off the engine. 'You can have a proper look at the outside tomorrow.'

As I climbed out and stretched my legs, he reached inside for my bag and headed for the front door. As he fumbled in his pockets for the keys, he chuckled to himself, looking back at me over his shoulder. The door opened and we stepped inside. We stood in a dark hallway that smelled of charity shops and old mail.

Caleb led the way upstairs and into his room, where the whiff of the old house was quickly suffocated by the familiar smell of leather, sweat and cheap aftershave that I recognised from Caleb's room back in Newark.

All his favourite things were in place: his rocket lava lamp, his weights, his 'I ♥ BEER' poster and the red and blue reversible tartan bedsheets. He had acquired a new portable wardrobe rack, which was loaded with his many bright shirt and tie combos. As he left for the bathroom, I walked over to the stereo and pressed play: *The Greatest Hits of Randy Crawford*. Of course. We had spent many nights together, talking while Randy's beautiful voice crooned softly in the background. Every time I heard one of her songs, I thought of Caleb.

Caleb came back in holding a beard trimmer and a dining-room chair, which he plonked down on the floor. 'I think it would be a good idea to change the way you look,' he said. He explained that he thought it would be for the best that I sell my jewellery and get rid of all the clothes that I'd brought with me. As he talked, I began to pull off my rings, placing them on the table. One was a huge ring, imbedded with twenty-six small diamonds (there should have been twenty-eight, but two had fallen out and I had cunningly replaced them with silver foil). The other was a large knot-shaped thing, dipped in gold.

There comes a point in every Gypsy boy's life, usually at about the age of ten, when toys are no longer seen as appropriate. After that, many a Christmas and birthday present will come in the shape of a piece of traditional jewellery such as a large diamond knot ring, a sovereign, a chain with some gold boxing gloves attached, or a ring with your initials carved into it that shows off your family name and doubles up nicely as a knuckleduster. Its suitability as a weapon is high on the list of considerations when buying a new ring.

For girls it's easier: as well as jewellery there's the option of perfume, shoes and designer clothes. And when it comes to the clothes, travellers like you to know that *whatever* they're wearing is by *this* person, so most of the time the girls wear outfits with the logos of Moschino, Chanel, Dolce & Gabbana, Vivienne Westwood and so on stamped all over them, from head to toe. While the girls can be as loud with their clothes as they wish, boys tend to stick to a good pair of smart jeans, a nice shirt and at least four digits, neck and a wrist adorned in weighty pieces of jewellery.

I was suddenly very aware of my Gypsy look. I only wished Caleb had mentioned getting rid of my clothes before, to save me the effort of lugging my bag all the way down to the phone box where he picked me up.

Caleb put a carrier bag onto the bed and took out three pairs of tracksuit bottoms, three plain white T-shirts and a hooded jumper. 'You can borrow my clothes too,' he said, 'but I think this would be a good start. We're going to have to take that off too,' he said, pointing at my hair.

I'd had the same Elvis hairstyle, with a big greased-up quiff, since I was able to grow hair. But Caleb explained that now it would make me look a little bit too obvious.

The only time I had ever taken a razor to my head was when I shaved off my eyebrows while listening to Cliff Richard's 'Wired for Sound' at full-blast in the bathroom when I was six years old and trying to imitate my father shaving.

'I'm not going to shave off all of it,' he said, trying to sound reassuring. 'I'll give you a number two with the beard trimmers, like an action man.'

Not only was I now feeling very self-conscious about the way I had looked my whole life, but I was also feeling very much like I was living out the first act of *My Fair Lady*. But I knew that I needed to blend in, so I sat on the chair while Caleb got to work and watched the stern concentration on his face as clumps of my hair fell about my shoulders and onto the floor.

When the cut was finished, Caleb steered me to the bathroom across the hall, where I got in the shower and stared into the cyclone in the plughole as soap, water and clumps of hair ran down into it. My aching muscles unfolded beneath the pressure of the hot water and I stayed there until my fingers wilted and my skin turned to a darkened pink. I held every part of myself beneath the hot water, obliterating the cracks of my dead skin, lifting it right off.

Then I wiped the steam from the mirror with my forearm and peered in. I ran my fingers through my thick eyebrows, pushing away the water. For the first time I could see the apple-like shape of my head. With the new action-man haircut, my Thunderbird eyebrows and huge eyes seemed to take over my face and my eyes shone greener than they ever had before.

I looked different – as if I'd aged five years in Caleb's car. Only my scars were still the same – three vivid red scars on my face, one of them down the side of my nose, reminding me that I was still the same boy . . . only minus a layer of skin.

I went back to Caleb's room. Our room. On the edge of the bed, some tracksuit bottoms and a T-shirt had been laid out. Caleb sat by the pillows, putting on a CD as I pulled the trousers on under the towel. I was, and always had been, terrible at being naked.

'Hurry up then, Mr Prude,' he laughed.

After I had put on my new clothes I looked at myself again in the mirror. Without my hair and jewellery, and in different clothes, my whole identity had changed. I was a Gypsy boy no longer, and it was a strange feeling. As if I hadn't just left my people behind, I had left myself.

I sat on the bed as Caleb took off his clothes, neatly and pointlessly folding them before putting them in the laundry basket, and then did his daily workout of press ups and sit ups before going for a shower. Thoughts of home started to seep into my head, and I turned to the CD stack for distraction and went through my trouser pockets for my cigarettes. I threw back the curtain and opened his window.

I looked down at the empty street below. A row of stone-clad houses, each with different shades of net curtain. A drunken group stumbled by, slurring random words to the tune of the Macarena as they danced down to the next drinking hole. In the distance I could hear the rumble of cars from the main road.

They would all know by now.

I felt a great collapsing in my chest. I had done it. I had finally left: my life, my home, my past, my family . . . everything that I had been before. I couldn't believe it, or see how I had even managed to do it. I looked at myself in the reflection of the window. Who was I? Who would I be from now on?

I loved Caleb so much, but the idea of losing my family and my culture for ever sent an avalanche of pain crashing through my chest. As I smoked, the tears began to fall. I thought of their faces, the sadness and the overwhelming pain I would be putting them all through.

I couldn't bring myself to tell Caleb how I felt. This was what we had planned. It was supposed to be the happiest night of our lives. The night we had spoken of for what felt like an eternity. I had to get this out of me before he returned. He had done so much to get me here – for at least this night, I would have to suppress my sadness and my fear of what might be to come.

I took my last drag and tossed the cigarette from the window. I smacked at my face and pinched at my cheeks to awaken some colour before Caleb came back into the room. An old trick I had picked up from Judy Garland in *Meet Me in St Louis*.

As I heard the click of the bathroom door I took a leap from the windowsill to the bed.

'Are you all right?'

'Yeah,' I replied, almost too enthusiastically.

Caleb leaned in and kissed me on the forehead. 'Welcome home, Mikey.'

That night was the first Caleb and I ever spent together. He was exhausted, and within moments of getting into bed he was asleep. Wide awake, I lay watching him breathe. In that moment, I loved him more than the very breath in my lungs. No matter what happened, I would go to the ends of the earth to be with him. He had saved me.

I thought of my mother finding that letter full of lies about the girl I had run off with and it impaled me. I missed her so much. The next day I would make the call. The one to say I was fine, but I was never coming home. I wished that I could tell her the truth, but that would have sent them straight to Caleb. I promised myself that I would keep it short. And I would tell her that she would someday see me again.

5

The Call

Caleb pulled the car over to a phone box on the pavement of a busy street. He came in with me. I knew he didn't trust me to be able to do this alone. He unfolded the piece of paper I passed over to him then, after rummaging in his pockets, he dropped a pound into the slot and entered a 'blocked number calling' code, before dialling the number I had scribbled down.

My father's mobile number.

After one ring he picked up, and Caleb passed me the receiver.

'Where are you?'

'Hello, Dad.'

'Fuck off hello – where are you?'

'I'm all right.'

'I didn't ask you that.'

'That's all I can tell you.'

'What! You're a selfish little bastard you are, my boy.'

Above the sound of gunshot, which I knew was coming from the television in the background, I could hear Frankie and the boys crying.

'Can't you hear what you've done to your bit of family?' my father said sternly. He must have pushed the phone right up to their mouths.

I heard Henry-Joe beg through his tears, 'Mikey, please come home, please.'

Frankie and Jimmy sobbed even harder as he spoke.

My throat and eyes filled. I glanced at Caleb, who looked panic-stricken.

I could feel myself cracking.

Caleb began to mime slamming down the phone, which I ignored, turning from him and holding on tight to the receiver. He started to pull it from my hand. Just as Caleb feared, I broke down and started to weep uncontrollably into the receiver.

'Please don't cry! You're better off without me, please, don't cry.'

My father's voice came back, calm and sympathetic. 'Mikey, my boy, you don't belong out there mate . . . you're not a Gorgia. What are you gonna do for a job? You won't survive.'

'I'll be all right, I'll find something,' I sobbed.

Caleb grabbed the phone and I snatched it back.

'Get off! Dad, I've gotta go now.'

'Who's there with you?'

'Nobody, I'll call again soon.'

'Don't be fucking stupid, Mikey!'

'I'm going now, Dad.'

'Mikey, please . . .' My father paused. 'For your mum, please come home. We'll forget any of this ever happened. Nobody will need to know. You can say you left the girl and that'll be that. Just say you're sorry. Mikey, you'll never hear me beg . . . but – please?'

I caught my breath. My father never, ever spoke like this. He was begging me. Had I misjudged him? Would he really forgive me and let it go? Did he love me and want me home?

Caleb made a throat-slitting gesture. My eyes met his.

'I'm sorry. I'll call again soon. Tell them I love them. Bye.'

'Mikey, no!'

I sobbed. 'I love you.'

Caleb grabbed the phone and I sank to the floor in tears. Then, from two feet away, I heard my father yelling, 'I know where you've gone, poofy bollocks! You won't take me for a cunt! I'll find you Mikey! I'll find you.'

That was the father I knew.

Caleb hung up the phone and I wept uncontrollably over the mess and the pain I had caused them. Never had I felt so awful. So guilty. So wrong. So selfish. So worthless.

'Come on,' Caleb whispered, holding out his hand. He opened the door and a gust of wind blew into the suffocating box.

But I sat in a heap on the floor and I couldn't stop crying. My cheeks, eyes and throat burned. I rubbed at my face with the sleeve of my jumper.

Caleb crouched down and put his arms under mine. 'Up you get,' he sighed, lifting me to my feet.

We stumbled back to the car and I crashed into the passenger seat like a heavy sack.

As Caleb made his way round to the driver's side, I reached for my cigarettes and lighter on the dashboard. I was shaking so much that I couldn't get a grip on either of them and as he started the car they fell to the floor.

I rubbed my eyes again and then opened the window, as far as it would go, sticking my head out of it, and taking in several deep breaths of air. As I leaned back inside, Caleb was holding out a lit cigarette. He detested the habit so much that he had never even attempted to put one to his lips before.

I took it from his hand. 'Thank you.'

He smiled and looked back at the road.

'I have to go home.'

He paused, then gave a nod.

I put the cigarette between my lips, sucking in the smoke every time I started to whimper again.

We said nothing more to each other for a whole hour as Caleb drove randomly about the town. Finally he swerved into a lay-by and parked. He yanked me towards him. 'I love you, Mikey, I love you so much.'

'I love you, Caleb. I'm so sorry.'

Through our tears we agreed that he would drop me back at the camp gates that night.

Then Caleb's phone rang. He ignored it at first but it kept ringing. He rubbed at his eyes with his wrists and pulled the phone from his pocket. I opened the car door and lit another cigarette as he answered. 'All right?'

It was his mum, and she was shouting.

Caleb pleaded with her to calm down.

'Where's Mikey?'

Caleb turned to me and pressed a silent finger to his lips, before responding to her. 'What?'

'Don't fuck about, Caleb.'

'I don't know, Mum.'

'Well, his dad's just been here you know, and his sister's bloke, and a couple of big-arse bastards!'

'You're joking?'

'No, I'm fucking not! They've torn the bloody house apart – I don't know what to do!'

'Oh God, are you all right?'

'Why do they think you're hiding him Caleb? Have you got him there with you now?'

I bit down on my fingers as Caleb blasted an angry denial. 'No, I haven't.'

She paused before replying in her calmest voice. 'You're lying. I know you are. I'm telling you now: give that boy up or send him on his way. They've been bribing and threatening everybody in town.'

I watched as Caleb's face drained to a deathly shade and he slumped in his seat.

'They're going to come back. And they know where you live. Someone has told them.'

'Don't worry, Mum.'

'Caleb, I think the boy is lovely, you know I do, but you don't want to upset these people.'

'I'll call you later.'

'They're on their way, Caleb.'

He hung up and rubbed his hands over his face.

'Did you hear that?'

'Yes.'

'Still want to go home?'

I realised how stupid I had been to think that my father would forgive me so easily. My phone call had done nothing but rouse his anger. God knows what he would do to me if he caught me.

I thought about the way he was when I phoned. I had believed his crocodile tears. I had believed he was still willing to take me back, in spite of everything. I thought

I knew him and all his devious, cruel ways, but he had fooled me and shown a side of himself that was darker than anything I had known before. I was his prey now, and he was determined to hunt me down. There was nothing I could do but run, and hide . . . and try to stay one step ahead of him.

Caleb was driving us back towards the house. 'We need to move you out for a couple of days.'

'Where to?'

'I'll have to get some money from someone. I'll put you in a bed and breakfast or something for a couple of days.'

'Where?'

Caleb thumped the steering wheel, fear and desperation turning to rage. 'I don't know, Mikey! Fucking hell – just shut up for a minute while I think.'

I shrank back into my seat.

After a long pause, Caleb spoke. 'We didn't think this through enough. You should have waited longer.'

I didn't answer, because as he was talking I was suddenly hit by an icy shiver that froze my very bones.

'Mikey, are you all right?'

My blood ran cold. A hand tightened about my throat. I could feel him, coming closer and closer to us. I grabbed the plastic cog on the side of the seat, spinning it as fast as my fingers could go, and as the seat back lowered below dashboard level, we stopped at the traffic lights.

At that moment I heard three familiar beeps of a horn.

'Oh fuck. Mikey, stay down.'

He must have been on his way even before Caleb's mother called us. We were seventy-nine miles from

Newark, an hour and a half's drive – less if you drove like my father.

The light turned green and Caleb took off. We turned a corner so sharply that I almost rolled onto his lap. But my father had done a U-turn and was on our tail.

'He's following us, he's fucking following us!'

I was too scared to speak.

Caleb ripped his way through the gearbox, screaming past howling car horns and bellowing pedestrians. 'They're right behind us!'

'Oh God.'

Caleb's voice sounded desperate. 'Mikey, I can't lose 'em.' Tears and sweat started to stream down his face.

Behind us the familiar horn was blaring as the van closed in on us.

Caleb took a corner so fast that two wheels lifted from the road, crashing back to the tarmac with a crunch. The little car swerved and collided with the kerb. He elbowed me several times, wielding and spinning the steering wheel like a helm on a storm-struck ship.

'He missed the turn, but he'll turn around. Mikey, I need you to listen, I'm pulling up to a pub, and when I stop, I need you to jump out and run inside. I'll come back for you, but whatever you do, don't come out, and don't get seen.'

'All right.'

'Open the door, ready.'

I did, holding the door in close, ready to swing it open and fall out.

The car skidded to a halt that almost threw me through the windscreen.

'GO-GO-GO-GO-GO!'

I jumped from the car and barely before I could put both feet to the ground, Caleb had gone.

I ran as quickly as I could towards the pub ahead of me. In my haste and terror I stumbled along the path through the crowded beer garden. Onlooking beer guzzlers jeered and clapped wildly at my stunt as I fell, smashing my chin on the steps. I didn't look back. I staggered to the heavy oak door, ramming it with my whole body weight as I charged in.

The unmistakable waft of crackling meat and hot bread was all around me.

I couldn't breathe, my chin was bleeding profusely, and I was dripping with cold sweat. I looked around. It was a typical English chain pub, full of families having lunch. And most of them were staring at this gasping apparition, with his bloody chin and hunted eyes.

I slunk between the tables and ducked below oak beams lined with copper pots and pans, until I spotted the door to the men's toilets, and dived in.

A row of yellow wooden doors mirrored a row of blue urinals. I hastily tapped along the cubicle doors to find an empty one and pushed it open. I pulled the brass lock across and sank onto the toilet seat, heaving for breath. Thankfully, there were no gaps below or above the door. The cubicle was a safe and secluded cell. The light above my head hummed and popped as my lungs began to settle. I pulled some paper from the roll, spitting on it several times before wiping it across my face and chin to remove the blood.

Without a watch, I judged my waiting time by the

number of cigarettes I smoked. At one point I got down onto the floor and rested my head against the door, listening for familiar steps across the tiled floor outside. In my head I went through every single move I had made the day before, when I left the camp. I wondered how he had managed to find us. Did I leave a clue? Caleb's mum said someone had blabbed, but if so, how could they have possibly known our precise location?

After ten cigarettes, which I guessed took five minutes each, I left the cubicle. Smoke poured from the open door as I casually stepped out from my cell, like a guest on *Stars in Their Eyes*. Luckily no one was around to point out that smoking in the toilets was not allowed.

With the coast clear, I went over to the mirror and looked at my grazed chin. It was the same kind of scrape I'd had on my knees as a kid. I splashed some water on my face, swilled the dry cigarette taste from my mouth and spat into the basin, before making my way back into the bar. The lighting had changed as night had drawn in, and bulky candles had been lit on every table, their reflected light flickering from the vast array of copper.

Cautiously I looked around the bar.

Caleb was sitting at a table, circling the rim of a pint of bitter with his finger. I walked over and stood beside him at the table. He didn't look up.

'Are you all right?'

His voice was a croak. 'No.'

I slid into the space opposite him. Caleb looked up. He had a burst lip and three large slits across his forehead. Those terrible rings.

'He caught up with you?'

'What do you think?' he answered sarcastically, before taking a large gulp of his beer.

I was so furious that they had hurt him, all I could do was cry. 'Caleb, I'm so sorry.'

'He warned me that I would be watched from now on. I don't know what to do.'

'What do you want to do?'

'He offered me five grand to set you up.'

'To be caught?'

'Yes.'

'Do you want to?'

He stared out into nothing, silent.

I took a sip of the bitter. 'You're gonna do it then?' I asked quietly.

He pulled me towards him. 'I told him to fuck off, Mikey. And that's when I got this,' he said, pointing to the wounds on his face.

'Oh, thank God!'

'And what's happened to you then, Mr Walsh? You been in a fight?'

'I fell over on the way in.'

He smiled, then spat a gob of blood into his sleeve, before taking another swig of bitter.

'Errgh – you dirty pig,' I laughed.

'Let's get out of here, Gypsy Boy,' he said, looking around at the bewildered punters. 'We look like Ike and Tina Turner.'

I slid out from the table, holding my ribs as I howled with relieved laughter. He downed the pint and climbed to his feet, then tucked me under his shoulder, knuckling my shaved head as we walked out of the pub.

6

In the Boot

We parked in a multi-storey car park near to where Caleb worked. He had a managers' meeting at seven.

'Do you have to go?' I asked.

'You know I have to. Besides, I need to tell them not to answer any questions from anyone who comes looking for me. You'll be all right here, just don't leave the car, OK?'

'OK,' I said quietly, knowing that the next few hours alone would send me into slow insanity.

He manoeuvred the rear-view mirror and peered in, arranging his collar and then licking his fingers and running them across his eyebrows.

'I'm just going to say I was mugged.'

'You sure you have to go?' I asked again, grabbing his arm.

He didn't reply. Just got out and went over to get a pay and display ticket. Moments later he leaned in and stuck the ticket to the front window. 'I'll be back in a couple of hours.'

He left the keys in the ignition, so that I could listen to the radio for company.

After only minutes without him I was struck by paranoia. I turned from left to right in my seat, looking around at the surrounding cars for the telltale signs of travellers' vehicles: souped-up vans, any kind of Merc or four by four, or anything that had baby boots, boxing gloves, horseshoes, rosaries or all of these hanging from the mirror.

The rosaries were a must-have in any Gypsy car; not a symbol of Catholicism, but a tag to let other Gypsies know it was a vehicle proudly earned and owned by a fellow traveller. There were still the odd few back then who would be stealing and rigging cars before selling them on, so the symbol served as a 'keep off' sign. They would never steal from their own.

My father had a lengthy career stealing cars, back when we lived in Warren Woods, in West Sussex. In those days he had a dossa named Wayne working for him. (Dossas were what we called the Gorgia men who worked for Gypsies.) Wayne had once been a professional car thief and his skills opened up a whole new line of business for my father.

The family would drive into places like this multi-storey and then my father and Wayne would scan the place, looking for a posh car that, as a bonus, had any hint of a bag with a credit card inside. Once they'd found one, Wayne would do his stuff and then follow us home in it. If they'd got a credit card out of it, the following week, after spending all night beforehand practising the signature on the card and getting into character, Wayne and my mother would pose as a rich couple, entering expensive stores and buying every household appliance and item of clothing we could possibly make a buck on, while my father followed them around the shops, pointing out his desired purchases.

Wayne was a typical class-A-drug fiend, with burnt lips and fingers, but after a major scrub up and in an Armani suit (also bought on the card) he could almost pass as a gentleman – unlike my father, who looked like the Godfather in the gutter in whatever he put on. My mother's costume was based on Krystle Carrington in *Dynasty*, her favourite show: a pink pencil-skirt suit with colossal shoulder pads, and a big-brimmed white hat.

As they hit the shops, we kids would be waiting in our ticking-over car, and once they had completed their purchases, they would hot-foot it, bags and boxes in hand, into the car and off. We kids thought it was exciting, we'd be whooping and bouncing up and down as my father hit the accelerator and roared away.

In the meantime, the stolen car would be 'ringed up': that was my father's term for changing the car's identity, after which he would sell it.

I was tortured by memories. I wound the seat back so that I was out of sight to anyone passing. I felt I should sleep to pass the time, but couldn't close my eyes. I listened to mindless chatter on the radio to calm myself but my mind began to play tricks on me. I imagined figures approaching the car, dragging me from it and beating me to death right there. Every few seconds I turned around in my seat to check for faces at the window.

I was overcome with guilt, and an overwhelming hatred of myself for what I had done. I told myself that if I had worked harder I would have been different. Normal. I envied every other Gypsy boy that there ever was: in that moment, they were the luckiest people alive to me. Their incredible masculinity, so primal that it surpassed my comprehension; their unfaltering courage; their pride in their race and their animal need for blood, sweat, family.

Even out of my father's clutches, I couldn't shake his horrible opinion of me. How many times had he looked at me with contempt in his eyes, called me a coward, spat at me in derision? It seemed to me that from the time I could walk, I had been disappointing and failing him. And now I could only agree with him. I was a waste of space. I may have got away from him, but he was still with me, poisoning my mind, like a curse I could never break.

Only my love for Caleb stopped me from giving up completely. He had given me recognition and meaning. He loved me, regardless of my past; he wanted to hear my voice when I spoke. He had brought me back to life.

I was afraid to draw attention to the car by turning on the engine, and over the next two hours I became so cold my teeth were chattering. Finally I heard the familiar tapping of Caleb's footsteps, and the door creaked open.

I looked for fresh bruises and, to my relief, there were none.

He said nothing as he started the engine. Dreading more bad news, I sat back and waited for him to speak. He didn't utter a word for several miles. Then he gave me a look from the corner of his eye. 'Your mum called me.'

'What? Where did she get your number?'

'I don't know. Through my work, I guess. She wanted to say sorry for your dad.'

'What did she say?' I asked, dragging the life out of a cigarette.

He said she had phoned with a warning. 'They're coming for him, Caleb. There's a price that's out, and no matter where he is, they are gonna find him. There's a lot of people looking for what his dad's offered. Horrible people. He's told 'em that Mikey has stole a ring worth ten grand, and there is a reward to get the ring back, no matter what it takes. I'm scared for my boy. Please, if you know where he is, please tell him that he has to hide. And you better hide, too. It's not safe for you.'

My heart broke and Caleb started to weep. 'I'm so scared, Mikey. I don't know what to do. She loves you so much. And she knows. I could feel it. I told her I hadn't seen you, but she wasn't fooled. She said they're coming back tonight. What are we going to do?'

I thought about what my mother had said. I knew exactly what ring my father was talking about. It was a gift from my grandfather to him a year ago: a thick gold band with a diamond in the centre of it as large as a penny. He hadn't taken it off his finger since he'd got it. Seemed now he had a good reason to. He'd found a clever way to spread hate for me and get other men hungry for my blood.

Caleb parked to give himself time to think, and his phone began to ring, almost non-stop. It was a new nightmare every time he answered: friends were ringing to warn him that Gypsy men were all over Newark, asking about him, and people had been scared into giving them information. Every Gypsy in the north knew where we were.

White-faced and grim, Caleb drove us home, raced

into the house and came out two minutes later with all my stuff, which he hurled into the back seat. Then he drove for twenty minutes, before stopping in the darkened car park of a pub. As he drove he told me what he wanted to do. We both got out and walked around to the rear of the car. A gust of biting wind cut through me as I pulled my arms up into my sleeves. Caleb opened the boot. A dim light flickered from inside. Caleb began to empty its contents, throwing his gym bag onto the back seat, the spare tyre over a nearby wall, and piles of old files and junk into a wooden waste bin at the side of the car park.

After the boot was clear he looked at me. I grabbed his shoulder for support and climbed inside. I could feel the tin ridges burying into my spine and hips as I swivelled into the most comfortable position I could find, my legs curled in front of me, in a foetal position.

'OK?'

I felt like a body in a Tarantino movie. 'No.'

He looked around, checking the coast was clear, then leaned in and patted my face. 'Sorry, Mikey. It's all I can think of. Goodnight.' He lowered the lid, and as it clicked into place, the light went out.

I curled into a ball and pulled my spare clothing around me to try to get warm. He started the engine and set off for our house, as I tried not to breathe in the fumes from the fuel. After a short while the car slowed to a halt, then rocked as Caleb jumped out. I heard the jingle of his keys, the opening of the door.

And then silence.

Realising that he would not be coming back out, I

tried to get myself into a less cramped sleeping position. To sleep took an eternity. My anxiety made me feel I was slipping into madness. I wanted to believe that we would make it through this, but I couldn't shake the fear that the worst of my father's wrath was yet to come.

Muffled whispers woke me from my doze and shot me straight into a state of panic. They had come. I could hear and feel them as they rustled through the bushes that surrounded the house and then circled the car. Each of the handles rattled and the car shook as they checked for an unlocked door. My heart leapt in my chest and I gripped my hands over my mouth as one grabbed the boot handle and began to rock the car.

'Locked.'

I could make out that there were three of them: two at the car, and one knocking at Caleb's front door. The two from the car listened to an order from the man at the door and scrambled out of sight, before he raised his voice. 'I just wanna talk to you.'

The door was unlocked and Caleb stepped out. I knew he was about to be jumped, and yet I could do nothing about it. I prayed that by some telepathic impossibility he could hear my silent screams to run back inside.

The other two re-emerged and the three of them dragged him out onto the drive. Caleb cursed just once, before thuds began crashing into his body.

Inside the boot, I put my hands over my ears to drown out the sounds of dragging gravel and groans. The car rocked as Caleb's body thumped across the boot. His grunts of pain and shouts of denial were an arm's length from me. My heart thumped like an uncontrollable machine, and my body went into total shock. I could feel every punch. And with each blow, they repeated, 'Where is he? Where is he?'

Caleb's groans stopped, but the punches did not. I wept through the fist that I had shoved into my mouth to keep me from crying out and curled into a ball, terrified and useless, locked inside my tin prison as the man I loved was flogged like an animal.

I knew he would rather be beaten to death than have these men take me away and hurt me.

'We know you have him,' rasped one of the voices.

'I don't mate, I really don't,' Caleb replied. 'You've come to the wrong place.'

'Liar! Listen, you Gorgia-bred bastard, we'll keep coming back, and that boy will be found – and till you bring him out, you, your family and everyone around you are gonna get the same as you got tonight.'

'I don't know where he is! Now leave me alone, or I'm going to call the police.'

A swinish laugh. 'Do you think that will help you? I saw your mum and sister the other day, did they tell you? If you don't cough him up, I'm going back there and I swear to God, I'll cut off your ugly mother's tits.'

I knew that voice now. Wisdom, my sister's husband.

The three men left the driveway and Caleb slid down from the boot. I waited for him to let me out. He didn't. He dragged himself back over to his door, and closed it behind him.

I couldn't stop shaking. My teeth rattled furiously with uncontrollable fear.

I woke the next morning to the choke of the engine starting up. Scared to call out Caleb's name, in case it wasn't him, I held my breath and lay as still as I could. After a few minutes on the road, the car ground to a halt. The jingling keys pushed into the lock and as the lid opened a beam of sunlight flooded in.

Caleb stood above me. The light masked the depths of his wounds as he lifted me out. As I landed on my feet, my legs gave way and I fell flat on my face. He leaned down and helped me over to the passenger side of the car.

We were in a supermarket car park.

I looked at his face and started to cry. One of his eyes was welded shut and his lips were busted in several directions.

'I'm going to get you some stuff from the shop. Wind that seat down, don't leave the car, and I'll be right back.'

A few minutes later he returned with a large bottle of Coke, two bacon sandwiches, a pasty and a bumper book of puzzles and word searches. He threw the bundle onto my lap.

'Thank you.'

'You're welcome.'

My eyes filled, as I looked at his wounds. 'Are you all right?'

He smiled, wincing as his lips cracked. 'Oh yeah, I'm fine. A pause. 'I had a call last night, from your brother.'

I was startled. 'Henry-Joe?'

'Yes. He had taken your father's mobile after everyone was asleep, he was crying, he wanted to warn me about the reward your father's offering. I told him I knew, and that he mustn't worry.'

'Thank you.' My poor little brother, worried sick. I should never have put this on him.

'Right, I'm off to work.'

I tried to laugh, and ended up crying. 'I'm so sorry, I'm so, so sorry.'

He disappeared, leaving me with my snacks and puzzle book.

I started with a 'spot the difference' on page one. I wished so hard that Caleb would turn out to be right.

7

A Witch and a Holy Place

As it turned out, he couldn't have been more wrong. That day Caleb had gone into a police station and reported what had happened. The police had interviewed my father, who denied any knowledge of the people who'd beaten up Caleb and said he simply wanted to know where his son was. The police had asked Caleb if he knew of my whereabouts, and he had said no.

After that, Caleb realised that going to the police would get him nowhere. The Gypsy men would cover for one another and, in any case, he couldn't identify his attackers because it had been dark. Not only that, but he was hiding a boy of fifteen who had been reported as a missing person.

We were on our own.

The late-night visits continued for three more weeks before Caleb finally caved.

We had decided that if he moved it would just look suspicious. Caleb was certain the only thing to do was to ride it out. And so I continued to spend my days in the car, parked in various car parks around the city, and my nights in the boot, cramped and claustrophobic and scared. The only time I saw Caleb was when he drove me to yet another car park in the morning – via a petrol station toilet, where I would brush my teeth and wash – and at the end of the day when, once he felt it was safe to come back to the car, we would go for a short drive and catch up on the events of the day. After that I would get out of the front seat and back into the boot before he headed back to the house.

As a trainee manager, Caleb wasn't making a lot. But he was able, for one night, to raise the money to put me up in a bed and breakfast. At least there I could have a proper shower and sleep in a real bed.

He couldn't stay with me. He was still getting visits every night from people my father had sent and he thought it best that he was there every time, so that they would presume he had nothing to hide.

'It's just *one* of you, isn't it?' asked the landlady as she scrunched the notes into her pocket. She looked like a white-faced witch, with her startling beehive of black hair, her long red nails and her angry scowl.

'Just him,' Caleb responded, rubbing my head. 'Look after him, won't you?'

I watched from the window of the room she showed me to as he sped off down the busy road. Every time he left me, I was afraid that I might never see him again. That he would have finally had his fill of me. And I wouldn't have blamed him.

The witch-landlady, who had a strong Northern Irish accent, came in with a pile of towels.

I hadn't thought that I'd burst into tears when she asked where I'd like them. I also hadn't thought that she would then sit herself on the bed and take me in her arms. 'There there,' she sighed, rubbing my back as I wept. 'It'll all be all right.'

I was cleaned up, cried out and had managed to eat some decent food before Caleb came for me the next morning. For over a week I had been unable to keep down a thing I swallowed. My appetite was non-existent and my weight had plummeted, while what was left of my hair had started to fall out in tiny clumps.

With no more money for bed and breakfast, for the next few days, I continued sleeping in the car boot, washing under a cold petrol station tap and filling every notebook, colouring book and jotter pad that the super-market had to offer. Colouring in the pictures was at least mind-numbing. I couldn't read well enough to manage a book – and in any case I couldn't have concen-trated on actual words. But ever since I was a kid I had loved colouring, drawing and doodling and now it gave me a way to help pass the endless hours.

As more time passed I got a little braver, leaving the car to stretch my legs and take short walks around the area close to the car park. One day I found a church, which loomed above the dull houses and second-hand shops like a great witch's hat. Hesitantly, I stepped inside. It seemed to be empty. My feet echoed across the great stone floor as I walked between the rows and rows of empty pews, each with woven cushions and bound Bibles perfectly placed. The ceilings stretched high above me and the dim rays of sunlight lit up a palette of colours in the vast stained-glass windows.

I was never a religious person. None of my family was. There was a popular culture of Born Again travel-ling people, though we were never any part of it. But this place held a calm that wrapped its arms around me. I sat upon the pew at the very front, and heaved a deep sigh. I thought of all the people who had come here to find help and the answers to their questions and problems. I walked over to a table, where for a small donation you could light a candle. I had no money for a donation, so I felt it would have been rude of me to even think of asking for help. But for the short time I was in there, I felt calmer and my aches seemed to hurt less. And for that I felt truly thankful.

I always associated churches with Christmas – a time of happiness and excitement. Sitting on the front pew, looking up at the statue of Jesus before me, I remembered a time when I was a small child, and my father came to see me sing a song as the Cheshire Cat in our school's Christmas bonanza.

My sister and I spent only a very short time in school. It was when my father had bought us a plot on a new Gypsy camp, Warren Woods, in West Sussex. Education for travellers was never considered important, especially back in the mid-eighties. But with the school board on our case, if we were going to stay in the area for a while the parents in the camp had no choice but to put us travelling kids in school.

One school, St Luke's, was willing to take us, though it hadn't gone down too well with the locals. But after an agreement to keep us away from the rest of the children for the majority of every school day, giving us a class of our own in the mornings with a special 'Gypsy trained' teacher, they were able to at least turn a blind eye.

The teacher, Mrs McAndrew, whose orange bird-nest

hair fascinated us, was keener on learning about us than actually teaching us anything, so our mornings were mostly spent chatting and colouring in pictures of Muppet babies, while she jotted down whatever she could glean of our language and tradition in a big notebook. To her and the school, we were Gypsy lab rats.

Being taught separately didn't stop the bullying or the fights at break times. It wasn't the children's fault; they were just bringing their parents' opinion of travelling people into the school with them. Our little group would always stick together and as far away from the other children as we possibly could.

In the afternoons we were sent to Mrs Kerr's class to learn with the other children. There were seven of us from our camp. My mother put my sister Frankie in as my twin, so that we would be kept together. We were with our cousins, Olive and Twizzel, also put in as twins, two Irish traveller sisters, Dolly and Colleen, who really were twins and whose accents were so thick that we could barely understand them, and finally the beautiful and terrible Jamie Lee Bowers – every teacher's nightmare, with a mouth dirtier than an old fishwife's. I adored Jamie Lee, who was the prettiest girl I had ever seen. While I sat silently, hoping no one would notice me, Jamie Lee was fearless, using the C-word in every sentence and farting violently at every opportunity. I thought she was amazing.

Mostly we hated school, and we certainly didn't learn much. But at Christmas the school plays would be put on, and I loved it. Our first year was 'The Twelve Days of Christmas'. My sister Frankie, Olive, Twizzel, Dolly, Colleen and Jamie Lee had been cast as all but two in the 'Eight Maids a-Milking' dance sequence. As a result, what was supposed to be a sedate little dance turned, on the night, into a Gypsy girl hoe-down, with the two 'odd' milkmaids running for their lives as the six others chased them in circles round the stage, before ending up in a great pile-up of Alice dresses with their milk pails on top of them.

I had been cast as a Leaping Lord, wearing a shirt of my father's and lying on the ground like a large rock as the school bully, Scott Leemer, leapfrogged over me. Just before we went on, he called me an ugly cunt, so rather than just lie there as I was supposed to do, every time he came back round to leap over me I bounced him off my back, sending him tumbling head first onto the boards. We ended up with our hands around each other's throats in the middle of the song, forcing Mrs Kerr and the headmaster to come onto the stage and drag us both off. All in all, it was not a success for the travelling kids, and the situation was only made worse by the howling and cackling from the back row where our mothers sat.

A year later Mrs Kerr, ever the optimist, asked if I would like to play the part of a wise owl in her latest Christmas masterpiece. Frankie and the girls had been banished to the chorus. Not that they cared; if anything it was an even better opportunity for sabotage, as they laid bets over who could put the word 'minge' into as many of the Christmas ditties as possible.

I was excited by my solo spot, and practised my song until I was word-perfect. On the night of our school performance, Aunt Olive, Uncle Tommy and my father came to watch. Or, at least, be there in time to take us home at the end of it. Our mother was unable to come: Henry-Joe was now a very excitable two-year-old, who was unable to sit still for the ants in his pants, and she had also just given birth to Jimmy.

I came on for my number, just after the real-life donkey that stopped to shit four times as it passed across the stage.

I was covered in paper feathers, I had cardboard wings and was wearing a pair of Granny Bettie's Nora Batty tights. I looked more like a trash heap than a wise owl. But still. I took centre stage and I sang my song, 'Memory' from the musical *Cats*. Mrs Kerr's idea, not mine. I had no real clue what the song was about, and now that I do, I am even more confused as to why I had to do it in an owl costume. But it went down very well; I got my first and last standing ovation. And right at the back, on his feet, whistling his head off was my father.

Frankie and the girls went off with Uncle Tommy and Aunt Olive, who were taking them to see *Snow White* at the pictures.

As we left the school, the smell of winter scorched my nose and the sky was already pitch black. My father and I walked out towards the car.

Mrs Kerr came chasing after us. 'Wasn't your son incredible, Mr Walsh?'

My father stopped and smiled. 'Yeah, he was really good.'

Mrs Kerr knelt down to me and took both of my hands into hers. 'Well done, little man,' she beamed. 'Right, I've got to go watch the Year Sixes,' she said, turning to go back in. 'Lovely to see you, Mr Walsh.'

I climbed into the passenger seat, and leaned back. The stars were already out, glowing like pieces of glass. 'What's the next show then?' my father asked. Next thing I knew, we were back out of the car, and sitting among the audience together watching the Year Six performance of *The Wizard of Oz*. The wicked witch made her entrance on roller-skates singing, 'I'm gonna wash that girl right outta my hair'. I loved every minute of it. And judging by his smile, so did my dad.

After an hour or so I slipped out of the church and made my way back to the car, where I coloured a squirrel in rainbow colours while waiting for Caleb to finish work.

When a car pulled up next to ours I leapt in shock – until I saw Caleb and his best mate David sitting in the front.

I waved to David as Caleb jumped out, opened the boot and took out my bag. He carried it over, placed it in the boot of David's Ford then jumped back into the front seat. David hadn't even turned off the engine and Caleb motioned to me to get in. I threw down the colouring book, jumped out and got into the back.

'Hello David,' I said, trying to sound cheerful as I slid across the fake leather seat.

'Hi, Mikey boy.'

'Hello, Cay. Where are we going?'

'Your dad came again today, Mikey. He's paid for a man to follow me. Tonight those men will be back again to look for you.'

'So what do we do?'

'I'm taking you to Leeds.'

My heart began to pound. 'Why Leeds?'

Caleb told me it was David's idea, and he had offered to drive us. I couldn't help but feel that David thought he would be doing Caleb a massive favour in helping him rid himself of me. Caleb explained that they would drop me in a street where I could get a cheap bed and breakfast for a week. Then I should get a cash-in-hand job, so that I wouldn't need a bank account or ID. He had cooked me a large shepherd's pie, which he had in a glass bowl, wrapped in clingfilm, at his feet. He picked it up, proudly, to show me. Judging by the size of the dish he had cooked it in, I would officially have more pie than luggage.

'I'm going to take a number from a phone box near where I drop you. I'm getting a transfer back to Newark in the meantime, so they can all see that I am not with you.'

'When will I see you?' I asked, feeling terrified that I was being deserted.

'I will call you a month from today at the phone box. By then you'll have turned sixteen and you can go to the police and let them know that you are all right. As long as you can prove you're safe and well and give them good reason why you ran away, they can't do anything else about it.'

My eyes welled up. 'There's no other way?'

They both spoke at the same time. 'No.'

'You want us to get through this don't you?' Caleb barked.

'Yes.'

'Good.'

Caleb pulled a large *A–Z* from the floor and started to give David directions as I hunched down in my seat and said a silent goodbye to Liverpool.

Two hours later we pulled up in a street of dingy stone-clad houses, many of them with bed and breakfast signs outside.

Caleb took me for a walk. 'Let's find a phone box, Mikey,' he said. Outside the bus station, a couple of streets away, we found several, well pickled with piss, but in good working order, and he took the numbers of two of them. Then he handed me fifty-five pounds and a little change. 'It's all I've got,' he said. 'It'll pay for a week's board with a bit over for food, and by then you'll have found work.'

We walked back to the car, where David was standing beside my bag.

'Remember what I said to you?'

I could almost taste Caleb's need to get away. He nodded at David, who started the engine.

'Now, you've got your money.'

'Yes.'

'You know the dates?'

'Yes. What if I don't find a job?'

'You *will* get a job . . . I know you will. Walk around today, ask on the building sites.'

I tried to smile, but it turned into a tearful whimper.

'Mikey, listen. If we're going to get through this, we have to go through the shit part first. Find a place to stay, find a job and if you get in real trouble, find a place called the Citizens Advice Bureau. Say it.'

'The Citizens Advice Bureau.'

He got into the car, winding down the window as he closed the door. 'In one month's time, this will all be sorted . . . I love you.'

I stood by my bag, clutching the pie dish in my arms as I watched the car pick up speed and vanish out of sight.

8

Alone

I had never believed Caleb would do this. There was a churning in my gut at the realisation that I had absolutely no way of getting in touch with him. The ball was in his court and, if he so decided, he would never have to see or hear of me again. Had he just dumped me here to rot?

Standing in the road in a trance, still staring after them, I didn't see the car approaching until a blast of the horn sent me flying onto the pavement – and in my panic I dropped the pie, which smashed and splattered. It was a good job I was yet to gain any kind of appetite.

I picked up my bag. Whatever happened, the fact was I had to get myself sorted out before the month was up, whether Caleb rang me at the end of it or not. I walked to the end of the street and started knocking on the doors of B&Bs, asking for quotes for a week-long stay.

'Eighty quid . . .' 'One hundred quid . . .' 'Ninety quid . . .'

After explaining that fifty was all I had, most people sucked in through their teeth and shook their heads. 'Sorry, love.' Others were blunter. 'You must be joking – I wouldn't give you the couch for that, mate.'

The last door on the street was that of the Claremont Hotel, a shabby pile of bricks with half its roof tiles missing and a worn-out canary yellow sign. The doorbell squealed like a pig several times before the door finally opened. A waft of putrid air hit me, as a heavily built transvestite in pink leggings and a red jumper decorated with pictures of kittens emerged from behind the door. She peered over my shoulder to see if I had come alone before inviting me inside.

'I've got two rooms, darlin',' she growled. It was a woman after all, vast and blond. All she needed was the horned hat and metal brassiere.

'I only have fifty pounds.'

'Sorry, darlin', but I can't do one for that. I could let these rooms go for at least a hundred a week.'

I stared at her in disbelief. I could see the threadbare carpets and yellowing wallpaper, and the smell made me gag. Yet the old bird had been going on as if I were standing in a five-star establishment.

'How about without breakfast?' I enquired.

'Without breakfast?' she squawked. She started counting her yellow fingers and muttering to herself. 'And you want to stay for a week, you say?'

I threw in a morsel to get her to bite. 'I hope that when I start my new job, I can stay on longer . . . maybe a couple of months?'

She hummed to herself, scratched her scalp and then disappeared into her living quarters. 'Be back in a minute, take a seat in there.'

She pointed towards a lounge area that was empty apart from a single faded blue settee that was occupied by two mangy felines. They stared me down as I walked through, licking their arses in between threatening glares and daring me to even try moving them. I stood in the centre of the room, listening through the wall as the landlady mumbled and barked at a husband she had hidden away in the back.

When she re-emerged she said, 'Fifty-five a week – no breakfast.'

It was two pounds less than I had.

'Thank you so much!'

We climbed the stairs to a small, scruffy room with the same yellowing wallpaper and faded furniture as the rest of the house. I didn't care about the state of the place; I was just relieved to have somewhere to stay. And with a real bed – after three weeks in a car boot any bed would be luxury.

I put down my bag, collected my key and made my way out. I needed to find a job. Fast.

For the next few hours I did the rounds of burger bars, arcades and shops. They all said the same thing. I needed a CV, whatever that was, a bank account, and experience.

The next morning, rested but desperately hungry, I remembered what Caleb had said about the Citizens Advice Bureau. I asked for directions and, after a long walk, found it.

Although they couldn't do much, the Bureau did tell me what I needed to do about locating a birth certificate in order to get some ID. I went to the local registrar and told them the name of the hospital I was born in and the date I was born. They chased up my birth certificate for me, and in the meantime I went to the Job Centre to get my national insurance number.

I was told that I had to wait for the next few days.

And in the meantime I was living on a couple of packets of instant mashed potato that I'd bought from the local food mart. I had not a penny left.

Three days into my first week I passed out in the shower. Hearing the bang, the landlady's Turkish husband came plodding upstairs to find me, naked and out cold on the bathroom floor. With a few good slaps he brought me round, helped me back to my room and brought me a large vodka and Coke. I told him I had been feeling ill. Not for a minute could I tell him that I was actually starving and exhausted.

I needed to find money. Any money I could. So, I swallowed my pride, went out into the streets, and begged for it.

Seven pounds into my begging trip, I spotted a familiar neon burger sign. Leeds Dyna Bowl.

I went in and dropped Caleb's name to the manager, a bird-like girl with tied-back hair, a large pecker of a nose and stalk-like legs. She had met him on a beer convention the year before.

'Oh my God, I love Caleb!'

After a bit of small talk about his drunken antics, she offered me a job on the spot. I would be sixteen the following week, and I could start after that. She told me her name was Jill, and handed me a form to fill in.

I had to confess to her that I couldn't read or write well. It almost killed me to say it, knowing that she would probably take back the job offer.

She looked at me in utter disbelief then, instead of throwing me out into the street for being so stupid, she got us both a coffee and talked me through the whole form, filling it in for me as we chatted. I was so touched by her kindness – but then we hit the next snag: I needed a bank account. Jill told me to go and get one, gave me a date to start work and said that I could pop in any time during the week with my bank details.

I left the Dyna Bowl and walked across the road into a high street bank. I waited for twenty minutes looking over at a buxom lady with backcombed hair, fake eyelashes and a purple neckerchief. I almost vomited with nerves when she called me over. I was sure she would laugh in my face.

'How can I help you?' she asked politely, as I sat before her desk. I couldn't think where to start, so I told her my whole life story. And we both cried.

Then, like a fairy godmother, she began to tap at her keyboard. She told me she could open an account for me, as long as I brought her my full address the next day. After that I would be sorted.

The next day I took the details in to Jill at the Dyna Bowl. She explained that I would have to work one week before I got my first pay. So I still had just over two weeks to go until I would see any money. And I needed to pay my rent.

'These are tough times, young man,' the landlady said, when I asked whether she could wait for the rent until I got paid. She wasn't unkind, but she said that she had been done over before by people staying there and had sworn not to let it happen again.

I sat in my room, on the edge of my bed. I had no mash left, no money, and two days until I would be out on my ear. There was nothing for it but to go begging again.

My line was simple and polite. 'Excuse me, I'm so sorry, but do you have any spare change please?' It wasn't as original as some of the lines other beggars used. Some would pretend they had been robbed, others would say they were short twenty pence for a bus fare. I just decided to look scraggy, be polite and hope for the best.

I had to get used to people looking at me as if I was something on the bottom of their shoe – that's if they looked at me at all. Most people would just grumble 'Getta job' or want to help me by giving advice but no money. I could hardly say that I had a job, but was waiting for some pay to come through. Then there were the people who would offer me leaflets on Jesus or Jehovah or whatever. The evenings when I made the most were when I kissed a couple of 'hens' in the numerous hen-night parties I came across in the city centre. They all chortled and said I was very cute, but it was also a dare to them, because I could have been a diseased crackhead.

I had to take the insults on the chin. I was desperate and I hoped – and was quite certain – that I would never see any of these faces ever again.

Two days before I started work it was my sixteenth birthday. I spent it begging, and celebrated in the evening with a bowl of instant mash, sitting alone in my room. I thought about my family, and about Caleb, and I felt my heart break. Where were they all now?

I managed to make my rent, but there was barely enough left for a meal a day. I was permanently hungry and had lost a ridiculous amount of weight. But at least my hair had stopped falling out. And when I started work I was given a mid-shift meal at the Dyna Bowl, which probably kept me alive.

I was so grateful to be working and off the streets. My first shift was spent scrubbing the floors, the fridges, and the whole front section that the customers looked at when they came to give orders. After that I learned to serve customers, make the burgers and clean the fryers. It was a quiet time, so I had two customers all day. Both at the same time and both requiring our special offer: burger and fries for a pound. Truth be told, the deal gave you about ten fries and a burger the size of a Galaxy Minstrel.

This Dyna Bowl was like a poor imitation of the brand-new one in Newark. It was falling apart at its 'circus tent' colour-schemed seams. And all the action that was supposed to be going on – the bowling and the bar – was in a different part of the building to my spot in the diner. I was yet to even see a bowling lane, which was on a completely different floor. I could hear it though. Around once an hour you heard the tumble of pins, confirmation that there was actually *someone* in the building doing something.

In the diner we had a few mocked-up fifties-style booths and a wide-open space of ripped carpet where a play centre for toddlers used to stand, before it became more danger zone than play area. Beyond the ripped carpet stood the Dyna Bowl's Sports Bar, covered in mock football trophies and signs that advertised Foster's lager.

Working behind the bar was a short fat girl who looked like Oliver Hardy, minus the bowler hat. Her name was Laura. And I knew straight away that she was a lesbian.

As we waited at our empty stations for customers, Laura and I spent hour after hour talking about everything except ourselves. But I knew what she was, and she knew what I was.

One night we were on the rotor to work together, catering for the local bank's staff night out. We had to prepare forty-two portions of deep-fried chicken and chips in a basket. Neither one of us had a clue how long it took to cook a frozen chicken leg, so we just drowned five chunks at a time in the vats of fat and guessed, then added extra time, just to be sure. Each piece finally made it onto the greasy piles of chips, but fried to half the size it should have been.

It was while we were both peering into an overflowing pan of chicken parts that she turned to me, smiled, and said, 'I know your secret.'

To which I replied, 'And I know yours.'

After that we opened up to one another. I told her of my escape with Caleb and where I had come from and she spoke of her three-year relationship with a sixty-year-old friend of her nan's. As the designated food-and-drink slaves, we created our own secret society away from the rest of the staff, who, to be fair, we barely ever saw.

There were five other staff: four 'small-town slags', as Laura put it, with bleached perms and a ton of dayglo foundation on their faces, and a totally bald sixteen-year-old who was shagging them all in shifts in the disabled toilet.

Then there was Jill, the assistant manager who had hired me, who was always very lovely, and would often spend part of her shift on our floor, chatting away with me and Laura while she scribbled out her stock-take. Jill dreamed of moving to Manchester to pursue a career in graphic design, which she had studied before economic circumstances forced her to take the job in Dyna Bowl.

The manager of the bar was Matt. He was so chunkily built that he looked as if he might be about to explode. We rarely saw him, since he spent the majority of his time hanging out with the bouncers at the bar next door.

After every shift, Laura would try to convince me to go and have a sneaky nightcap with her down at her local, a gay bar named The Clapperhouse. But in my financial state I was in no position to go out drinking. How do you explain to someone at work that you actually have no money whatsoever and have to beg for change after your shift to make the rent? I had just received a letter from the bank with my first bankcard inside it. Of course, with nothing in the account yet there was no point going to a cash-point to try it out.

I walked around the main town square at nights, politely asking for any change that people could spare.

One night I was approached by a guy who spotted me asking for change outside a theatre. He asked me if I wanted to have a drink with him for a tenner. The thought of earning ten pounds just for keeping someone company was amazing. I could have done with the coffee and conversation myself, since the only people I ever spoke to outside work were the ones I was asking for change. But of course I was being a fool. The drink, it turned out, was not in a bar but in his house, and I found myself running for his front door when he started taking his clothes off.

That first week was long and hard. I spent my days working at the Bowl, my evenings begging, and my nights trying not to think about how hungry I was. And then there was Caleb. Every hour I wondered if he would call me, if he was safe, if we would make it through together, if he would be proud of how hard I had worked to make a go of things on my own.

I could only wait and see.

At the end of my first week's work, Jill came down to hand me my wage slip. She gave it to me with a knowing smile. 'I knew you'd do well,' she said.

I opened the small envelope. My name was all typed out in bold letters, and below it, the amount paid into my bank account: one hundred and ten pounds. One week's rent and some money for food. With any luck I would never have to beg for my rent again.

I couldn't wait to go and try out my new bankcard, and actually draw out a chunk of my first ever pay cheque. I could finally buy more than a bag of eight-pence instant mash. It felt thrilling.

'Congratulations,' said Laura as she rushed into the kitchen, throwing her apron to the floor. She looked over my shoulder at the slip. 'Your first pay! This calls for a little celebration, I think.'

'What shall we do?' I asked.

'First, we're gonna go to the bank so you can use your card and I can get my money out before my overdraft does, then,' she winked, 'I'm gonna take you to your very first gay bar.'

I nodded, my eyes lighting up with excitement.

Could there really be places where it was OK – even a good thing – to be gay?

Laura whipped round the floor with the mop as I changed out of my Dyna Bowl shirt, put on my coat and we ran out the door. We went to the cashpoint, where she showed me how I could change my PIN to something I could remember and how to take out money. When that twenty-pound note came out, I felt so proud of myself. I had officially earned it . . . all by myself.

'Come on,' Laura grinned. 'It's time to party.'

From the outside, The Clapperhouse didn't look like any kind of bar at all. There was no sign – just a large door that opened on to complete blackness. Laura took my hand and led me down some stairs. As we got further down there were bursts of music and pink light flashed and crackled along the edge of the stairs. I had butterflies in my stomach as we pushed through the red double doors at the bottom to a burst of Carpenters disco remix.

Inside it was dully lit with a navy blue light that shone through the shiny glass bottles that rested at the rear of the bar shelf. Around the walls were several booths with dark red couches in them. As Laura ordered drinks for us, I looked around. The place was full of people and I marvelled to think that they were all gay, and all able to just be who they were. I had never believed I would actually meet another gay person, apart from Caleb. I couldn't wait to bring him here, to be in a public place where our affection towards each other would be fine, and he wouldn't have to fret or worry.

Laura passed over my pint and we toasted to officially being normal.

'Do you know any gay slang at all, Mikey?' she asked.

'Nope,' I said, laughing.

She leaned against the bar and went through pretty much every term she could think of. I was amazed, and so pleased to have my first 'gay lesson' over that drink. And Laura, shocked that I knew so little about anything, was delighted to be my teacher.

It was during a rundown on gay history that Laura spotted someone coming in, yelped and ran over to hug him. She brought him over and introduced us. His name was Simon Douglas and as I went to shake his hand, he pulled me to him and asked if I was an angel.

I laughed it off. 'I'm afraid not.'

As Simon went to order drinks, Laura explained that he was a popular face on the scene and a good person to know. He was also a drug dealer, and I was shocked when she told me he had supplied her ex-girlfriend with drugs and that while under the influence, she had killed herself. Laura clearly didn't blame Simon, but I couldn't understand her warmth towards him. I had never taken hard drugs – my only vices so far had been beer and cigarettes. But I knew about wanting to kill yourself and my heart went out to Laura's ex. As Simon and Laura chatted, I found myself feeling terrible for a girl I had never met. Brought to the point of death and now just someone's thirty-second story.

Simon said he was here to meet a friend and minutes later a tall slim figure appeared with a bottle of beer wedged between his fingers.

'Hello, all,' he said, before turning to me and taking my hand. 'I'm Tim'.

I was mesmerised. His hair fell about his pointed ears in thick black curtains and his face looked as if it were carved from ivory. He was the kind of glamorous man I had only ever seen in TV commercials. And he seemed to be interested in me, because as he sat next to me at the table, he put his hand on my thigh. I slid as far away from him as I could, but it didn't stop him. I had no intention of being unfaithful to Caleb. But I couldn't help being flattered. It was only later that Laura explained to me I was 'fresh meat': a new young guy on the scene, and fair game.

As we all chatted, Laura told them who I was and where I had come from. I felt worried. Had I said too much? I was on the run after all, and started to feel increasingly paranoid that I had given myself away and would be found by my father and his men.

I slipped out to the toilet to escape from Tim and to get my head together. When I came back, Simon said, 'Mikey, I've just moved into a new house, and I'm letting out a couple of the rooms. If you need a place to stay, you're welcome to have one of them.'

I smiled. 'Thanks, but I'm fine where I am.'

'You said your place is a shithole!' Laura piped up.

'It's fine,' I said. 'But thanks for the offer.'

'Do you want to come for a drink with us?' Simon said.

I felt it was time to make my excuses and leave. I wasn't sure I trusted Simon – or Tim. 'I've got to get up really early,' I said with a fake yawn. 'But it was really lovely to meet you both.'

Before I left, Simon pressed a silver business card into my hand and said, 'Call me if you change your mind.'

Gobsmacked by my first gay bar experience and feeling a bit more drunk than I thought I had been, I stumbled up the street back to the guesthouse, and fell onto my bed in a heap.

9

Caleb's Call

Four weeks had passed and the date of Caleb's call finally arrived. It seemed like forever since I had last seen or spoken to him. He was yet to hear of all I had been through, how I had found a job and a place to stay, got myself a bank account, my birth certificate and a National Insurance number. I felt I had done him proud and I couldn't wait to tell him about it all.

The worry that haunted me was whether he would actually call me. I couldn't even imagine what I would do if he didn't. As the hour of his call approached and I walked towards the phone box, my heart was pounding. I was twenty minutes early, just to make doubly sure, having worried that his watch might not be on exactly the same time as the clock at the guesthouse.

I stood leaning against the phone box smoking a cigarette and watching the buses going in and out of the bus station as people hurried past, dragging cases or clutching bags. There was a cold wind, so I wrapped my coat tighter around me as pigeons pecked at the chip-wrappers and fast-food cartons littering the pavement.

At eleven on the dot – the hour Caleb was due to call – a girl the size of a truck, in a velour tracksuit, pushed past me and wedged herself into the box, just as the phone rang. She picked up. 'What? Hold on.'

She stuck her head out of the box. 'Are you Mikey Walsh?'

'Yes,' I replied, holding out my hand for the phone.

She spoke into the receiver. 'You're gonna have to wait, cause I got a call to make.' And with that she slammed down the phone.

I screamed.

'Sorry mate,' she said, with a smug smirk across her fat cheeks. I was about to grab a pigeon and beat her over the head with it when the phone in the next box along rang.

I darted to pick it up. 'Hello?'

'Hello darling,' Caleb said, with a bounce in his voice.

'I love you!' I cried. 'I thought I'd never see you again.'

'Can't get rid of me that easily, Mr Walsh,' he laughed.

I was so happy just to hear his voice, and to have him refer to me as his 'Mr' in the familiar way he always did. For the next few minutes I garbled into the phone, pouring out my news in a haphazard stream.

Caleb laughed loudly when I told him I was working for Dyna Bowl and wearing the uniform he'd been wearing when we first met in Newark. But most of the time he was strangely muted and he said nothing of what he had been doing, or what had happened with my family or the people looking for me.

Every time I asked, 'How have you been? Has anything happened? Have you seen any of them?' all he would say was, 'I'll tell you when I see you.' His voice was distant, unemotional and almost cold. I became afraid that he was trying to protect me from some kind of hideous news. 'Caleb, you need to tell me right now, please. I need to know.'

He changed the subject. 'Sixteen now, aren't you, Mr.'

I sighed, realising that to get any information from him would be impossible. 'Yes, I am.'

'Well,' he said. 'I've got a surprise holiday sorted out for us to celebrate it.'

'Really?' I yelped.

'Can you get this weekend off?'

'Of course,' I said, knowing full well that I had been put down for double shifts on both Saturday and Sunday. I gave him the address of the guesthouse.

'I've got to go now,' he said abruptly. I had hoped that this conversation would last at least an hour. Sadly it had been barely ten minutes.

'I'll be up on Friday night, OK? I miss you, Mikey, so much it's killing me. I've got an amazing trip planned for us. Away from everything and everyone else.'

'OK.'

'Bye then, Mr.'

'Caleb . . .' I was desperate to keep him on the line.

'What?'

'I dropped the pie.'

He laughed. 'Never mind, I'll bake you another one.'

The phone clicked. He was gone.

I couldn't bring myself to go back to my room, so I walked through the city until I got to the river, and then I followed it past wharves and blocks of flats until I came to a grassy space with a bench, where I sat down to have a cigarette.

A few minutes later an old lady with horn-rimmed glasses and dyed red hair sat next to me.

'You look like you're thinking very deeply there,' she

croaked, digging into her bag and pulling out a large tuna baguette. 'Always liked to sit here, lovely view isn't it?' she said, pointing to where the river snaked into the distance.

'It really is,' I said, with a sigh.

'Full o' shit though, this river,' she chuckled.

I let out a laugh. There was something so refreshing about hearing an old biddy swear. It made me feel I was amongst my family again. She tore her sandwich in two halves and passed one to me. 'Here, eat that,' she said with a nod. 'You need to build up your energy.'

I didn't know what she meant, but I accepted it politely and took a bite. We sat on the bench in silence, enjoying the solace of one another's company, looking at the river as geese cackled overhead and tugs chugged by.

I thought of my family. Where were they now? Were they all right?

I stared into the river. I had been frightened of water ever since I was nine when we had been taken on a trip to the seaside at Chichester and I almost drowned. My father had swum so far out into the distance that I could no longer see him. His body rippled up and down through the waves like a great sea monster. I couldn't swim, but I tried to follow him, feeling the sand falling away from beneath my feet. I was up to my neck when a mighty wave hit me and the water swallowed me whole, dragging me beneath it. I panicked as the water consumed me and as I grew tired of struggling, I went further and further down, until my body was cradled in the sand below. I stared up at the light for what felt like an eternity, listening to the water flow around and through me. It was my father who lifted me from the water and rushed me to the shore. I could not respond, but I could see everything that was going on. I saw the panic-stricken faces of my mother and my aunts as a strange man breathed life into my mouth. Then suddenly a surge of energy shot through me and I sat up, vomiting a bucket of water into my lap.

It was the last time I ever went in the sea and afterwards I wouldn't even get in a bath. As the years passed my phobia of water escalated so much that I have become convinced that the way I'm going to die is in a watery grave. It's a phobia I've yet to get over, and until I do, I will always look on seas and rivers as if looking death in the face.

Remembering this incident always used to make me certain that my father really did love me. I knew he did. It was only shame that had stopped him from being able to admit it. It was no surprise to me that he had put out a reward for people to hurt me. I had proved him wrong. I had taken myself out of his grip and left behind a lesson to be learned by all travelling men who tried too hard to make their child into something they could never be.

Caleb might think my father a monster. Anyone hearing my story might think it too. But my father was a great, great man. And despite his anger and shame, I knew that he loved me. At nine I had already failed him in many ways. If he didn't love me, if he really felt all the terrible things he claimed to feel towards me, then he would have left me to die in the sea long ago.

Friday came and I had yet to find a way to get time off work. I didn't have the courage to phone in and put on a 'sickly' voice. So I went in on Friday morning, ran to the bathroom, shoved my fingers down my throat and then went straight to see Jill, while I still had the look of a sick man on my face.

'Oh my God, you look terrible,' she sympathised, stepping out from behind her desk to rub my back. 'Go home and get some rest and call me when you're feeling up to coming back.'

'OK,' I whispered, milking the moment for all it was worth.

I hobbled out of the Dyna Bowl as far as the security cameras could see me, then picked up my pace, running as quickly as I could through the town and back home, where I bounded around my room with excitement, knowing it would only be a short time before I would see Caleb again. And not only that, but he was taking me on holiday!

I had no idea where it was going to be. At this point I was yet to board anything bigger than my father's lorry. I'd never been on a train or a plane, though as kids we used to spend hours parked up watching the planes take off from Heathrow. My mother had an obsession with planes, just like the one I had with water. She loved to watch but she was sure that if she ever got on one, it would crash and burn.

I showered and changed. I had bought a brand-new polo shirt and jeans in the Top Man sale and I had shaved every part of my head, minus a long fringe at the very front, which I had gelled up in electric-shock spikes. I felt it was a good look, and I couldn't wait for Caleb to see it. After a last check in the mirror I packed my rucksack and stuck on some Randy Crawford, then sat on the sill of the window in my room, looking out for Caleb's little orange car.

It was early summer but tiny drops of rain tapped against the window and a chilly wind blew the last of the blossom from a candyfloss pink tree across the street.

I was desperate to know what was going on. Why had Caleb refused to tell me anything over the phone? I hoped and prayed that he did not have bad news. As his car pulled up outside, I grabbed my bag, and rushed down the stairs.

'Hello, Tin-Tin,' he laughed, as I hugged him.

I climbed into the passenger seat, absorbing the familiar smell of leather and cheap aftershave. I looked at him – his face had healed and he looked well. 'So?' I asked, as he drove out of the city. 'How are things?'

He looked back at me and winked. 'All right, Mr, all right.'

I leaned against the window and lit a cigarette. 'You have to tell me sooner or later, Caleb,' I said.

'What do you mean?' he said. 'Everything's all right.'

'Caleb, I'm not being funny, but you have to fill me in on what's happened with my family and the people following you. I need to know.'

'Mikey, I'm sick to death of talking about the fucking travellers. Every fucking day of every fucking week, all I get is fucking traveller talk and, to be honest, I'm sick of it and I'm sick of them. I've come up here to see you and I don't want to spend one moment wasting my breath on a load of idiots.'

I felt furious. How dare he keep me in the dark?

And how dare he talk about my people in that way? 'Don't you ever talk about them like that . . . ever. They're my family and I want to know what's going on! I've been driving myself mental thinking about it, and I have a right to know. It's not up to you to shut me out.'

He was silent for a moment, then he asked me to open his large blue sports bag that was on the rear seat. Inside was a padded envelope that had been opened and stuck back together with tape. My name was on the front. I tore it open. Inside was a blank cassette in a blank case. I took it out and put it into the tape deck. It hissed for a few seconds, and then came the distinct sound of a tap tap tap, and a throat clearing. I knew who it was before she said a word, and something cracked inside me.

'Dear son. I just wanted to tell you that I knew . . . I know. I could see you were unhappy, my baby. I hoped, so much, that things would change for you, my boy. But now you've gone.'

Caleb looked blankly out at the road as I choked back tears. I could see her sitting in front of her stack system recording herself, just as she used to with Frankie and me when we were kids. She was calm and collected, but between the lines, in her long pauses, I could hear her pain.

'They're coming for you, you know? He's put the word about this morning. He's offered five grand to the man who catches you. And I'm frightened. I'm scared to death they're gonna find you. And what do I do? You think I don't understand, don't you? You think I don't know what it's like to be lonely, unhappy, trapped. I do . . . and I know you . . . because you're a part of me. I want so much for you to be happy . . . I want so much for you to live a life that's full of everything you've ever dreamed of . . . but I dream . . . I wish . . . I wish so hard that I could have you back in my arms . . . just one more time. I want you to be a child again . . . I want to be able to start again.

'You'll always be my little boy. And as much as you try to change . . . you'll always be what you are . . . you're my little boy . . . my little travelling boy . . . I wanted to do this message as a birthday present for you. Because I love you, Mikey.'

I could hear her tears through the hiss of the tape.

'How many years will I have to wait to see you again? You can keep yourself out of my sight, Mikey . . . but you'll never keep yourself out of my heart.'

And with that, the tape clicked and she was gone.

I sobbed into my sleeves.

Caleb placed his hand on my leg. 'I didn't know whether to give it to you or not.'

I was shocked that he would even contemplate keeping my mother's voice from me. 'Why would you keep that from me Caleb?'

He looked at me for a split second, then turned back to the road. 'Because I knew it would make you feel like shit.'

'How did you get it?'

'She gave it to me. Now that I'm back in Newark she's been coming into the Dyna Bowl every other night. She waits till your father leaves for the pub, then she drives down. She's been sitting with me, asking me things.'

He went on to say that she would tell him what she knew of my father's plans to track me down. She would speak of her worries for me, and her fears, and she would ask him about us. Not about whether we had any kind of romance, but simple things about what I liked, what kind of things made me smile. But Caleb stuck to the story that he knew nothing of my whereabouts.

On my birthday she had been in to see him again. She said to him that as the only person in her son's life who ever made him really smile, she was sure he would hear from me again. She gave him the envelope for me, 'Just in case,' she said.

I couldn't say a thing. I was so angry that he had even considered keeping all this from me. I turned to the window, focusing on the scenery, my mind overflowing with thoughts.

'I feel so fucking horrible,' he said. 'That woman loves you so much. The guilt, Mikey . . . the fucking guilt; to sit there night after night and lie to her was awful.'

I picked the envelope back off the floor and shook it over my lap. Out fell a small gold chain and a photo. It was of me and my mother, her arms wrapped tightly around me, on my eighth birthday. The day I received the greatest present I had ever been given. You could see in the picture, from my big gappy-toothed grin and red eyes, that I had been crying with the sheer joy of receiving it. I was holding a tiny puppy in my arms. My first and last pet, a scruffy little Jack Russell that Frankie and I named KC – an abbreviation for a name that sent a shock wave through school when we stood up in assembly to speak about our pets.

We had spent the morning of my birthday peering through the window as the rain poured down in great buckets from the sky. It crashed against the tin roof of the trailer like gunshot, and the whole plot began to fill with hundreds of tiny dark brown spots. And as we peered through the waterfall that ran down the windows, we could see that the brown spots were moving. Tiny toads, the size of a fingernail, were crawling and hopping all over the ground outside.

'It's raining frogs!' Frankie screamed.

'Don't be silly,' our mother said, rushing over to take a look, holding Henry-Joe in her arms.

With a look of utter disbelief, she stared at the little creatures. Whether they had fallen from the sky, or crawled out from every nook and cranny, they had arrived – and there were hordes of them.

As the clouds parted and the rain stopped, Olive, Twizzel and Jamie Lee swung open the gate and came running to call for us to come out and play. By the time I had got my coat on, Frankie and Jamie Lee had already decided that they were going to start a toad hospital, for all the ones they could find that were injured. It wasn't a hard job, since Olive and Twizzel, in their matching Little Red Riding-Hood coats, were already stomping on several of the toads and gathering them up in their pockets.

I grabbed a bucket from under the trailer and started to help out. Meanwhile, Frankie and Jamie Lee had put together a contraption that would make doubly sure that the toads they were taking into their 'hospital' were actually injured to start with. Jamie Lee had removed one of her shoelaces and Frankie tied it to a little wooden toy train cart that belonged to Henry-Joe. Once attached, the piles of toads were emptied out of the girls' pockets and my bucket and they would place one toad at a time inside the cart. Then, grabbing the end of the shoelace, they would spin the cart around in the air as fast as they could, with only the pressure of gravity keeping the toad in his seat, before slamming it hard to the ground. The result: one petrified toad, ready for hospital and recovery.

After that they wrapped each toad in little squares of toilet tissue and placed them in a line in the 'ward' along the back of Frankie's Wendy house. After about an hour or so, the frogs that were petrified but not actually crushed would be released into the huge mud pile that loomed over the back of our fence. 'Released' meant they would be catapulted over to it, hopefully landing safely and regaining their freedom. The ones that didn't survive the crush, the whirling or the hospital ward, were mummified, also in toilet tissue, and buried in the newly established Toad Graveyard.

This game continued right through until tea, for which our mother had prepared a small banquet of burgers and lemonade under the trailer awning. Exhausted from their nursing duties, the girls tucked in, as my mother came in with a burger with a candle in it. Gypsy boys usually never had a full-on birthday party, presents, cards or a cake (those were for girls), so the burger was a substitute, and I was happy that we were all together and having a good old feast.

My mother had put on an eighties Cliff Richard CD, which Frankie and I loved to sing along to, just as my father came back from work. 'Happy Birthday, boy,' he said, rubbing my head. He was covered in tar and had been working non-stop since he had conned his way into getting a full-page ad in the local directory without even paying for it.

We finished our food and made our way back outside, to find that all but one flat and very dead toad had discharged themselves while we were on our break. Jamie Lee, feeling rather low about the escape, decided it would be a good idea to dig up the dead ones just to check if they were still there. Strangely, one of them wasn't, and another, that we had managed to find a matchbox for, was completely recovered. Twizzel claimed that this toad had to have been the Jesus Christ of toads, since she was certain she had stomped him good and hard before putting him in there.

As the girls carried on digging, an old Ford Estate pulled up in front of the gates and out climbed a chunky girl with jet-black hair. In her arms she was holding a small bundle. She pushed the gate open with her shoulder before making her way to our trailer. We all ran over to investigate and before I could wipe the mud from my knees, all the girls were already inside, making baby noises and sighing loudly. 'Is it mine?' I could hear my sister shouting over and over, raising her voice a little bit more every time she was ignored.

'There he is,' said my father as I stepped inside. 'Your mum got you something.' Before I could ask what, the visitor advanced through the gang of girls and stretched out her arms to me. She was holding a tiny black and white puppy, all wrapped up in a tea towel.

'Take her then,' grinned my mother. The girl dropped the bundle into my arms, causing the tiny thing to make a little squeak. I nestled it like a baby as a silence fell in the awning.

'It's not fair!' screamed Frankie, running by me and out into the Wendy house, screaming her head off all the way. Through the silence, all we could hear was Frankie beating it down from the inside, in a rage.

'It's for you,' my father said, looking out of the window and laughing at Frankie's reaction. I looked at my mother, my father and the girls, in total shock. Then I looked down into the eyes of the little dog that looked back up at me, and I started to cry. I had never, in my whole life, felt so overwhelmed with happiness as I did in that moment. 'It's mine?' I asked with a crack in my voice.

'Yes, you big fool,' said my mother with a laugh.

I looked down at the little puppy again, unwrapping her from the tea towel and holding her tightly in my arms. Knowing that it was not looked upon very kindly if I ever shed a tear, I hid my face in her coat as I cried.

'Well,' said the girl. 'I better go, me dad's outside waiting.' She walked to me and gave me a kiss on the cheek. 'Happy Birthday, Mikey,' she said, stroking the puppy one last time before leaving.

The girls all gathered around the new arrival, patting her as she licked our hands and wagged her stumpy tail. After taking some photos with my new puppy, I took her outside to the Wendy house. Frankie's tantrum had calmed to a mere tirade of swear words, which wasn't too far from her usual self, anyway.

'What do you wanna call her then?' I asked. And in her fury, she blurted out the name that stuck for good.

After that, Frankie instantly brightened, chuckling at the speed of her own wit. We spent the next hour listening to Madonna's 'Dear Jessie' on repeat, as the girls were positive Katie Cunt found it relaxing.

10

Trailer Heaven

I shook myself back to the present as Caleb drew into a motorway service station where we bought cigarettes, a couple of pasties and a bag of jelly babies for the second leg of the journey.

'Where are we going, then?' I asked him.

Caleb gave a cheeky grin. 'I'll tell you now if you really want to know.'

I was never good with surprises, so of course I said yes. It turned out that the company that owned Dyna Bowl also ran a resort down in a place on the Welsh coast. As Dyna Bowl employees, we got a cut-price deal for a trailer with telly, heating, coastal walks and plenty of local pubs to visit.

'So . . . we're going on holiday to a caravan site?'

'Yup,' he said, and grinned. I had spent my entire life bar the few weeks I'd lived in Leeds living in different trailers and now, for a break, I was going to be spending a long weekend re-visiting the travelling life. I had to laugh. And Caleb was very pleased that I got the joke. Only it wasn't a joke. As we pulled up inside the gates, I just couldn't believe my eyes. He returned a few minutes later with our trailer keys, in actual tears from laughing so much.

I took it quite well. I was excited at the fact that I could have a little dip back into my roots, only this time with Caleb rather than my sister, who had a tendency to freak out and sleepwalk in the middle of the night.

In the centre of the camp was a complex with a swimming pool, a bowling alley, an army of children carrying cheap teddy bears, and their parents, swigging back pints.

'You think there's a gay bar in there?' Caleb laughed.

Somehow I thought it was more likely that there would be a big fire and a stake that they burned people like us on, somewhere between the coconut shy and the bar.

The inside of our trailer reminded me of the first one I ever lived in: veneered in fake wood, with the curtains, the bedding and the couch all shades of psychedelic orange and brown. The television stood in the centre with a coat hanger stuffed into the top of it.

Caleb unpacked as I set up the bed, then we gathered up our funds and headed into town for supplies. As we walked along the beachfront we smiled and joked in a way that we hadn't for months, and I didn't care where we were. All that mattered was being here together, without a soul around who knew who we were. No hiding, no jumping into bushes, no darting into nearby shops – just us, together.

Caleb made a pact with me not to talk about any of what had happened while we were there, and the pain of missing my family, I chose to keep to myself. There was nothing Caleb could do and it would only make him feel even more guilty.

For the next couple of days we just talked, ate, slept, watched TV and walked on the beaches. It was bliss. Caleb had bought a TV guide and a copy of the *Sun*, and he made me read each article and listing out to him.

After no more than two years of schooling in all, my reading was not good. I could recognise words such as 'and', 'cat', 'sat', 'on', 'the' and 'mat' and I knew my alphabet, so I could sound out simple words. But I had problems when words like 'night' and 'through' appeared. I just couldn't get my head around them at all. Caleb sat and wrote down every single word he could think of that had one of the crazy combination sounds within it, showing me that there were many words that used the exact same pattern. I still struggled, but I was determined to learn to read properly.

I must have bored Caleb half to death with question upon question about words and meanings, because he quickly became a very keen napper. Every afternoon he would be out for the count from 2 p.m. right up until seven. During this time I'd sit in the lounge of the trailer, looking out of the window beyond the sea of caravans and down to the seafront. The weather was terrible – the rain hammered against the tin walls, and the winds rocked the trailer back and forth – but I didn't mind. Although I had begun to get used to living in a place with a staircase and stone walls, I would never give up the love I had for the travelling life. As Caleb slept, the trailer rocked us like a cradle. No house could ever give us that feeling of sailing in a boat upon dry land. What Caleb had seen as a prank turned out to be just what I needed. I couldn't speak of my home to him. I couldn't speak of my family to him. But right here, as he slept, I could reflect upon what I was. The person within me that, no matter how much education or knowledge I absorbed, I could never shake off. I am a Gypsy. And I am very proud to say that I am.

Caleb had brought me two presents. One was a long, Inspector Gadget-style trench coat that he had got from a catalogue, and the other was a pager. I wasn't sure at first whether it looked more like a calculator or a bomb. It was a solid square lump of see-through plastic with two red buttons and a calculator strip across the front.

Caleb sat next to me and explained exactly how it worked and why it was the ideal present. The idea was that, no matter where I was, he could always leave me messages. He would call a number for the pager, leave me a message, and a few minutes later, it would scroll across the strip for me to see and read. I was over the moon to know that I wouldn't need to worry about having to set days and times to be able to talk to him. Caleb could simply page me whenever he was free to talk, and I could run down to the phone box. What I didn't realise at the time was that it would only work one way. He told me it was one step back from the mobile phone that neither of us could afford and I thought it was a wonderful present.

Caleb popped out to get us some groceries while I had a shower. As I got out, the pager beeped and there was my first message: 'I love you more than you'll ever know'. It was almost magical to see it scrolling across, like the adverts in Piccadilly Circus, and it made me smile.

Our time together in the seaside retreat came to an abrupt end a day early when Caleb got a phone call from one of his staff. My sister and her husband had been in with two other travelling men asking where he was and a staff member let slip that he had gone away on a long weekend break. Suspecting that he was with me, they had begun questioning, offering bribes and calling on anyone who knew Caleb.

'I've got to get back before anything else happens,' Caleb said, his face furious as he threw clothes into his sports bag and kicked at cupboards. It was then, in his frustration, that he started to tell me everything that had been going on, not to me but in a furious soliloquy to himself.

I learned that because word had got round about the five thousand pound reward, everyone who had ever known anything about him was jumping at the chance to pass it on. So much information had poured in that my father couldn't decipher the truth from gossip, so he had hired a private detective to follow Caleb. Not only had Caleb been trailed night and day, wherever he went, but the detective had found a girl who looked like the one in the photo I had left behind with my note, living only seven miles from Newark centre. Some poor girl out there, who had nothing to do with me, was being followed and photographed. It seemed that my father was throwing his money away to people willy-nilly, but there was not a single person who was able to supply him with any direct information.

As he ranted about being followed all the time, I realised that everything he had been through was taking a huge toll on him mentally. I just prayed that, with no solid information, my father would eventually give up and back off. We grabbed our things and left, barely pausing to pay the bill on the way out before heading back towards Leeds.

I asked Caleb if he thought we might have been followed to the holiday camp.

'No,' he said.

'How do you know?' I asked him.

He punched the roof of the car and screamed, 'Because I fucking know, all right?'

I couldn't really argue with that. As we drove along the motorway, his heavy breathing was louder than the music that blared from the cassette player. I felt it best not to say a thing because I was sure even one word or question would tip him over the edge.

After an hour or so of me chain-smoking nervously through the silence, Caleb, in a very direct tone, started a conversation to divert him from his thoughts.

'Made any mates then?'

I told him about Laura and how she had helped me with using my bankcard and had taken me for a drink after work.

'That's nice,' he smiled.

I chatted on, telling him the story of her girlfriend's suicide.

'She's a lesbian, then?'

'Yes,' I answered.

'So you went to a gay bar with her?'

'Yes. Perhaps we can go there before you leave tonight.'

I started to tell him about the place, but he pushed his hand in my face, cutting me off. 'I don't want to hear it. And I don't want you ever to go out with that girl again.'

'Why?' I asked, bewildered.

'I don't know her, and I don't like you going to those kinds of places without me there with you,' he said. He pulled over onto the hard shoulder of the motorway, switching off the ignition before turning to me. 'How many times have you been?'

'Just once,' I said.

He stared at me silently. 'You're a liar; I can tell you're lying to me.'

He could see I was hiding something from him, but given his mood, I didn't think it would be a good idea to tell him about meeting Simon and Tim. 'I swear, Caleb, I went there with her once the other week. We had a few drinks and that was it.'

'Did anyone chat you up?'

The halt in my breath was confirmation enough for Caleb. 'I can't believe it,' he screamed, before pounding his fist several times on the dashboard, his thick Irish accent getting broader as his anger rose. 'I can't fucking believe it. I've been going fucking mental and you've been out making new friends and chatting up men in a fucking gay bar!'

I tried to reassure him, but he wasn't having any of it. I told him how much I had missed him, how much I loved him, how it wasn't right being there without him, how much I longed for him to come with me, so that we could be open together without people judging us. But it wasn't enough. As we drove, he ranted and battered his hands against the steering wheel, sending a shudder through me with every thud.

I promised him that I wouldn't ever go again. He ordered that not only should I not go to a gay bar, I should not go anywhere at all with Laura. I would see her at work and that was it.

I agreed.

When we got back to Leeds we pulled over outside the Claremont. 'Are you coming in?' I asked.

He was so angry he couldn't even look me in the face. 'No,' he shouted.

I had barely closed the passenger side door before he stomped his foot on the accelerator and was gone.

I trudged up the tatty stairs, dropped my bag down in my room and sat on the bed. I hated myself for upsetting him so much. I could only hope that next time he came to see me, he could meet Laura and see that she was a very sweet and fun girl to be around and she cared about me as a friend.

I took myself down to the Dyna Bowl to tell Jill that I was OK, and maybe do a shift, just to save myself from sitting alone and thinking about what had happened. Not just about Caleb's terrible mood, but the worry that he would be hurt again, or I would be found.

Laura was rushed off her feet when I arrived, juggling the diner and the bar area and, for once, we actually had quite a few people in, all wanting cheap food and beer.

'Thank God you're here,' she shouted from the bar. I leaped the counter into the kitchen to dish up three burgers that she had cooking. We cleared the rush of customers, and then she came to join me.

'So?' she grinned. 'How was it?'

'Good,' I smiled back. 'Really nice.'

Laura looked at me with wide eyes. 'Is that all I'm getting?'

I forced a laugh and shrugged. 'That's all there is. He

came, we had a lovely time, and he bought me a pager for my birthday.'

On my way home that night I found three messages on the pager. The first said, 'I'm gonna phone the box in ten minutes.' The second said, 'Where are you?' And the third said, 'I knew you would do this to me.'

I didn't know what to do. I wasn't allowed to call his work and that was the only number I had for him. I could only wait for him to send another message. It was now past one in the morning, but I was afraid to leave the pager for even a moment, just in case he sent a message. Fully clothed I lay on the bed, staring into the blank screen, until eventually I fell asleep.

It was five o'clock the next afternoon when I finally got another message asking me to go to the phone box. No sooner had I picked the phone up than he began to blast me with a catalogue of rules that I had broken. I tried to explain that I had been working and hadn't got the messages until I was on my way home, but he didn't believe me and I felt distraught.

Caleb came back to see me three days later. It was midnight when he arrived, his black hair glistening as the light from the street lamps rolled over him, and he stayed for only an hour before he had to go back to Newark.

When he parked the car I went out to greet him. He didn't reciprocate, just said, 'Go up and get your coat,' as he locked the car. He said that we should go for a walk. What I hoped would be a romantic stroll around Leeds turned out to be a mission to find the numbers of convenient phone boxes in the area. He entered each one as we passed it, writing down the number and location in a little Filofax© he had in his coat pocket. Once he had all the numbers he needed we headed back to the guesthouse, but he didn't come in. I sat with him in the car park as he explained how he was going to be able to keep a watch over me and make sure I wouldn't be able to miss a call from him again. In future, when he wanted to call me, he would first phone my work. If I wasn't working, then he would page me and I'd have ten minutes to be at the phone box at the bus station, or one of the other phone boxes we had passed.

It was insulting and unfair. He wasn't going to take my word for it that I was being loyal to him. I loved him – I had never loved anyone as much. But he had started to change towards me. He was unravelling before my very eyes. I could only do as he asked and hope that he would come back to me, that things would somehow work out, that despite everything, we had a future together.

After his fleeting visit, just to check up on me and tighten my shackles, he left.

As the days passed, Laura would frequently ask if I was up for a drink after work, or a look around the shops, or even if I'd like to go back to her house to watch a video with her housemates. I said no, and told her I was seeing Caleb pretty much every other day. The truth was, I was spending my evenings alone, waiting for him to page me. How had it come to this?

11

Under Arrest

Feeling in need of cheering up, I decided to go and buy myself the latest Mariah Carey CD as a belated sixteenth birthday present. It was a few weeks after our weekend away and Caleb was coming up that evening for our first night out on the town together. I was excited and looking forward to introducing him to my friends. I was also desperate for him to see that I wasn't doing anything to undermine our relationship.

After buying a copy of the CD in Woolworths, I went into a high street chemist to see what cosmetic samples were on offer. My mother always used to say to us, 'Moisturise every day, and you'll never age.' And though most Gypsy men wouldn't dream of using beauty products, I had always loved watching on as my mother went through her routine as if she were in a Max Factor commercial.

With my CD and pager in the pocket of my new Inspector Gadget coat, I wandered the shop floor, picking up and sampling the tester pots of pretty much every product I could get my hands on. After around thirty minutes of browsing, I decided to head home. But as I walked through the main doors, I was accosted by two hefty men, who grabbed my arms as one of them snarled, 'Not so fast sonny.' I was convinced they had been sent by my father and were after the reward. My heart pounded as I struggled and screamed my head off. But the men dragged me back into the shop, and I realised they were a security guard and the shop manager, who had been watching me and was convinced I had nabbed a load of products.

As people looked on in horrified fascination, I was marched through the shop and upstairs into an office.

'We've watched you on our screens for the last thirty minutes, filling those pockets of yours with everything you could get your hands on,' the grim-faced manager said. 'So you're going to stay up here until the police arrive.'

'But I've got nothing!' I exclaimed, pulling out the CD and the pager.

'Well, what's this then?' the manager said triumphantly, waving the CD in my face. The shop had a music section, although I hadn't even been near it.

'I bought it before I even got in here!' I shouted.

But he was having none of it. 'We'll see about that, won't we?'

There was nothing I could do – he wasn't about to admit to being wrong. In shock, not even comprehending that the key to my release – the receipt that I had tucked into the CD case – was within my grasp, I sat silently until two policemen arrived and marched me out of the store and into the back of a police car.

I had been in the same police station only ten days earlier. Caleb had phoned to say that I should go and report myself alive and well because my mother had told him that all sorts of crazy stories were beginning to circulate, including that I had been seen dressed as a woman, I had fathered the baby of a local girl who was claiming her child was mine, and even that my head had been found in a bin after a psychopath had murdered me. My mother knew that these rumours were all ludicrous but she told Caleb that if I proved I was fine, all the stories would die down.

Now that I was sixteen the police couldn't make me go back. I was entitled to do as I wished, providing I had a roof over my head and was safe. I wasn't keen on the police – no Gypsy really was, as our experience of them was mostly not good – but I plucked up my courage one evening after work, walked into the station and announced that I might be listed as a missing person.

I sat in a tiny grey room with two sympathetic policemen and told them all about my life, showed them my scars and explained why I had to escape. I begged them not to report my whereabouts back to my father. They asked if I had done it all alone and I said I had. My only lie. After giving them details of where I was now working and where I lived, I was told I was free to leave. Their only advice was that I check in with them regularly, stay out of trouble, and take care of myself.

Three days later, Caleb called me at work. He told me that my mother had been to see him to tell him that she had heard I'd reported myself safe at a police station in Leeds. The police had not kept their word and my father and a couple of other men had already taken to the motorway to come and search for me.

The news hit me like a strike from a Great White and

I sank to the floor of the kitchen. 'That's it,' I howled. 'They've found me.'

Laura came running and, alarmed by my frenzy of tears, she panicked and sent for Gary the general manager to come and help calm me. He marched into the kitchen and picked me up in a fireman's lift, taking me out through the diner doors and up into his office, where he sat me down, handed me a tissue and asked me what was going on. After wiping my eyes and taking a deep breath, I told him everything, even though I was sure I would probably lose my job as a result.

When I'd finished, Gary passed me a cigarette. 'Listen to me, Mikey,' he said. 'I've heard from everyone here how hard you've worked and how much you put into this job. If anyone comes in looking for you, they won't get past me and the boys downstairs, I promise you.'

I was astonished. I had expected that he would think I was more trouble than I was worth. I grinned. It was a real comfort to know that my manager, in his smart suit and tie, was just a bruiser of a bouncer at heart. Even though I knew that he and the security guards couldn't stop a bunch of travelling men if they tried.

He told me he thought it would be best if I went home and came back the next day, and he was more than willing to have one of the security staff walk me home if I wished.

I declined, but thanked him all the same for being so kind. I could only hope that they wouldn't turn up – or if they did, that it would be when I wasn't on duty.

For the next couple of days I constantly looked over my shoulder, and tried to stay out of sight as much as possible. Then Caleb phoned to say that my mother had told him my father and the rest of the group had only stayed in Leeds for one night. They didn't have an address for me, so they'd started going into every bar, restaurant and shop, with a photo of me – until my mother told my father that she thought I would be too sneaky to report myself safe in the very town I was actually staying in. She convinced him I must really be living somewhere else, and saved me once again.

Now here I was, heading back to the police station for the second time in a fortnight.

As we pulled away in the police car I broke down, trying to explain through my tears that I had done absolutely nothing. But they said that if the manager was sure I had stolen from his store then they had to act on it.

I was put in an open cell, along with a drunken tramp who looked like the Penguin from the Batman movies. A policewoman asked us both to empty our pockets and remove our belts and shoelaces and place them in the bags she gave us and then we were put into separate cells. I did as I was told, while the Penguin sang 'The Wind Beneath My Wings' at the top of his lungs throughout the whole process.

I was escorted to a small room with no windows and a large iron door. A mattress on the floor was the only place to sit, and the only sound was the annoying buzz from the neon light high up on the ceiling. I sat on the mattress and pictured my father, already on his way to collect me, and Caleb's fury with me for getting myself into this mess. I just couldn't understand why no one would listen to me.

For an hour I waited and fretted, before the two policemen who had brought me to the station collected me from my cell, took my fingerprints and then took me to another small room where I was asked to remove my items of clothing and pass each one to them as I did. Embarrassed and humiliated, I stood awkwardly in my pants as they searched the pockets and linings of everything I had.

After that ordeal was over I got dressed and was escorted back to the cell, while they waited for an interview room to become available. Three hours later they came to escort me to my interview. As the door opened, I expected to see my father, and I was almost sick with fear. But there was just a tape recorder on a desk, three chairs and something bulky on the floor, under a blanket.

After a short explanation of the recording process, one of the policemen pressed the record button and announced the date and my name, before holding up the CD and asking where I had got it. The receipt for the damn thing was inside the case, and after I had shown it to them, there was absolutely nothing more to say on the matter.

I sat silent, expecting a 'thank you and goodbye', but to my surprise they lifted the blanket to reveal a box they had brought from my room back at the guesthouse. Inside were three large bottles of alcohol that Caleb had bought when we went on the trailer weekend. I had put them under the sink for when he visited.

The police wanted to know how a sixteen-year-old would have several bottles of spirits. I wondered what this was about, since I was perfectly entitled to keep alcohol if I wanted to, although not of course to buy it.

Then I realised that they thought I might have stolen the bottles from work. I explained that I had a friend who lived in another town and who had bought the bottles for himself, since we didn't have a lot of money to go out drinking.

'Is he the one in the photo?' enquired one of my interrogators.

I was shocked. I had a bag of photos under my bed. Some were family photos of my mother's that I had brought with me as keepsakes and others were jokey photos of me, Caleb and some of his friends on nights out in Newark. I couldn't believe that the police had gone through all my things. Had they found Caleb's love letters to me? I felt ill, but I kept calm.

'Yes, that's Caleb,' I said.

'Is he a good friend?' asked the other policeman.

'Yes,' I replied.

'Is he a special friend?'

I decided to appear as stupid as possible and pretend not to get what he was hinting at. 'Yes, he's a special friend.'

We stared one another out for the next few moments. Finally I broke the silence by asking what all this was about, and why I was still being kept there, since it was clear that I had absolutely nothing on my person that was stolen.

I was informed that the guesthouse I was living in was well-known to them as the landlady had been harbouring criminals for a number of years. My address, it seemed, was not only a hellhole of a B&B, but was also black-listed for having housed some of Leeds's most notorious thieves and drug dealers. The only resident I'd seen was the man who lived in the room next to mine. I had also smelled him. A waft of putrid air was emitted every time he opened the door to go and use the bathroom we shared. On one occasion he had even left his false teeth on the floor of the shower. They looked like a cluster of rotting popcorn. I had thought he must be the worst of my fellow lodgers, but clearly I was wrong.

Eventually the police told me that I was free to go, but they wanted to keep the bottles of alcohol, to check with my employers and see if they were missing from the stock.

I collected the Mariah Carey CD and the pager and left. There was no apology, no offer of a lift home, and no explanation as to why the last time I was there, and *gave* them my address, they had said nothing about it being a den of criminals.

Shocked and upset, I made my way home. I got back twenty minutes before Caleb was due to arrive, to find my room had been ransacked. My mattress had been thrown to the floor, my photos scattered all over the carpet and just about every single thing that wasn't bolted down had been thrown around the room. It was as if a cyclone had passed through. I felt sick. The whole awful experience had left me feeling worthless, victimised and dirty.

I couldn't bring myself to clean the mess or get ready for Caleb's visit, and I was most definitely not in the mood to play the CD. I sat on the windowsill and smoked one cigarette after another, as the sky darkened.

An hour later Caleb's car pulled up outside. 'My God, what happened?' he said when he saw the room.

I explained, but he couldn't understand why they would ransack my room when they had taken me in on suspicion of theft, and shouted at me as if I was a naughty six-year-old.

Next thing I knew, we were in the car and on the way to the police station. Like an angry mother, Caleb yanked me from the car, across the car park and up to the reception, demanding to see the two officers who had taken me in. One of the interviewing officers appeared and went to shake Caleb's hand, but he ignored it. He said that the alcohol was indeed his, and they had absolutely no right to confiscate it or to have kept me in the station for most of the day, when I had done nothing wrong. Within ten minutes we were back in the car with the bottles of spirits on the rear seat.

Once in my room, Caleb poured himself a very large whisky as I tidied up. His mood was dark and I kept as quiet as possible. I noticed two raised blood-red patches on the side of his head; it was clear that he'd had another visit from the travelling men, but we didn't talk about it. When he saw me looking at his injuries he scowled. 'What?' he said, through the bottom of his glass.

I could tell by his tone that *anytime* was not a good time to ask about it.

12

Heartbreak

At first, the idea of having a pager had seemed great. But I was beginning to understand the real reason Caleb had bought it for me: he wanted to control my every move. He would call me at work, and if I wasn't there, he would page me. From that moment I had fifteen minutes to get myself to a phone box for his call.

Mostly he didn't page me during the day, when we were both at work. But at night he paged me frequently, checking up on me to make sure that I wasn't going out. My social life with Laura had ended as soon as it started, and after that I didn't go anywhere. But Caleb didn't believe it, and he would page me at one, two or even three in the morning, expecting me to get to the phone box. I began sleeping fully clothed, just so that I could make it on time.

The green-eyed monster had started to take him over. And the more it consumed him, the less I was able to speak openly to him. It wasn't enough to assure him that I loved him. He was convinced that I had made a friend of someone who wanted to separate us. This person existed only in his imagination, but nothing I said could persuade him to trust me. As he saw it, I could get on with my life while he was being harassed, followed, threatened and physically attacked. On top of that, he had to lie to my mother, who was still visiting him most days.

I wasn't living the fun life that Caleb imagined – far from it. I went to work and spent almost all the rest of my time sitting in my little room tense with anxiety, watching mind-numbing TV, eating junk and missing him. But compared to what he was going through, I was still the lucky one. Caleb was under such pressure that it was destroying his life – and his sanity too.

I did everything I could to reassure him and go along with whatever he wanted, hoping that it would help, but things were getting steadily worse. In the past he had always looked at me so lovingly, but now the love in his eyes was turning to hate and I began to fear that he was disgusted with himself for getting mixed up with a person like me.

'Why didn't you tell me it would be like this?' he would ask.

I had no answer. I felt terrible. Because he was right, I should have known what my father would do, I knew, after all, what he was capable of. I loved Caleb more than anything in the world, but I was starting to wonder if we could survive what was happening.

That night we had planned to go out together for the first time in Leeds, to a local gay pub. And despite the miserable events of the day, we decided to go anyway. I hoped it would lift the mood. When Caleb had agreed to go out, I had been so excited about us being together in public, at last. So as Caleb poured himself another drink, I gelled my hair up into spikes and put on an electric blue polo shirt I knew he liked.

The pub was ten minutes away. As we walked I talked about my awful day, but Caleb was silent, his mind elsewhere.

The Grapes of Wrath was a bit like the Rover's Return from *Coronation Street*, only with inflatable sex dolls and posters of orange men in shiny pants stapled all over the walls. Inside were no more than a handful of people, while behind the bar a chinless girl wearing army-fatigues watched a soap on the oversized TV screen as she munched through a packet of Scampi Fries.

I sat at one of the small wooden tables while Caleb went to get the drinks. As he waited I watched him in the mirror over the bar. Silent and morose, he was in his own world. When he got to the table I attempted to be as upbeat as possible, making funny comments about our surroundings. Caleb picked up his beer, took a sip and turned to face the window. I took his hand and asked if he was OK.

'Why wouldn't I be?' he replied, pushing my hand away.

I ignored the gesture and ploughed on, telling him how wonderful it was to have him here for a whole two days and how much I'd been looking forward to it all week.

He gave me a cold stare, then got up and went to the toilet.

While he was gone the barmaid came over and handed me a beer mat. 'This is for you,' she said.

Someone had written on it, *To the green-eyed boy. I find you very attractive. I'd like to buy you a drink. If you're interested, lay this on the table, if not, you can throw it away.*

Surprised, I looked around, and spotted the culprit: a portly, forty-something guy in a beige business suit, sitting at the side of the bar, looking my way.

At that moment the mat was snatched out of my hand by Caleb. He read it, looked over at the man, turned on his heel and strode over to him. He grabbed the man and threw him to the floor, then began to stuff the beer mat into the poor guy's mouth as he screamed for help. I jumped up and tried to prise Caleb off the horrified man, while the barmaid ran for the bouncer, who pushed me out of the way, grabbed Caleb and hurled him out into the street.

Caleb marched ahead as I chased him along the pavement back towards the room. I had never seen him in this state before. He had never been a violent person and I was frightened. When we got into my room he poured himself a whisky and knocked it back in one as he stared into the mirror above the basin.

'What's happened to you, Caleb?' I said. 'I only had to tell the guy I wasn't interested. Why are you being like this?'

Caleb dropped the glass into the sink, spun round and grabbed me by the shirt. 'You!' he screamed. 'You and your fucking lies, and your fucking family are what's wrong with me. You have NO IDEA what I've done and what I've had to go through to get you here, to your comfy little job and your new little friends. You've ruined my life!'

He dropped me to the bed and turned back to the mirror. I didn't want to hear what he was saying, though I knew that all of this had been hard on him too.

Unable to contain myself any longer, I lost my temper. 'I left my family for you, I left my whole life for you and I can't ever go back. Do you think I'm having fun? Do you think I don't walk around here every single day, pining for you, worrying to death about what might be happening to you, and all the time, feeling like a complete stranger in this town? And now you're punishing me, with your endless pages and calls in the middle of the night and your silent treatment.'

He turned and pushed me. 'Shut up.'

I was angry and pushed him too. 'No, I won't.'

'Shut up right now, or I'll make you.'

I had to do the stupid thing and get the last word in. 'You can't make me,' I whispered.

And with that, Caleb grabbed me, and with one hand round my throat, began punching me. I hit him back but I had lost a dramatic amount of weight over the previous couple of months, and at that moment I realised just how weak I had become. All I could do was wait for him to stop. When he did, I was bloody and bruised.

As soon as he had stopped, Caleb was in pieces.

'Oh my God, I'm so sorry. What have I done, Mikey? I don't know what's happening to me. I never wanted to hurt you.'

He was desperate to make amends, to bathe my cuts and bruises and have me forgive him. But as I lay in bed dazed and aching, his words seemed to bounce off me. I would survive the beating – I had survived so many in the past. But what was happening to Caleb shocked and frightened me. He had never been aggressive before. When we first met he was the most gentle, tender and affectionate man I'd ever known. But the events of the past few months had transformed him into someone I felt I didn't know: a man who was moody, unpredictable and angry. Often I would look at him, hoping to see the old Caleb, the one who teased me and gave me a cheeky grin, the one who loved me and looked at me as though I were special. But I couldn't see that man any longer. And the more irritable and morose he became, the more anxious I became. I was afraid of upsetting him, afraid of his cruel comments and angry silences. Now his anger had erupted into violence. How could we ever get over that, or go back?

The love between us was dying. I knew it, and it broke my heart.

The next morning, to apologise, Caleb went out to the pet shop and brought me back a lovebird, a little beauty in rainbow colours, in a bell-shaped cage. He said it was a token of how much he loved me, but I couldn't help suspecting that it was just another way to keep me occupied while he was away. Apparently this lovely little thing could be trained to perch on my finger, eat out of my hand and even speak. What a mug I was to believe that! I spent a whole week trying, but I couldn't even put my finger in the cage without him biting it as hard as he could. He was like a miniature pit-bull, and each time I had to prise him off me by flicking him as hard as I could in the face.

Every morning, from six till nine, he would screech and chirp the iconic music from the shower scene in *Psycho*. I had to leave the room after the first hour, to avoid going demented. When I told Caleb, he said I just wasn't patient enough, and lovebirds were known to be wonderful pets. 'Maybe he just needs a partner?' he said. That afternoon I went down to the pet shop and picked up a friend for him. Not another lovebird, because I couldn't afford one, but the next best thing: a plastic budgie the same size, with a weight on the bottom that made it jerk and wobble around if it was touched.

I went home and attached the little friend to the perch while Damien (no lovebird was ever more aptly named) hung back in the corner of the cage, waiting to pounce. As I stepped away, he climbed up to investigate. He chirped politely, slowly sidestepping closer and closer to his new plastic friend. He went to curl around him, as lovebirds do, but the plastic bird leaned in the opposite direction. Damien paused for thought, then went back in for another go, but sadly every time Damien touched him, his plastic friend gave him the cold shoulder. Increasingly frustrated, Damien began laying into his new chum, pecking at its fixed little face and sending it spinning round and round the bar. I couldn't help but laugh out loud. After the injuries he'd inflicted on me, I had to admit that I was kind of enjoying his little temper tantrum.

As the days passed, I kept trying to make friends with him, but Damien wouldn't give in, just as he never gave up trying to befriend the plastic budgie, who by now had only half a face and seemed to hate Damien even more than I did.

Caleb came to visit and didn't believe for a second that I had been trying to train him. And he laughed when

I told him about the morning *Psycho* music. 'You take him then!' I shouted. 'See if you can do any better.' Two weeks later, Caleb told me that Damien had driven his whole family crazy, and he'd had no choice but to let it out into the wild. I couldn't help but ponder on how well he'd survive out in the big wide world.

I had been in Leeds for three months and Caleb was unravelling more and more each day. The stress and torment he was still getting back in Newark was destroying him, his family, and us. He was being eaten up by jealousy, convinced that if he wasn't with me, I was with someone else, and he was having increasingly violent outbursts, frightening me and himself. I usually gave as good as I got, but I never started the violence and I was so sad that the love I'd treasured and believed in could become so ugly.

After each episode Caleb would seem calmer – but not for long. Every time he came up to see me he would promise to get his demons under control, but he was fighting a losing battle. Just walking down the street became hazardous. It only took one half-decent-looking guy – or even girl – to pass by and he would ask, 'Were you checking them out?' Of course I wasn't and I would always say that I hadn't even noticed them. But he would be convinced that I was sharing glances with strangers. We would eventually go back to my room, where he would hit the drink, begin to cry, talk about ending it all and then, because I 'wasn't supportive enough' of what he was going through for me, he would get angry. There was nothing I could say that would calm him or save him from the 'other place' he went to in his mind.

The bruises got harder to conceal. One day, when I arrived at work with a nasty black eye, Gary said that he had no choice but to send me home, because it didn't look professional having a guy who looked like he liked to get into fights working behind the food counter.

The messages from the dreaded pager got more and more frequent, and I constantly had to run down to the phone box, just to reassure him. It was in a 3 a.m. call that, after yet another visit from some travelling people, he flew into a rage and said that I had always lied to him. He used the fact that I had kept my real age from him against me. 'How could I ever trust you, when I know what a liar you are?' he said.

Time after time I forgave his anger because I knew it came from his frustration at our situation. But after yet another midnight rant at me for not warning him how things would be, I finally lost my temper. I told him that I loved him, but I could no longer deal with his anger towards me. I explained that ever since he had dropped me in Leeds I had done everything that he had asked me to do, even dragging myself out of bed two, three or four times a night, just to answer his calls. He had to change this behaviour, because it was destroying us both. He fell silent. Then he began to cry, and I hated myself. Not because I had hurt him, but because for the first time, listening to him cry, I felt nothing.

He promised to come up at the weekend and prove to me that he was going to change. Of course, I had heard it all before. But this was the first time I had ever given him an ultimatum. Perhaps this time things really would be different. He told me that he wanted to meet Laura, go to a bar with her, meet her friends, see how I lived and stop trying to keep me locked away. As I walked home from the phone box I hoped, with all my heart, that he meant it.

That Saturday night, as Caleb had promised, we went to the gay bar and met Laura, who was with her two friends, Bev and Gail. I was so happy; I was desperate for them to like each other. We lasted all of fifteen minutes before Caleb was ranting at Gail for flirting with me. Gail was a very butch lesbian, with absolutely no interest in me whatsoever, but she was, as many lovely people are, very tactile. A huge argument broke out and Laura began to spout home truths about our relationship, sending Caleb into a frenzy.

Unable to physically drag him out of the bar, I left, and he followed. We made our way back to my room and once we got there, Caleb hit his bottle of whisky. I sat and watched as the very last of his sanity unravelled before my eyes. How could I save him now? It had become clear that the part of him that hated me for ruining his life had overwhelmed the part that had any kind of love for me.

I knew this was it. The end of our brave, defiant, desperate love-against-the-odds relationship. And it was my fault. Caleb should have known better than to get caught up in a world which he knew nothing about. But I should have told him more about it. I knew my people. I knew my father. Now we were losing what we had fought so hard for. Sadness overwhelmed me. Caleb was no longer the man I fell in love with, the man who loved me enough to steal me from my people, to risk everything to have me with him, to teach me how to live in his world and make me a part of his life.

He told me he wanted to finish his whisky then head down to the river and finish himself off. He could no longer deal with what was happening to him. When he dropped the bottle at his feet, clutching his head in his hands, I picked it up and started to pour the contents down the sink.

He snatched it from my hand and smashed it across my head.

Dizzy and reeling with pain, blood pouring down my face from a cut above my eye, Caleb and I began to beat into each other with every bit of anger and strength we had left.

My body must have gone into shock, because I couldn't feel a thing except the burn of the blood that filled my eye.

I thought of my grandfather's prophecy that I would be the one to fail the family line, and how I'd wasted my life trying to prove him wrong. He knew all along there was something not right about me. I couldn't cut it as a Gypsy man, not even as a Gypsy boy.

I thought of my father, his brothers, my grandfather and every man I had ever had to put my hands up to and fight. All for a family name and my father's honour. Not mine.

I thought of my father's curse. 'You'll never be nothing, you'll never amount to nothing. You'll live off me for the rest of your fucking life.'

He thought he had beaten everything out of me. But I had told him I would have the last laugh.

And there and then, lying in a pool of blood on the floor, as Caleb slammed his fist into me, I proclaimed *myself* a King of the Gypsies: the one who was brave enough to turn my back on them, without even knowing a thing about the world I would find myself in.

I made it.

Me.

Caleb smacked down on my collarbone and pain seared through me.

Mikey Walsh: the sickly, mollycoddled, whimpering, effeminate, pathetic people-fearer.

I was drowning in my own blood. But I knew I would get back up.

13

Moving On

We had been on such a journey, Caleb and I, but there was no hope left for us now.

After his anger was spent he wept and apologised, but I was beyond hearing him.

We held one another and sobbed.

'I don't want to leave you,' he said. But we both knew there was no choice.

'Take care of yourself,' was all I could say. To say goodbye was beyond me. I loved him so much that, despite everything, I was afraid I would always regret this parting.

As he walked out of the door he turned to me and said, 'Remember, Mikey, no one will ever love you as much as I do'.

I watched from the window as he started the car and drove away, and my heart broke. I stood there for a long time before turning and limping painfully into the shower, where I stared at the cyclone of dried blood running into the plughole.

With Caleb gone I would no longer have any news of my family. From here on in it would just be me.

I didn't go to hospital. I didn't want to be asked questions. I nursed my injuries alone, in my room. And I threw the pager into the bin. I had been beaten up so many times in my life, and I had never been to hospital. That wasn't the Gypsy way. Not for my family, anyway. We just ignored most injuries until they healed. My mother would try to help things along with one of her famous poultices or remedies. She fancied herself as a witch. It made me smile as I lay in bed that week, willing myself to get better, forcing myself not to give in to the feelings of heartbreak, to think of the time she rubbed a slug into Frankie's warts. She reckoned they were the revenge of a toad Frankie had stepped on. She was amazed when it didn't work.

A week after Caleb left my room for the last time, I decided I was ready for a new start.

I pulled Simon Douglas's card from my drawer. He had offered me a room to rent and I was sorely tempted. I couldn't wait to get out of this place that was so full of agonising memories. But I wasn't sure I trusted Simon. Laura had said he gave her girlfriend drugs. I had never taken drugs and didn't plan to. But Laura had also said he was a nice guy, and he had been friendly to me. I decided to take a chance. I walked down to the phone box, and called him.

'Hi Simon,' I said, as chirpily as I could. 'I don't know if you remember me but I was wondering if you still have a room free?'

'Of course I remember you, Mikey. And yes, I've still got a room. You can move in today.'

Ten minutes later I was on my way back to the guest-house to say goodbye to the landlady, pack my bags and make my way round to my new home.

Simon lived a good half-hour's bus journey away, and

by the time I got there it was growing dark. Before I rang the doorbell I checked the address I had carefully written down. This was it. A tall, white house in a middle-class street of respectable terraced houses. There was a tree in the front yard, full of fairy lights, and the house had a red front door.

The doorbell gave an ever so polite chime. As the door opened I heard a cheer coming from Simon and Tim, who were in the kitchen popping champagne corks. Out from behind the door peered a tiny boy, around my age, with a face that appeared to have years of worry etched into it. His hair was white blond, brushed into a little 'Mr Whippy' shape on top of his head, and wedged behind his ears were two enormous hearing aids, in flesh-toned plastic. Holding onto the door and staring at the floor, he held out a shy hand.

'Hi,' he said quietly. 'I'm Harry.'

I reached out, grabbed his hand and shook it enthusiastically. 'Hello, Harry, I'm Mikey. Do you live here too?'

He raised his eyes. 'I moved in today. Simon's a friend of my sister and I've come to Leeds to go to college.'

'Let the boy in, for Christ's sake,' shouted Simon.

'Sorry,' Harry muttered, opening the door wider and backing himself in behind it so that he vanished from sight.

I wiped my feet on the doormat and, wide-eyed, took in Simon's astonishing home. The walls were high and painted in brilliant white, with white carpets, a white staircase, and a vast crystal chandelier that hung down from the top floor to the hall below.

I turned and closed the door, but Harry remained squashed against the wall. 'Are you OK?' I asked.

'Yeah, I'm fine,' he chuckled as I pulled him from the wall and we made our way down the hall and into the kitchen. Purest white, with black wood surfaces, spotlights and hanging copper pots that seemed to contain bunch after bunch of lucky heather. At the end of the kitchen sat Tim and Simon at a black table, already halfway through a large bottle of champagne.

'Welcome,' Simon said, and smiled, pouring me and Harry each a glass. After we'd drunk a toast he showed me to my room. White – of course – and simply furnished; it was a thousand times cleaner and more elegant than the room I had just left.

'Harry's across the hall,' Simon said. 'The rent won't be high, I'll charge you forty pounds a week, but in return you and Harry do the cleaning and some cooking.'

'Fine by me.' I grinned, wondering if he would be interested in trying the pig's head stew my mother had learned to make from her father. We used to have to eat jam roly-poly afterwards to take away the taste. Or there was my midget Granny Ivy's speciality, known as Joe Grey: swede, onions, animal fat, chicken, beefsteak, pork and liver, all shallow-fried and served up with crusty bread and, in my father's case, the ladleful of salt he added to all his meals. Looking round at the lovely room that was now mine, I realised I had already come a long way from Granny Ivy's trailer.

I soon settled into Simon's house and became good friends with Harry, who had a sweet-natured and gentle personality. The two of us would put on loud music and dance around as we did the cleaning. All those years watching my mother busy in the trailer with a duster and her Marigolds paid off after all. I smiled to myself, thinking about how hard she tried to teach Frankie to be domesticated. Frankie should definitely have been the boy. She was solid as a tree, kicked like a donkey, and was about as much help to my mother as a wooden bar of soap. I, on the other hand, while being a failure as a good Gypsy man, took to domesticity like a natural and was in my element doing my Doris Day routine around the kitchen.

Simon owned a clothes shop in town, although he didn't seem to spend a lot of time there. He had inherited money and always had plenty of it, so he didn't really need to work. He liked to take recreational drugs but he never offered me any, and I was glad of that. I began to realise that, while people would ask him for drugs because he had a steady supply, he wasn't a dealer and he wasn't interested in making money selling them. He would just get drugs for people as a favour. While I lived there, I never got involved in the drugs side of things, and as a landlord and friend Simon was a nice guy.

Tim didn't live in our house but he was around a lot. He lived and worked with his partner, a much older man, in a local hotel, but he never talked much about it and we never met his boyfriend. As for Harry, he never did start college. He said he had changed his mind, and he went out and got a job as a shelf-stacker in the local supermarket.

A few days after we moved in, Simon and Tim invited

me and Harry to come with them on a night out around the Leeds scene. I was delighted to have company and a social life after months of being practically housebound because of Caleb's jealousy. I was also grateful for the distraction from my own thoughts. My life was getting better, that was for sure, but I couldn't stop wishing that it hadn't turned out this way. This wasn't what I'd had in mind when I abandoned my family and my culture.

But I threw myself into the plan. Harry and I spent the whole day getting ready for it, digging through Simon's wardrobe while listening to the *Rocky Horror* soundtrack. Amongst the piles of Gaultier and Westwood, I found a T-shirt of Simon's that at the time I was convinced made me look gorgeous. It was skin-tight leopard-print Lycra. Yep. Hideous.

Meanwhile, Harry made the decision that he was going to completely change his image, now he was living away from home. For starters he decided to dye his hair post-box red. As he pranced about with the towel on his head, he marched into my room, yanked the two honking great hearing aids out of his ears and threw them on the floor, before stomping all over them.

He seemed quite certain that when the towel came off, his thinning blond hair would have transformed into locks like Nicole Kidman's. But he must have picked up the wrong box of dye, because it had gone from Warhol white, to SpongeBob SquarePants yellow. But he was pleased, so I told him it looked great.

As we entered The Bar with Simon and Tim, Harry and I grabbed each other's arms. I had been in a gay place a couple of times before, but never as a single guy.

This was officially the beginning of my life as a gay man in the Gorgia world. As we swept through draped tinsel and inflatable hula-girls, Harry's grip got tighter. 'I can't believe I'm actually in a gay bar,' he whispered.

'You'll be OK,' I answered, squeezing his arm back. 'Let's just not leave each other and we'll be fine.'

Harry said nothing, and after a second I realised it was because he wasn't watching my lips move. It suddenly dawned on me that the little guy had just destroyed his only mode of hearing.

As the drinks flowed, my confidence grew. It was just the boost I needed. We all joked, laughed and danced along to track after track of incredible eighties standards. Harry was perfect company; we shared the same music taste, were moved by exactly the same songs, and mimicked each other's gawky dance moves.

During the chorus of an Annie Lennox track, I looked out across the sea of heads. Everyone looked so happy, so incredibly free to express whatever they wanted, without comment or judgement from anyone. And suddenly, my wonderful mood fell away. I missed Caleb. I had found somewhere I belonged, yet I couldn't have felt lonelier. I didn't know how I'd ever be able to stop thinking of Caleb and couldn't help but ask myself where he was now. I wondered if he was still being hounded and if he would ever be able to think of me without regret. I just hoped that one day the pain would go away. And in the meantime, I would have to find a way to live with the decision I had made. I would dance even harder, smile even wider, and do just as Annie Lennox told me to and 'put these wings to the test'.

After The Bar, Simon and Tim said they would take us to the Cockpit, where pretty much everyone out on the scene ended up. The club was only a five-minute walk away, but Tim and Simon warned us that after eleven on a Saturday night, Leeds was not a safe place for gay people, because of the number of lager louts and stag parties wandering the streets.

We flagged down a taxi and then stopped at a cash-point, where Simon and Harry jumped out to get some money. Simon grabbed his cash and made a dash for the back of the cab, just as a group of seven half-cut men swaggered around the corner. As Harry typed his numbers into the cashpoint, the group piled up behind him, making crude gestures and falling around laughing.

'Oh hell,' said Tim, winding down the window. 'Come on, Harry, leave it, I've got some money.' But as Harry turned around, the group of men closed in on him, pushing him back against the wall.

'Here we go,' groaned Simon. Harry reappeared, making towards the cab, before two of the men pulled him to the ground by the back of his shirt. As Simon and Tim shouted for the men to leave him alone, I jumped out of the cab, ran to Harry, pulled him up from the ground and practically catapulted him into the back of the cab.

As I turned to get into the cab, I was spun round and punched, hard and flat, on the bridge of my nose. My nose had already been broken several times before, including – I was pretty sure – a couple of weeks earlier by Caleb, so it was not in the best of shape, but this one hit sent it spattering right out of its joint and off to the side of my face. I fell backward against the cab as three men from the group all jumped on me at once, laughing hysterically as they punched my face and ripped my 'faggot's shirt'.

'I got him, John,' cheered one of the crew, laughing like a hyena, 'look at the fucking faggot's face. I gotcha,' he laughed, 'I fucking gotcha!' He leaped about as if he had just won the lottery, while two others continued to punch and kick me up against the cab and Simon, Tim, Harry and the cab driver shouted abuse from inside it. As my head turned from side to side, I could feel the joint of my nose swinging as if it were hanging off my face.

Through the punches I could see the guy who had done this to me. And once he was in my reach, I leapt onto him, grabbing him by his ears. 'I may get beaten to death tonight,' I thought, 'but I'm going to kill you first.' And with that I began to headbutt him in the face, over and over and over again. With every hit from my forehead, I could feel his teeth bite, his nose squeal, and his cheeks flatten beneath it. I was more furious than I had ever felt before. My looks might have been beyond repair, but I would be damned if this guy ever went home to tell his friends about the night he and his mates beat up a bunch of faggots. As the other men crawled all over my back and pulled at their friend to get him loose, I tightened my grip on his ears, nearly pulling them off his head, as he screamed and gurgled.

The next moment, a gang of policemen appeared from nowhere, prising the man from me and taking hold of the others, throwing them down on the pavement and against nearby parked cars.

I howled as two police officers tried to calm me down. One of them, a tall man with a red beard, said that he had seen what had happened and I had every right to press charges against the group.

Right up until the moment they were piled into a police van and taken away, they continued to hurl drunken homophobic abuse at us. Simon, Tim, Harry and the cab driver all climbed out of the car, each more than willing to give their accounts. The tall policeman asked if I would like a lift to the hospital, but I was just so overwhelmed with fury and sadness: I was still doing what I hated most – fighting.

'It's OK,' I said. 'I just want to go home.'

As the others stayed to give their stories, Simon and I got into a police car and were dropped back at his house. I was in agony, and didn't say a word all the way there. As the car pulled up to a halt, the police officer gave me his card, telling me that these people should not be allowed to get away with what they had done and that I should really think about pressing charges, while they were all still being kept at the police station.

Simon unlocked the front door and I made my way up to my room and crept over to the full-length mirror that Harry and I had propped up against the wall earlier that day, while getting ready for our big night out.

I looked at my face. It seemed that every scar I had ever earned in my life was highlighted in that moment. So many scars . . . so many stupid acts of violence that had done this to me. My nose had become an unrecognisable mound. My eyes had already started to bulge and darken from the impact, and my forehead was covered in tiny pockmarks from the teeth of the man who had done this to me. I had tried so very hard in my life to avoid violence. And yet somehow, even in the place where I had gone to escape it, the spectre of it still caught up with me time and time again.

Simon walked in quietly and sat down on the bed. He had changed into a tracksuit and was carrying two large cups of coffee. 'Are you all right?' he asked quietly.

I nodded, still facing myself in the mirror. After everything that had happened – the fights with my father, the fights in the playground, the fights with man after man wanting to beat me to a pulp just for being me, not to mention the beating I had received from Caleb . . . I came to the conclusion that this was who I was. This man that I was looking at in that moment was the man I was born to be, and no amount of beauty treatments or haircuts were ever going to disguise that. I was Mikey Walsh, the son of a great fighting man. And I would never escape it. A tear rolled down my face, but I wasn't going to cry any more. There was no point. I was brought up to know that to cry was a sign of weakness. And so I tightened my throat, held my breath, and wiped it away.

'Come on,' said Simon, standing up. 'Let's go to the hospital.'

'It's OK,' I said, reaching for the coffee. 'I'm going to leave it.'

Simon turned me to him, placing a large hand on each shoulder. 'Listen, Mikey, get your coat, because I'm going to call us a cab and we are going to fix your nose.'

'No, that's all right,' I answered. 'I deserved it.'

Simon's voice reached a pitch that could have broken

glass. 'What? You listen to me, Mikey, what you did tonight was nothing short of amazing, and I'm not going to have you walking around for the rest of your life knowing that your face was ruined by a bunch of fucking homophobic bastards on a crappy night out. If you don't come downstairs immediately and get in a cab you can just move out right now, because I couldn't look at you for making such a foolish decision.'

I was so touched. 'You'd really throw me out?' I asked, and despite my injuries, I smiled.

'Yes,' he answered. 'I do NOT have ugly friends. Now get your coat on.'

Simon sat with me the whole time in accident and emergency, telling silly jokes and quoting lines from *Absolutely Fabulous* until it was my turn to go in. When the nurses came to wheel me through to the operating theatre, he walked by the bed as far as he could. The nurses above my head laughed and joked with me, making light of the whole situation, which was exactly what I needed. 'It's not the first time it's been broken,' I said to the doctor, who prodded it around. 'Well,' she smiled as she stuck in a needle and asked me to count to ten, 'maybe the little sods have done you a favour, eh?'

The next thing I remember is being wheeled back into the ward, where all three of my new friends and Laura and Jill from the Dyna Bowl were waiting, with a bunch of bright yellow roses, tied in a red bow. Each of the group leaned in to give me a kiss. Harry was last, and he whispered, 'Thank you.'

As Tim retold the story to the two girls, with fully animated gestures, Simon stood in the background and gave me a knowing wink. I was so grateful that he had been there to talk me into going to hospital. For the first time, away from home, away from Caleb and away from everything I'd known before, I felt I had found a family here. And it was absolutely wonderful to have one.

14

A New Nose

After a few hours in the ward I was released back into the wild with a large fibreglass 'duck beak' over the bridge of my nose that they said had to stay on for two weeks. When I turned up for work in it a couple of days later, Gary was horrified and told me I couldn't work in the diner looking like that. There wasn't a lot I could do behind the scenes, but Jill came up with a cunning plan. She dug out an eight-foot tall bear outfit for Dyna Bear, Dyna Bowl's mascot, and suggested I wore it out and about, drumming up custom. The suit was ancient and stank with the sweat of a thousand men, but I put it on and with Jill and Laura – in crisp Dyna Bowl uniforms – set out to coax people to come along for a game of bowling and a bargain burger.

The suit was hot and ridiculously heavy and I couldn't see a thing from inside it, so walking around wasn't exactly easy. The girls thought it especially hilarious when I was accosted by a group of children who sent me plummeting to the ground. I was saved from injury by my padding, but my bear head rolled off and into the main road. Without the head on, the only part of me that was visible was the top of my hair, so the children thought they had decapitated Dyna Bear and ran screaming into a nearby arcade. The girls laughed so much it took them twenty minutes to get me up off the ground. After that, Dyna Bear was demoted to greeting people around the bowling alley, scaring children, performing lewd dances for hen nights and being manhandled by groups of drunken guys who wanted to take photos of themselves with Dyna Bear in dodgy poses.

As the days passed, my bruises faded and my nose hurt less and less. The boys in the house and my bowling alley chums had decided there would be a grand unveiling of my new nose, followed by a night out – this time with cabs both ways and no stops-offs.

When the big day came we all gathered in Simon's living room and as I began to peel off the tape that secured the beak to my face, they sipped excitedly on homemade cocktails. When it finally came off there was a gasp and a cheer. I turned to look in the mirror that Tim passed me and was astounded. Not only had my nose been fixed, but it looked once again as it had when I was twelve years old. There was no sign that it had ever been broken. I was so overwhelmed; I jumped for joy around the lounge, throwing my arms around everyone. I took a large swig of Laura's vodka and Coke and made my way upstairs to the bathroom where I looked in the mirror again. It was so strange to look into my face without the bent and lumpy nose I had grown accustomed to. For the first time in my life, I felt quite handsome.

That night, wearing yet another of Simon's Lycra T-shirts, I finally made it to the Cockpit nightclub where, between the meetings, the hello kisses, the toasts and the shaking of strangers' hands, Harry and I saved every cheesy pop song just for us and leaped and bounded about the dance floor.

Simon introduced us to the Leeds' gay scene as the drinks flowed and a once great lady of the eighties pop scene performed a medley of all her hits. As her act came to a finish, the club played its final song before we were all sent home. The whole gang of us performed a drunken routine to Whigfield's 'Saturday Night', which, to our giggling shame, we knew every step of, as did the majority of people in the club.

After that we moved on to another smaller club that Simon wanted us to see. It was just a large lounge in a house, with a wooden bar in the corner. And it was absolutely packed. We managed to find a table and Simon got the drinks in, while I looked around at the dancers.

Across the other side of the room, through the crowd, I could see two men leaning against the wall, laughing themselves into a stupor as they groped at every half decent guy that tried to pass them. They had dark complexions, brightly coloured designer clothes and the kind of jewellery that was only too familiar to me. It was very clear that not only were these two the most predatory looking gay men I had ever seen, but by they way they held themselves, they could only be travelling people, and what sent a deathly chill down my spine was that one of them was looking at me with a knowing smirk on his face. I looked away, hoping I was just being paranoid. When I looked again, the men had gone. I hoped they had left, but a few minutes later, as I made my way to the toilets and joined the queue behind a large man dressed as Nana Mouskouri, one of the travellers reappeared beside me. He rested his huge hairy arms either side of my head against the wall, leaned into my face and smiled, showing an overcrowded mouth full of jagged teeth, then said. 'Hello, beautiful.'

'All right,' I nodded, trying to duck under his arm and back out into the bar.

As I walked away he called out, 'Where you going, Mikey?'

I turned back. 'Do I know you?'

His friend came up behind me and laughed, as the hairy man curled his arm around my shoulder and pulled me towards him, before pressing his mouth against my face and licking my cheeck. 'I know who you are,' he whispered. 'They'll find you, Mikey.'

'What are you doing here, then?' I asked.

He laughed. The second man grabbed me by the arm. 'You's nothing but a dirty poof,' he whispered, crushing my wrist. 'I hope they fucking kick the cunt outta you.'

I pulled my arm from his grip and walked to our table. The travellers followed, and the hairy man stopped and grabbed my shoulder, gripping it tightly. 'They'll find you, my boy,' he said. 'And I can't wait to hear about it.'

I watched as he walked through the crowd, turned to mime a boxing jab at me, and went out of the door.

'Who was that?' asked Simon.

I shrugged it off as best I could. 'I have no idea.' My night out had turned into a nightmare, so I asked if they would mind if I went home. I could only be reassured that the two men, being two closeted men on a night on the pull, had just as much to lose as I did, if the events of this night were ever to come out.

Harry was relieved to see an opportunity to escape

with me and said that he'd go home too. I had no money for a cab, so looking around to make sure no one was following us, we walked home along the backstreets, away from the crowds. Both the worse for wear, we supported one another along the empty streets. Harry was in a happy mood and he began singing one of his favourite Disney songs – 'Part of Your World' from *The Little Mermaid*. He had grown up a fan, too. I was still anxious and scared after my encounter with the two men, but I joined in with the song, belting it out defiantly and lightening my mood with every corny line.

When I got into bed I lay awake thinking about my encounter with the two travelling men. It had been several weeks since my father and his friends had come to Leeds to look for me, and in that time I had begun to hope that he might be backing off. Although I was still wary, I had stopped looking over my shoulder every five minutes and begun to feel a bit less like a hunted animal. Now my spirits plunged. I was crazy to think that my father would give up. He was a determined man and he was angry. Was I going to be constantly frightened that he, or some other Gypsy man, would be around the next corner, waiting for me?

That night I decided that I wouldn't give up either. I was beginning to make a life for myself, and it felt good. I had friends, a job, a nice place to live and I was proud of that. My father might be a dogged, defiant Gypsy man, but so was I.

A few days later, as Jill and I took a break to sip coffee over the bar counter, Laura excitedly announced her brilliant news: she was leaving Dyna Bowl to become a dominatrix. As she beamed, Jill choked on her coffee. 'You what?'

'That's right,' said Laura. 'I've already had my first client. He gave me fifty quid just to have me come over and make him clean his house.'

As she chattered on I couldn't help laughing at the idea of Laura, a stocky little lesbian, all dressed in rubber, whipping some strange guy around his house as he scrubbed the floors. But she seemed thrilled. There was no sex involved, the guy would just call up pretending to be his mother, saying that her son had been 'incredibly naughty' and needed Laura to come over right away to sort him out.

Jill was baffled. 'So he doesn't even touch you then?' she asked.

'Nope,' said Laura with a grin. 'There was just one time, when I was whipping him as he scrubbed the floor under his fridge, that he jumped up, waving his rubber gloves in my face and asked if I was ticklish. I soon whipped him back down to the floor again.' She went on to tell us that the guy's 'mother' had called to say that her son had several other friends who deserved the same treatment. Laura would be off beating guys with a stick before emptying their pockets three times a week, and that was more than enough to pay her rent and give her a reasonable social life.

Jill was clearly less than confident about Laura's new career choice, and was convinced that she would be back in a few weeks' time when she came to her senses. But Laura never did come back. And although I saw her once or twice out in the clubs, mostly the guys stuck to their nightspots and the women to theirs, so she slipped quietly out of my life.

My first Christmas away from home was spent at Simon's house with Harry, Tim and an old Cockney lady, who was a good friend of Simon's and had once been a famous madam. She was clearly very proud of the fact. In her leopard-print clothes, red shoes and with a fag in her mouth, she was a dead-ringer for Bet Lynch from *Coronation Street*.

Harry and I were cooking the Christmas feast since Simon was giving us a rent-free week as our Christmas present and had paid for all the ingredients. One of them being a lobster, which neither Harry nor I could bring ourselves to kill. Simon did that, plunging a knife down through its spine, while simultaneously lighting a Dunhill off the stove. I spent the day hating him for not letting me go to the river and release the poor thing. Harry took over the boiling of the victim, while I stuffed the turkey and shoved it, plus potatoes, into the oven. I'd spent many Christmases watching my mother pull off a perfectly horrific, burnt roast, so I watched mine like a hawk and got it out well before it started to blacken.

Tim, Simon and the Madam popped cork after cork of champagne as Harry and I slaved like a couple of Cinderfellas. When the phone rang I wiped my hands on my Christmas apron and picked up the receiver. An ancient and very deep voice shouted down the line, 'Hello, Simon?'

I couldn't tell if it was a man or a woman. 'I'll just go and get him for you, who shall I say it is?'

'It's Bea,' the voice growled. 'And who's this? Are you his lover?'

I chuckled politely. 'No, I'm his lodger, Mikey – I'll just get him for you. Merry Christmas.'

'And merry Christmas to you, Mikey,' the voice replied.

It was around an hour later, over the triumphant Christmas lunch, that Simon spoke about his friendship with one of the famous Golden Girls. I nearly died of shock. 'That was her?' My jaw was on the table.

'Yes,' Simon said calmly, 'I thought you knew'.

I choked for the next ten minutes, completely overwhelmed by the fact that I had been wished a merry Christmas by my favourite Golden Girl, without even knowing it. I had loved their show ever since I was a kid. I knew I would probably never speak to her again, but I also knew I'd never forget the day Bea Arthur wished me a merry Christmas.

All I wanted to do was call my mother and tell her. We had watched *The Golden Girls* together so many times. I missed her terribly – I missed them all. I wouldn't be there for my mother's appalling roast, my father's hogging of the remote, the visits from every member of the family, and the boys opening their presents. I just hoped so much that they were able to have a good Christmas.

What I didn't know, and didn't hear until a long time afterwards, was that at that time almost the whole family had stopped talking to my father, blaming him for driving me away. Not only that but Frankie was pregnant and was being kept a virtual prisoner in her trailer by her husband Wisdom, who had decided that she would not see our family any more. She was having to take money from his pockets as he slept and sneak off to the local phone box to call our mother, who was taking care of the three younger kids, while my father was spending most of his time away, looking for me. So my family was not together, and not happy.

I asked everyone at the table if I could raise a toast to them. And in that toast, I told them how very much I missed them. It was the hardest mouthful of wine I have ever had to swallow. Life seemed so very strange and different without them. In a matter of months, every-thing that I was and that I'd had before was gone. It was as though I had been born again.

On New Year's Eve I decided to stay at home. For the past few months I had been out with the boys to the same clubs, seeing the same faces, and I was now at the point of exhaustion. I needed a break from it, and them. So I sat in front of the television in my pyjamas and watched Simon's top three must-see films that he couldn't believe I had never seen: *A Star is Born*, with Judy Garland, *What Ever Happened to Baby Jane?* with Bette Davis and Joan Crawford, and *Death Becomes Her*, with Meryl Streep and Goldie Hawn.

I had promised to watch all three by the time they came back, but I was only halfway through the second film, *Baby Jane*, when Harry arrived home. It wasn't even ten o'clock, but he insisted that he didn't want to see in the New Year without me. He rushed into the lounge, grabbed me by the ears, and kissed me hard on the fore-head, before darting off towards the kitchen to open some wine. He had brought a friend with him, and I could hear them talking as Harry pulled corks and poured.

The friend came in carrying a couple of bottles of wine, followed by Harry, who had brought out Simon's best crystal. Harry introduced us. Glyn was 6´ 3˝ and had an enormous build. He was a giant of a man, a ginger Terminator, with hands as large as dinner plates, who greeted me in a thick Welsh accent.

Harry and Glyn had just met in a club where both had lost their friends, and they'd got on like a house on fire and decided to come back and party with me. I wasn't sure why Glyn had come along. It was clear he didn't fancy Harry since he winced every time Harry stepped close to him. I could only assume he was either a nutcase or a robber. But I played along, knowing full well that as long as he was here I wasn't going to be sleeping a wink for fear of waking up to an empty house and finding Harry smothered under a cushion in the bedroom.

For the next few hours we mimed to songs, did tequila shots and drank our way through Simon's wine cupboard, right through the strike of midnight. I wasn't sure if it was the drink or not, but as the night went on, Glyn grew more and more fascinating, with his wild sense of humour and wicked laugh.

'I think he likes you,' slurred Harry, just as he dropped to the floor, smashing three of Simon's best glasses and passing out in a heap.

Not long afterwards, Big Ben had counted Harry out for the night, and Glyn picked him up as though he was a kitten and laid him on the couch, while I laid a blanket over him.

Glyn and I talked through the night. I was still unable

to wean myself off Caleb's taste in music, and Celine Dion roared and howled in the background as we smoked and filled in the details of our lives. And crazy as it seems looking back on it, by the time the sun came up, we had both confessed our absolute undying love for each other.

As Glyn left the house, promising to see me again that evening, I was certain I had discovered love at first sight. I saw him every day for the next week, introducing him to my friends and inviting him out with us, regardless of the fact that they all seemed to loathe him. He was odd, an enigma of a person who seemed to get people's backs up before he'd even said a word. But I thought him enchanting and refused to listen to warnings that he was actually completely insane and someone to avoid.

It was a classic case of a rebound relationship. Blinded by desperation, I ploughed on.

'What a *loon*,' Tim announced, as Glyn left the house after a dinner party.

Simon was quick to agree. 'Who are you now, the bride of Frankenstein?' he threw at me.

I chose to think that they were not happy that I had found someone outside our circle of friends. So I started spending more and more time with Glyn, away from the others, and by the end of January I had decided to move in with him.

Simon made it clear that it was the kind of decision that only a love-struck, rebounding fool of a teenager would even contemplate. He told me, 'You're a lovely boy, Mikey, but if you walk out that door with him, I swear to God, I'll never speak to you again. Your choice.'

I was so infatuated with Glyn by this point that I was

unable to see even one of the many cracks in his bizarre personality. Harry backed me up when I told him I thought it was all down to simple jealousy and told me I should go for it and move out. And so, despite Tim and Simon's advice, I followed my heart.

Glyn had been living with his parents, but he called one day at the Dyna Bowl to tell me that he had found us the perfect home. It was a dirt-cheap ground floor flat in a great location, owned by an old lady with a passion for doing her own painting and decorating. My only qualm when looking at the place was that the Artex she had slapped on the walls and the ceiling was layered so thickly and unevenly that it looked like the interior of the Flintstones' house. It was a fixer-upper. And I was happy to take on the job of Wilma.

Tim gave me a hug and called me a fool when I said my goodbyes, and Harry arranged to come over to our new flat for a visit in a few days' time, once we had settled in. But Simon refused to leave the lounge to wave me off. And he kept to his word. Although I saw him out and about round Leeds many times afterwards, he never spoke to me again.

15

Dreaming of a Fresh Start

It was only after we moved in together that the blinkers came off and I began to see what everyone else had seen from the start – Glyn was certifiably mad. His behaviour was eccentric at the best of times. He would lock himself in our bedroom for hours, fantasising about his life and coming out with bizarre theories, imaginings and questions that didn't make any sense.

One morning he walked into the kitchen, sat down at the table very calmly and told me that he had discovered for a fact that neither I nor anyone else around him was in fact real; we were all just a figment of his imagination. I nearly choked on my cornflakes. Where did that leave me?

He began to spend hours at a time just standing, prodding at himself in the mirror as I watched TV, and some days he would choose not to speak to me at all. He began to have violent mood swings: one moment he was elated, the next he was utterly depressed. Some days the sane Glyn would come back to me, and I would begin to believe things were fine – but then he would crack again.

Over weeks and then months he became more secretive, and more critical of me. And it was the same the other way round. I began to think that everything he said was drivel. The moments when I found him funny or clever or charming were increasingly a thing of the past. Most worrying of all, Glyn was addicted to drama. He had to create a drama, just to get through the day. And it was exhausting following in his wake.

One day I got a call at work. I wasn't used to receiving personal calls since I'd split up with Caleb and when the call came through my heart leapt and for a second I thought it might be him. Sometimes I still missed him with a pain that seared through my whole body.

I picked up the phone to a weirdly unruffled and almost euphoric Glyn. We had got into a pointless argument that morning, which had escalated to the point where I said that I regretted moving in with him so soon. Now he let out a laugh down the phone. 'There's been a fire in the flat. You need to come home,' he said. I told Jill the news and she panicked, practically pushing me out from behind the bar and sending me on my way. I was aware that Glyn had a flair for the absurd, but at this point it still hadn't occurred to me that he could have done something as reckless as burn down our little Flintstone flat. I was just too shocked to think clearly at all, but I did have a funny feeling about everything.

When I arrived at the scene Glyn and our landlady greeted me. His mood had changed and now he was looking distraught and teary, clutching his laptop and a pair of Gucci plimsolls – the only things I wished had been burned to a cinder.

Our flat looked as though the Marshmallow Man from *Ghostbusters* had just exploded all over it. Great blobs of melted Artex were splattered all over everything. As

I searched through the mess, it didn't take long for me to notice that Glyn's possessions were nowhere to be seen, and I was quite certain that it wasn't because they had been burnt to ashes. But everything I had – my clothes, my photos of my family, even a snow globe that Caleb had bought for me – was destroyed. This was a planned piece of drama on his part that I could not bring myself to even comprehend. What I had was so little, but it meant everything to me, and he knew it.

As I searched through the scorched rubble I came across my precious bundle of photographs. The faces of my family were blackened and charred. As I shuffled through the photos, they crumbled and fell to pieces in my hands. The few memories I had, gone up in smoke. I tried to piece together the remnants: my father sitting with me on his lap when I was four, my little brothers opening their presents on Christmas morning, my mother cuddling baby Minnie, me and Frankie with our cousins Olive and Twizzel. We were a gang: me and Frankie, with Olive, Twizzel and Jamie-Lee Bowers. We used to sneak off into the woods near the Warren Woods camp to smoke, to spy on the old woman in a rundown trailer, who we simply called 'the Minge', and to creep up to the fence around the local mental hospital. I was devastated about this photo in particular because Olive and Twizzel had both died in a car crash. Olive, just thirteen, was already driving. She was at the wheel with Twizzel beside her, when they were hit by a lorry. I had missed them terribly. I still did. The picture of us all at school on Red Nose day, where I went as The Artful Dodger and Frankie, Olive and Twizzel all went dressed as Samantha Fox was nothing now but a sticky black lump.

Then there was my grandfather, Old Noah, asleep in the lace-covered armchair in his pink trailer, wearing a witch's hat with green permed hair attached and a full face of make-up that we kids, in fits of giggles, had painted on while he dozed, totally unawares. I would always remember those Sunday get-togethers as if I had only just come back from one. Every single week we would all go over to my granny and granddad's pink trailer for Sunday dinner. Pink as a 'My Little Pony', and yet on the inside it was a shrine to the family and its achievements, the walls lined with family photos, boxing gloves signed by celebrities and the various trophies Old Noah, his sons and grandsons had won. In the centre of the lounge was Granny Ivy's chair. She was so small that she'd had to have it made specially for her, with a foot-stool to help her climb up to the cushioned seat that put her at the same height as everyone else. From this lofty height she would survey us all with regal dignity.

Tall tales of all kinds would be spun, and then one by one we'd get up and sing. My mother's voice was a wonder – she could do a spine-tingling imitation of Patsy Cline that always won her rapturous applause. The men would sing a Johnny Cash or Slim Whitman number, while Frankie's speciality was Limahl's 'Never Ending Story' and mine was Dean Martin's 'Bumming Around'. The two of us always finished the party with 'Show Me the Way to go Home'.

There were photos of Caleb too, the two of us out with his friends, laughing together and fooling around.

I knew for sure in that moment that I still loved him so much, and now I couldn't even look at his face.

Those photos were the last remnants of my past. It felt as though my whole history had been ripped away from me. From that moment on I had no evidence at all that I ever was a Gypsy, and the only images I would have of my family or the man I had loved so much would be the ones in my head.

That night, Glyn and I stayed with his family, and even though he continued to act out the drama of our little home being ruined, I just didn't buy it. His laugh on the phone remained in my mind and grated on me. As he sobbed crocodile tears and asked the gods how on earth the fire had started, I sat and hated him.

Eventually I just couldn't keep it in any longer. 'You know full well how it started.'

He paused for a second. 'How dare you even insinuate that I did this on purpose?'

I was ready for that one. I pointed out that not only had he been laughing when he called me but, by apparent coincidence, every single possession of his that meant something to him had somehow managed to make its way back to the safety of his parents' place, while everything I cared about was lost.

He shrugged. Then he admitted to me that 'yes' it was all pre-planned and 'yes' he did destroy my stuff on purpose.

'Why?' I asked.

His face turned to stone. Because, he said, he had grown sick of us, sick of our boring routine and our relationship, and sick to the hind teeth of hearing me constantly reflect on the past and the things I couldn't let go of. And so he decided that he was going to rid me of the past and everything that bound me to it.

I was so flabbergasted that I just couldn't believe what I was hearing. I thought of the friends I had lost because I couldn't accept their dislike and distrust of him. They all saw in Glyn what I had constantly tried to block out, simply because I was a fool on the rebound. Not only was he absolutely, positively one hundred per cent insane, but he was also a self-obsessed maniac to boot.

Realising how badly I had judged Glyn and the whole situation, I felt any remnants of self-esteem drain from me. I had nowhere else to go, so I stayed with him. But I knew it would not be for long. I just didn't know what my next move would be.

For three weeks we lived with his parents before moving back to our flat, where the smell of smoke never did go away. The first time I told him I wanted to move out, he grabbed a carving knife from the kitchen drawer and screamed his head off, wielding the thing around his head like a sword. I ran and locked myself in the bathroom and sat in there for the next two hours, as he waited outside the door. Finally, when I promised never to leave him, he put the knife away and I was able to come out.

I felt trapped. I remembered all that he had told me when we first met. How sad he was, how lonely he was, and how he never felt that he fitted in with his own life. And I had sympathised with him. I understood those feelings so well. It had taken nine months for me to finally see that I would never be able to help him, or to bring him back from the lost place where he chose to go. I had to get out.

The night I left, I had to literally run out the front door as he chased me into the street to drag me back inside. Luckily I was faster than he was. 'You'll be back,' he bawled after me.

Shakily, I made my way down to the Dyna Bowl. I had nothing but the clothes I was wearing and a small bag. The guys at work had seen it coming for months, and weren't surprised at all. I am not ashamed to say that I felt like an absolute mug.

The gang at work had become real friends to me. A new girl, Karen, had replaced Laura. She was pure Scouse, wide as a log and with the face of a startled cockerel. Gary had given her the job instantly, after reading on her CV that she had been a backing dancer for Michael Jackson on his BAD tour. Not only that, but she had also been a female wrestler. She had the stories to back all this up and I guess she was pretty certain that no one from a local bowling alley was ever going to call Mr Jackson for a reference.

Karen soon proved to be a compulsive liar, but she told very funny stories that, true or not, had us all in stitches. And she was the first to make an effort to get the staff from all the areas of the Dyna Bowl to start socialising together. I was so glad she did, because it turned out that the guy who worked in the bowling alley, Colin, and his 'slags' were an absolute hoot and when they were around staff drinks after work would carry on for hours.

After I explained what had happened with Glyn, it was Colin who offered to put me up in his flat that night. I had thought he was a fool, but I had never been more wrong about a person. That night, I sat and played Nintendo with him and his cousin, before being set up on his sofa bed with a hot drink and a soothing chat. He asked me the simple questions that I had forgotten to ask myself: What do you want to do? Where do you want to go? What do you plan to do with your future and is Leeds the place where you are going to do it? He also said that I could stay with him for as long as I needed to.

I could never have thanked him enough for such a lovely gesture, and for opening my mind.

The next day I went for a walk in the city centre, hugging my coat to me in the autumn cold and thinking about what Colin had asked me: What was it I wanted, and what would I have to do to make it happen?

Suddenly I knew: I wanted a fresh start, somewhere new.

I called Harry and asked him to come and see me to discuss a big move. When he arrived at Dyna Bowl the following day, I asked what he thought of the idea of moving to Manchester. While thumbing through a gay magazine with Jill a week earlier, I had come across an ad from a housing association, asking for gay people to move to the city and promising to supply a great flat. I told Harry that I had left Glyn and wanted to make a drastic change. Harry jumped at the idea, exclaiming that he was going to come with me and start a new life too. We sat with Jill and Karen all afternoon, going over the thrills of Manchester life. Jill's sister lived there with her husband, and Karen had dated a Manchester guy. Though he had turned out to be gay, as had most of Karen's exes. It was only an hour or so away by train, so we wouldn't be far, and visits and nights out could be a regular thing for all of us.

That night I had a call from Glyn, begging me to come back, shouting, sobbing and threatening to kill himself. I told him I wasn't coming back, and he became angry, yelling that he would come after me.

The call shook me. I couldn't wait to get away.

The following day I called the number in the magazine, and a few days later I went to Manchester to have a meeting with the housing association. They told me that they could find a place for Harry and me within a few weeks, but it would be an unfurnished flat with absolutely nothing in it. I was fine with that.

After the meeting I walked to Canal Street, which I had heard was one of the most famous gay scenes in the UK. Along the canal was bar after bar with rainbow-coloured flags in the windows. I wanted to get myself a job as a waiter, to make sure I had work lined up when I moved. I went into every bar, and three of them took my phone number, while others were keen for me to come back another time with a CV to show them.

When I arrived back in Leeds, I arranged to meet Harry. We met in a pub next to the station, where Harry bought me a pint of Guinness and buzzed with questions about what Manchester was like. After making it sound like the Disneyland that we had both hoped it would be,

I calmed Harry down and told him we'd be able to go the moment a flat came up.

One evening, while I was waiting to hear from the housing association and dreaming of my new life in Manchester, I sat down and wrote a letter to my mother. It wasn't a long one – my writing wasn't good enough, and anyway I couldn't say a lot about where I was or what I was doing. I just said that I was safe and that I loved her. I addressed the letter to Granny Bettie's house – one of the few permanent addresses I knew. Wherever my family moved to, I knew my mother would always go back to see her mother regularly, and she would be able to pick up the letter.

After I lost the photos of my family in the fire I became more desperate than ever to reconnect with them. I longed to see them, but I knew that wasn't possible – I wasn't sure it ever would be. So writing the letter gave me a link, and a way of feeling close to my mother, just for a little while. I knew she wouldn't tell my father about it. The next day I posted it, and for the whole of that day I pictured her opening it and reading that I was safe and well and I felt happier than I had in a long while.

Two weeks went by and then I got a call from the housing association in Manchester, asking if I'd be able to come and look at a flat that afternoon. I almost squealed with excitement, before leaping out of bed to get ready for the trip. I called Jill just before I boarded the train, to explain that I wouldn't be in to work till later. 'Don't worry for a second,' she said. 'I just hope you get a nice one. You deserve it.'

When I arrived at the housing office, they walked me

around the corner to a high-rise block that looked like a wedding cake before the icing goes on. It was truly ugly, but I didn't care. And when I was shown around the tenth-floor flat, with its bare floor and stark, empty rooms, I said yes, right away, and went down and signed the papers. After that I took a walk down to Canal Street and handed out copies of the CV that Jill had helped me with.

Everything was falling into place. I felt I was on a roll. I met Harry that night and we agreed to move to Manchester in a week's time. Three days after my trip, I got a call from the manager of a bar named Battlefield Eight. It was a brand new bar on Canal Street that doubled as a café in the afternoons. He offered me a full-time job as a waiter by day and glass collector by night. I could start work the following Saturday, on the very evening of the day that we were due to move.

I was thrilled.

Neither of us had a lot of possessions to move. With a bag each, me and Harry boarded the train that Saturday morning, waving goodbye to Leeds and wildly excited about our new life. Jill, Karen and the gang from work had kissed me goodbye and wished me luck when I left the evening before. I would miss them. When we arrived we caught a bus to the high-rise, where we trudged up to the tenth floor and our new home. It was even grimmer than it had seemed the week before. And we had nothing but our bags – not even a bed, a chair or a cooker. But to us it was a palace. This was where we would both find the new life we longed for.

16

Manchester

That evening, I worked my first shift at Battlefield Eight while Harry wandered Canal Street, looking for a job of his own. We arranged to meet at midnight, once I'd finished work, at the Old Navy, one of Canal Street's most popular cabaret bars, with plenty of trashy clientele and drag queens reminiscent of every old biddy that ever graced a soap.

When I arrived at work, Adrian, a dark and handsome Scot with pepper-coloured hair and an adorable little stutter, showed me around the bar, before handing me my Cadbury-purple work shirt and apron. The whole bar was decked out in deep oranges and purples, with a great chandelier in the centre, covered with glass bulbs that hung and twirled like frozen tentacles. The bar's unisex toilets were part of a new fad, thanks largely to the hugely popular *Ally McBeal*, and gave the place an extra edge.

I was given a quick introduction to each of the staff and then sent to do the rest of my shift shadowing the other glass collector. 'You'll pick it up quickly enough,' said Adrian.

The other glass collector, Leigh, seemed appalled at the idea of having to train someone. I gathered that he was used to spending much of his shift skiving outside with the guy who worked the door. 'It'll give you something to do tonight, Leigh,' chuckled Adrian as he introduced us. Leigh heaved a deep sigh, gave me a nod and then took me behind the bar. The place had started to fill and the staff were leaping around, trying to control the crowds of people coming in for their weekend booze-up. Leigh pointed to the dishwasher. 'The glasses go in there, then when they're clean, you put 'em on the shelves . . . all right?'

I couldn't help but laugh. 'Is that it?'

Leigh gave a shrug. 'Yup . . . Right, I'll see you in a bit.' And with that, he wandered off into the crowd carrying a large glass holder a bit like a milkman's crate.

I grabbed another from next to the dishwasher, just as a buxom blonde crashed into me. 'Sorry,' she yelped, bending down to pick up the handful of change she had dropped. 'You're very pretty,' she smiled, tilting her head at me.

'Thank you,' I laughed. 'So are you.'

As I walked through the bar with my holder, she called out, 'What's your name?'

'Mikey,' I yelled back.

'Oh!' she exclaimed, 'That's SO pretty . . . I'm Lisa!'

Collecting glasses was easy, and as I wandered from table to table, I soaked up the buzzy atmosphere. I was going to enjoy my new job – and Manchester.

After my shift I made my way to the Old Navy. Harry, it appeared, had already started to get settled in, having found a bunch of new friends. He was barely one shot away from being out for the count, and was dancing to 'Barbie Girl'. Of course, I was obliged to join in. We drank every kind of shot that was available, danced every step to every Spice Girls track they played and said hello to dozens of new people by the time the bar closed at 2 a.m.

It was only when we got back to our flat that night that I remembered that, not only did the place have absolutely nothing in it, but we had also just spent the last of our money on a night out. We didn't even have any coins left for the electric meter. All we had was a blow-up mattress that Harry had the good sense to have brought from Leeds, so we set it up in the lounge and made our bed there.

We woke the following morning to find that the mattress had punctured during the night, leaving us huddled on a freezing cold floor. It was so cold that we could see our breath and when we stepped out onto our balcony a blanket of fog had covered the whole city, with only the tallest buildings poking up above it like mountains poking through clouds. I set off for my first day shift at Battlefield Eight, where I would thankfully find warmth and something to eat. And Harry promised to go job-hunting again.

When I arrived, Lisa was there to show me how to use the coffee machine and introduce me to the chef, Norma, a self-proclaimed wench who was the spitting image of the serial killer Myra Hindley. Her kitchen porter was Alan, who was the straight man, and the butt of Norma's jokes, which were always to do with his terrible toupee.

The bar was dead, so we spent most of the morning sipping coffee as I ended up telling the whole group my life story. I felt that by now I had told it a thousand times. It was always impossible for me to end a conversation that started with 'Where do you come from?' without having to go into every detail. Every question I answered would be followed with another and another, until I had told the person about my whole life. The thing was that most people, knowing very little about my people and culture, were interested and wanted to know more. I was happy and proud to talk about being a Romany to people who were genuinely interested, but at times I felt sad too, thinking of all I had left behind.

That afternoon the bar was still very quiet, so we did a bit of half-hearted cleaning and tried out some samples of free hair gel that had come with various gay magazines. Lisa filled my hair with gold and styled it up into two devil-like horns as we sipped our way through a bottle of Taboo. As Leigh, the bouncers and the night staff began to arrive, I started clearing the crockery and cutlery off the tables.

At that moment I looked up as Glyn walked in.

My heart sank. He had phoned me many times before I left Leeds, begging me to come back to him. I had hoped that moving away would be my chance to escape him, but he had somehow found out where I was, and, judging by the furious scowl on his face, he wasn't happy about it. Knowing Glyn as I did, I was prepared for this to turn into a confrontation, but I was still taken aback by his next move. He picked up a plate from the nearest table and threw it at me like a Frisbee, following it up with another and another, as he shouted, 'Did you think I wouldn't find you?'

It took the bouncer, the manager and several other staff to remove him from the place, as I cowered behind the counter trying to avoid the flying crockery.

'Don't worry,' Adrian told me, when they came back in. 'We've warned him that if he ever sets foot in the place again we'll have him arrested.'

'Thanks,' I said, feeling dreadfully embarrassed. What sort of a first impression was I creating? I explained that he was an ex I was trying to avoid.

I couldn't believe Glyn had found me. The whole thing left me feeling shaken and a bit panicky. Part of the reason for moving out of Leeds was to escape the last location that my father had known about. I was tired of feeling that I was being watched. Now I had someone else on my tail. I tried to pull myself together.

'That was weird,' Leigh said, as he crouched down and began to sweep up bits of broken plate. He helped me clean everything up and by the time we'd finished, my shift was over and he still had an hour before he was officially meant to start, so he asked if I fancied going for a White Russian in his favourite bar, to steady my nerves.

Manto was all eggshell and spotlights, with a great balcony that hung over the bar and staff in sandals with pointed boy-band hair. It was bright and nice and I could see why Leigh liked it, though I did feel very out of place with my gold devil-horn hairdo. But I was grateful for the company after the unsettling afternoon I'd had. Leigh and I sat with our drinks and cigarettes and talked. And in that one short hour, I knew that I had found a soul-mate.

Like me, he was seventeen. He didn't live in Manchester and was still at school doing his A levels. But he said that he couldn't wait to get out of class on a Friday and make his way here, to work in the bar, meet friends and see the scene. He wanted to come to Manchester to live as soon as he could.

It was easy to see that Leigh was made for a place like this. He was just about the most handsome, trendy, graceful, quirky guy that I had ever met. He drew me in completely. He spoke about how he hadn't enjoyed school, how he dreamed of being a great writer, of having a lovely flat, of moving to this beautiful city and finding the man of his dreams.

I told Leigh about Glyn. I felt I owed him a bit of an explanation since he'd cleared up so many smashed plates! I found it so easy to talk to him that I even told him about my passion for Caleb, how it had given me the courage to run away from home, and how heart-broken I'd been when it didn't work out. The conversation calmed my nerves. I told myself to forget about Glyn's crazy reappearance in my life and to just get on with things as before.

After that first drink together we became inseparable. We worked the same shifts, went out to the same places, shared the same love of movies and music and, true to form, time after time, fell for all the wrong kinds of men. But regardless of it all, we were there for each other, to pick up the pieces, listen, offer comfort, make each other laugh and – if it came to it – share our last crust.

*

Three weeks into our new life, Harry had given up on trying to find a job and was signing on the dole. It just about covered his share of the rent, and seemed to suit him fine. He had made his own group of friends at the Old Navy, while I spent more and more time with the staff at Battlefield Eight. The two of us would catch up at the end of each day, telling each other what we'd been up to.

One night he told me he had found a job, one that didn't pay, but did, however, supply him with drinks. He was going to join the cabaret group at the Old Navy and dance Spice Girls and Steps routines on stage, while pounding away on a tambourine. It was hardly a West End role; in fact it wasn't even real cabaret. But Harry loved it. With his new, blood-red hair and 'Barbie is a Slut' T-shirt, he would stand in the line-up between the drag queen with no neck and the fat male stripper in a G-string, grinning away and doing his thing. I was thrilled that he seemed to have found his niche. Our new life was working out for both of us.

Then, one afternoon we arrived home from a trip to the local supermarket to find that a box had been left with the security guard. It had my name written on it in fancy calligraphy, and I knew right away that it was from Glyn. When we got up to the flat, I opened it, and inside, wrapped in paper was a brick-sized slab of meat, which on closer inspection turned out to be the tongue of a cow. A card lying next to it said, 'You are nothing. You are worthless. You know it, your father always knew it, and now so do I. One day soon, when you least expect it, you will see me again. I promise you.'

This gesture really gave me the creeps. Once again

Glyn had shown himself to be completely unstable. And he had hit me where it hurt the most.

I put the card back inside with the tongue and closed the box. I walked out onto the balcony and lit a cigarette. The sky was steel grey and rain had begun to hammer down.

The gruesome gift and those cruel words had carved wounds into my chest.

Harry came out and stood on the balcony next to me. We smoked in silence, looking out over the city. Harry was never very good with words, but as he flicked his cigarette he eventually said, 'Mikey, you know as well as I do that he's wrong. Don't let him win. You could put an end to his games right now by going to the police.'

I looked at him, stunned. Every now and then, Harry amazed me with his clear-sightedness.

'OK,' I said. 'You're right, let's do it.'

I had never liked the police, and my encounter with them over the supposed shoplifting was still fresh in my mind. But I had also seen them in a different light when I was attacked in Leeds and the police officer had urged me to press charges. I just had to hope that this time they would be on my side.

We packed up the box containing the tongue and set off for the local police station. It was pouring with rain and Harry's lime-green umbrella, with a great pair of frog's eyes that poked out the top, was not the most inconspicuous of accessories. I looked around, wary of some of the locals who were not the most accepting of our kind. But the rain kept them at bay and our platform 'Spice' shoes kept us from getting our jeans wet.

When we got to the police station I explained to the duty

officer that I was being stalked and harassed by an unstable man. I showed him the contents of the box, which definitely got his attention. I was taken to an interview room and I gave them Glyn's details and told them the whole story. After talking to Harry too, they promised to follow it up.

We headed home, hoping that a visit from the police would be enough to scare Glyn off. We laughed at the thought of his face – he would never have believed I'd go to the police, but he might have enjoyed the drama of the whole occasion.

That night, Harry and I got dressed in the dark – we still had no electricity – then went out to his workplace for some well-earned free drinks. I was so grateful to him for helping me to see that I didn't need to be terrified and passive, just waiting for the next awful thing to happen. It had felt empowering to report the harassment, like I was drawing a line under an old version of myself.

I never did hear what happened back in Leeds, but something must have worked, because Glyn didn't show up again.

17

Eddie

Every bar has its regulars and Battlefield Eight had three: a chicken-faced prostitute who cleaned us out of all our free 'safe sex' condom packs, a six-foot lesbian who was the living image of Arnold Schwarzenegger, and Eddie, the managing director of one of Manchester's leading hotel chains and an absolute howl to listen to.

He was incredibly camp, constantly lengthening his vowels and using his hand as a fan whenever he felt he'd said something witty. He looked like Mrs Doubtfire in a suit, but swore he was only thirty. We never argued, because he was always such fun to have around the bar. Eddie had only been in Manchester for a year; he moved in after the heartbreaking loss of his partner. One evening he told us what happened.

Eddie and Matt had been together since they met as student and teacher at university. With a start like that, they were bound to be a controversial couple, especially as Matt's homophobic parents disowned him the moment he came out to them. He never spoke to them again. When Matt graduated, Eddie left his job and they began an empire of their own, opening a chain of florists across the country. They made a lot of money, very fast. Then, after five years of blissful success, with a huge house and a love like no other, they got into an argument. Nothing big, just the kind of spat that most couples have.

Matt went out for a walk but was queer-bashed by a gang, and attacked so badly that they had to take the awful step to turn off his life-support. Eddie was obviously devastated and his grief was made even more terrible when Matt's family took him to court for a chunk of their wealth. Eddie had to stand in court and listen to accusations of all kinds of horrific behaviour. They said he had groomed Matt from a young age and manipulated him into his way of life and his bed. Believing he was about to lose everything, he sold their businesses.

The day before the verdict, Eddie's lawyer told him that he was not going to win the case. That night, heartbroken and determined not to let Matt's family take everything they had worked so hard for, he got steaming drunk and trashed the house. Furniture, clothes, ornaments, even their photos were destroyed.

The next day, Eddie won the case.

He moved into a flat in Manchester and became a recluse. He fell into a state he thought he'd never escape from and the money from the business was all spent on alcohol. Then one day he woke up and the pain had subsided. He could never explain how – he used to say he thought it must have been a gift from Matt. He suddenly felt free to live again. Within another year, Eddie had landed his new job and claimed back his social life. Now here he was, propping up the bar, and just as I had sat and told my story to Norma, Alan and Lisa, Eddie did too. 'It's getting like fucking *Jackanory* in this place,' said Norma with a cackle.

Eddie would be in the bar every day and was always willing to join the staff for a drink after closing time. One night over some drinks after work, Leigh and I began talking about finding a place to move into together. I was finding life with Harry difficult because he wasn't earning and I was paying the lion's share of our rent, food and bills. Harry wasn't doing a thing to help himself, and I was beginning to feel suffocated. Not only that, but we still hadn't got a stick of furniture in the flat. We were still sleeping together on an old mattress on the floor.

I was having a good old moan about all this when Eddie butted in. 'I live in a lovely flat you know, and I have a large spare room. You can rent that if you like and share it.'

Leigh and I looked at one another in amazement, before leaping over the table to hug Eddie. It was the most incredible offer. At this point we both felt that neither of us could have picked a nicer landlord, or a better person to share a room with.

The next day, I took Harry for a drink. It would be four weeks until Leigh left school and came to Manchester and I wanted to give Harry as long as I could to either find a way of paying the rent himself, or ask around to see if any of his friends wanted to move in with him and split the costs. When I explained that I would be moving out, Harry was very calm and very sweet. He said that he understood and that he was glad I had found somewhere that was better than where we were. I knew he was sad. And I knew that he felt as if he was being left behind. I only wished that he had the drive and confidence to get out and do something for himself. He could stand on a crappy stage every night with his tambourine and yet he felt totally incapable of walking into a job interview. I promised I would always be there for him. But I could no longer afford to keep him, knowing full well that as long as I did, he would never change.

Four weeks later Leigh and I moved into Eddie's incredible flat, right on the waterside in Canal Street. We couldn't believe our luck. After three months in the empty high-rise flat with Harry, I thought I'd landed in paradise. The flat was decorated in different shades of green, with dark green chiffon draped from the ceiling and walls, like a scene from the Arabian Nights. Our room was huge and creamy white, with a king-size bed, high ceilings and a great bay window that looked out towards the student flats across the road.

The only minus point was Eddie's two huge cats, Gin and Tonic. They lazed around like a couple of fat slobs and engulfed the entire flat in a tang that stung your eyes. I had never been a cat person. In fact, there has never been a Gypsy in the whole of the UK I've ever known of who has owned one, or thought of a cat as a decent pet. They are seen as unlucky. But putting up with a couple of cats was a small price to pay for such a great place to live.

The night we moved in, we ate a slap-up dinner that Eddie had prepared and drank three bottles of red wine. After what seemed like hours of camp conversation, Eddie left the room, only to return wrapped in bed sheets and wearing a Joan Collins-style hat. He introduced himself as his alter-ego, 'Lady Astor'. He was holding a platinum tray with eight lines of cocaine laid out neatly upon it. He put it down on the table and gave us each a twenty-pound note to roll.

I'd never taken drugs of any sort before, and I don't think Leigh had either. We looked at each other and I knew we were both thinking the same thing: 'why not?' It was scary, but daring and exciting too. So I snorted back the powder, tasting it as it worked its way back through my nose and down my throat. I felt as if I had just inhaled popping candy and toothpaste.

As Eddie piled up more lines and Leigh and I topped up our glasses, Eddie chopped at the coke with his credit card while simultaneously fending off his cats, who he claimed had got a taste for drugs when he once left a tray out, while going to meet his friend at the front door. When he came back, they had licked it dry. He told us his previous two cats, Bacardi and Coke, had met their end after hoovering up some Ecstasy and cocaine when Eddie popped out for a quick drink. He arrived back at the flat with friends to find Bacardi stretched out dead on the floor. Soon afterwards Coke leapt from his fifth floor window, and when Eddie looked out, there was not a trace of him. Eddie might have had a very professional job, but we realised that night that he had not exactly sorted his life out, and was certainly in no position to be an owner of pets.

When he saw how surprised we were, he told us he thought we knew that he sold drugs, since he was well known around the street. But we were both new to the scene, and had no idea. Still, it didn't worry us. We were young and optimistic and everything seemed new and exciting.

That night the three of us went out onto Canal Street, to celebrate our moving in. Our favourite bars were now on our doorstep, and Eddie refused to let us pay for a single drink. As for the effects of the cocaine, my nose was running, my eyes were rolling, I was sweating like a pig and I was churning out monologues at the speed of Alvin the Chipmunk.

I also felt confident. More confident than I thought I ever could be in a busy gay bar filled with strange and beautiful people. When Leigh and I finally crawled into bed that night, we kept looking at each other in the semi-darkness, squealing inwardly at how incredibly our luck had turned.

Over the next couple of weeks we settled in happily. Our rent was peanuts, so we made up the difference by doing the chores and making the food – and we argued constantly over whose turn it was to clean out the awful cats' litter tray. Eddie was great company, and he loved having us around. But what neither Leigh nor I fully grasped, despite the liberal quantities of drugs provided for our welcome dinner, was that we had moved into the home of the area's resident drug baron.

Within a few months we had cemented ourselves as regular faces on the scene and both found new jobs, just for the fun of a change. Leigh went to work in a different bar, and I started working at the Disney Store. I'd always wanted to work there, if only to see if the staff were really as happy as they always appeared to be at the front of the shop. When I went for my interview, I was called in as part of a group. You had to be able to quote fluently from a selection of Disney movies to get the position. Luckily, I had always loved Disney movies; my sister and I had watched so many that we'd grown up using quotes from them in our everyday conversation, so I walked into the job.

And yes, the staff were all just as happy and cheerful as they always seemed. I had half expected the staffroom to have a brainwashing machine in it and was disappointed that it was all very normal. Though there was a large, poster-sized print of Walt Disney reading a storybook to a crowd of very Aryan children, which was a bit creepy.

I also got to meet Mickey Mouse once, when he was brought over to have a photo taken with a local boy with leukaemia. We closed the shop for the event and our manager, Trish, asked me to stay to help with the event, which I was more than thrilled to do, if only to meet Mickey himself.

The Disney Store was a brilliant place to work, and I had a lot of fun.

The manager at Leigh's new bar was called Julian. With his chubby cheeks, beady little eyes set deep in his face, and since he was always dressed from head to toe in bright pink, he resembled a pig more than any human being I have seen before or since. He was great fun though, although he could be very cutting, and only an apparent crush spared me from his vicious wrath. I never really took to him, but Leigh liked him and we hung out with him for a few weeks – until Leigh and I woke one day to discover that in return for our friendship, he had given us both scabies. I just knew from his constant itching and red raw skin that there had to be something up, but Julian used to say he was allergic to his washing powder. Leigh was a little too trusting, but being the Jessica Fletcher of the unit, I knew the 'allergy' didn't sound right. And allowing him to stay over at our place one night gave me the proof I needed. We ended up housebound and covered in bright pink lotion that had to stay on for twenty-four hours, while we boil-washed everything we owned to get rid of the scabie mites. Julian called and played dumb, saying it must have been from somewhere else and how dare we make such an assumption. But we knew it was him.

That night Leigh came up with a idea to get our revenge. He was positive that Julian was so smitten that he would do pretty much anything I told him to. I didn't believe it for a minute, so I went along with Leigh's plan. Julian had a tattoo of a whole load of Chinese writing up one arm, which he had long since forgotten the meaning of. He also had a massive crush on actress and newly formed pop star Martine McCutcheon, so the next time I saw him, I suggested he get a picture of her tattooed on his other arm.

The next day I was on the 'meeting and greeting' shift at the Disney Store, enthusiastically waving hello and goodbye to anyone who passed through the doorway, when Julian appeared, with a great big bandage around his forearm.

'Guess what?' he shrieked joyfully. I felt sick when I looked at the bandage, praying that he had seen sense and picked something – anything – else. But he hadn't. He unwrapped the bandage and there, in thick black ink and smudged shading, with her name inscribed above her head, was Martine, dressed as Tiffany, her famous

EastEnders character, gracing Julian's arm, from elbow to wrist. I tried to sound enthusiastic, but I felt as if I had done the cruellest deed.

The gay scene had accepted and welcomed me. It showed me faces just like mine; people who had been through similar difficulties and faced the same rejection from families and loved ones who could never understand. It was a place where I could learn to love myself again.

As a boy I had prayed for a compassionate god to 'cure' me of the disease my people despised. But living amongst men and women just like me, I began to find self-acceptance. And as time passed I realised that if I was asked, 'If there was a pill to make you straight, would you take it?' I would say no. Because being gay was a part of who I was, a part I would not change.

I thought a lot about my past. If I hadn't been gay, I would have stayed at home. I would have got married. I would have had children. I would have been doing the same as every other red-blooded travelling man out there. But that wasn't meant to be. I left home because I had to, not because I wanted to. I knew that being the way I was would destroy me at home. But here in this city, amongst liberal people who understood and who didn't see my sexuality as a disease or a god-hating life choice, I had finally found somewhere to settle and belong.

After a year in Manchester, with no word from my father or his people, I began to think that maybe he had called off the hunt. That was a huge relief, but I missed my family so much. I blotted them out as best I could, with any kind of upper or downer I could get my hands on, and I blotted out my ache for Caleb with any man who would give me the slightest bit of attention. I was always unlucky in love, simply because I was always so desperate for it. I had Leigh, I had Harry, and I had my friends at the bar. But to feel love . . . actual mind-bending, heart-leaping love, seemed impossible. And so I took more party drugs, I drank more alcopops, I smoked more cigarettes, I wore even stupider outfits, just to disguise myself as someone who didn't give a damn. I wore a purple velvet coat, shaved my hair into a Mohican and wore platform shoes. I was a cartoon-like mess, dipped in club drugs and alcohol. I stopped speaking about my family to people altogether. But I was still writing to my mother: after that first letter I had written to her every month. I never included a return address and I hated that I could never say in my letters what I had been up to. They were all very short, with just one message, 'I love you, and I think about you every day.'

Canal Street had become famous through the Channel Four series *Queer as Folk,* which was set there. But when the filming ended after several months, the fairy lights, street performers and wonderful decorations that made the street look so appealing all disappeared. And without them, the whole street looked dark and melancholy. The TV show brought new people to the area: we'd see gangs of girls on hen nights and groups of straight men walking along the street at night, for a dare, or just to start trouble with the regulars. The gay people of Manchester were in mourning for what it had become.

For me it had been a wonderful escape. But I knew the time was coming when I needed to move on. As I walked along the street I would see the faces of people that I had been out with the previous night. In a night-club, high on drink and drugs, we had been dancing shirtless, screaming our love and appreciation for each other, but in the sober light of day we were practically strangers with nothing to say, but a shy 'hello'.

On those few nights when the pills failed to take effect, I would leave whatever club I was in early, go back to my room and think to myself, was it all worth it? What had I done with my life? Had I wasted everything? Sometimes I felt I could die of loneliness and heartbreak, so I would try to blot it out again, by going back out, to talk to anyone, to sleep with anyone. Just to forget for a little longer.

I was lonely. I missed my family. I missed my life back home. I missed what I was. And I hated what I had become. The incident with Julian left me feeling that Leigh and I were becoming the kind of people we disliked most: unkind and uncaring. The dazzle was beginning to fade. We were out at least four nights a week, and always fuelled with alcohol and drugs. But the truth was we weren't enjoying any of it any more.

The only person who seemed never to tire was Eddie, who would finish off a bottle of scotch a day, shell out drugs to all areas of the street, snort and swallow just as much as he would sell and then be able to pull on a suit and run a major hotel. And as Leigh and I started to refuse his offers of drug-fuelled binges, Eddie began to run cold. He was not happy to get intoxicated by himself, and we were no longer fun. And that meant that he was becoming increasingly rude to us, sometimes even spending whole days in the flat blatantly ignoring us. I felt like the shine was well and truly coming off my life.

18

An Education

Leigh had always wanted to be a writer. As for me, I knew I wanted something more, but I wasn't sure what. I wanted to learn and to push myself to achieve something. Without that sense of purpose there was just too much time for me to miss everything and everyone I had lost.

My education so far had been negligible. Gypsies had been suspicious of schooling and didn't see the point of it. Our parents reluctantly put us into school when the local education officer arrived on the Warren Woods site and said we had to go. Even then, I only went for a couple of years, three or four days a week, and before I was ten my father had hauled me out, saying it was a waste of time.

During that patchy bit of education I did receive, I learned the alphabet and how to read and write very simple words. But far more importantly, I found I loved school. It was a safe place, away from my father's authority, where I could do things I never did at home, like paint and listen to stories.

Mrs Kerr was the teacher who had given me my starring role as a singing owl in our school's Christmas bonanza. And in the relatively short time I knew her, she changed my life. She believed in me, encouraged me and, despite knowing what my future as a Gypsy man would be, she sat me down and told me, that if I really wanted to, I could be anything that I wanted. She was a warm and kind woman, and I soaked up her tenderness and affection like a sponge. She probably didn't treat me differently to the other kids – she was kind to all of us – but I thought she was an angel. She even fought for me to go on school outings, and although my parents would never let me, since they didn't trust the Gorgia teachers to take care of me, it meant a lot to me that she cared enough to come down to our trailer and ask them if I could go.

I had always wanted to go back and finish the education I had barely even begun as a kid, but I had no idea how to go about it. I had taught myself how to read, with help from Caleb, and could now read reasonably well, but that was it.

Leigh had done A levels at school and he decided to apply to college. I was thrilled for him when he got a place on a course in creative writing, but I didn't think I would have a chance to do anything similar.

One day, he met me after work and brought me a prospectus from his college. We sipped White Russians as he flicked through the pages, showing me all the courses that were available and what qualifications and A levels were needed to get into them. Unfortunately, there wasn't a course that would accept someone like me, who had taken no exams at all. Then, towards the back of the prospectus, we came across two performing arts courses: one took two years and required three A levels, but the other was only a year long and didn't require any, as it was just an introductory course.

Leigh said that I should at least apply for it and maybe even do the A levels I needed to get into the two-year course at the same time. I had always loved film – which was the closest I ever came to drama – but I was alarmed at the idea of standing up in front of an audience. I was still very shy and it had taken everything I had just to stand in the doorway of the Disney Store and say hello to strangers. But I loved the idea of performing arts, and here was a course I just might have a chance of getting onto.

That night, we sat in our room and Leigh helped me draft a letter to send in along with my application. I wrote it as he stood over my shoulder, slapping my wrist and making sure that I did my very neatest writing and spelt everything correctly. Leigh thought it best that I simply state the truth: that I was a Gypsy, that I had never been to school and had no O or A levels, but would be more than willing to take night courses to get the grades I needed to be considered for a place at the college.

Three weeks later I got a letter asking me to come in for an interview. It was there that I met a tutor who would make a lasting difference to my self-confidence, encouraging me to believe in myself and reach for things I had always thought were impossible.

Robert was the head of the Princess Street College drama department. He sat down with me at a long beige table in a whiter than white room and told me that after reading my letter, he felt it would be a crime not to let me audition for the two-year course, regardless of my lack of education. He asked me to come back in a week's time, and, in the meantime, to learn Romeo's famous balcony scene speech from *Romeo and Juliet*.

I was so moved by what he said, I nearly burst into tears. But the idea of learning a chunk of Shakespeare was daunting, to say the least. I went to the library to get a copy of the play, and once I got home I pored over it, wondering how I was going to memorise something so long and in words so unfamiliar. I couldn't have done it without Leigh. He sat with me night after night, going over the speech with me and making sure I understood every ounce of meaning and memorised every single word correctly.

A week later I went back and after watching dozens of other people audition, and taking part in some very strange vocal and physical workshops, my turn came. As I walked up out of the crowd of teenagers seated in rows of chairs, onto the stage, I thought about the one person I had ever felt such love for in my life.

Caleb.

I thought of him until it burned my guts. And then I said my speech, to an imaginary balcony above the tutor's head. The rest was a blur.

I went home, feeling baffled by the whole experience. The workshops, the crowds, the auditions. But I knew I wanted more of it.

The wait to hear whether I had got in was hard. This was my chance to change my future. I didn't want to be one of the people stuck in the gay teen scene. I didn't want to be just another familiar drugged up face, or an ex-shag of so-and-so. I didn't know if the stage would be my future, but I wanted to try. I wanted to do something that I'd never imagined myself doing.

Three days later I got a letter from the tutor. I had

won a place on a BTEC national diploma course in acting. Leigh was so overjoyed, he cried. Eddie was less impressed, saying sarcastically that it was a step into a world of gays not worth talking to. I didn't care, though, I was so proud and excited I danced around the room.

That night Leigh announced that we would be going out – one last mighty blow-out before we made leaps and bounds towards our new professional futures. First Manchester. Then London. That was the plan. We had spoken about it a thousand times. Leigh suggested it should be a night for the two of us, as he threw me his favourite trousers. 'Put them on. And don't wear that ugly purple coat. Tonight you're gonna look great.'

I laughed. 'Like you?'

He pushed his feet into a pair of Nike trainers. 'Like me,' he said.

As we went out, Eddie was sitting on the couch with a face like a codfish. He took one look at me and said, 'You look fucking hideous.'

It was at times like this that I knew how little confidence I really had. Underneath all the hectic social whirl, I had never felt anything other than ugly, unapproachable, awkward and out of place wherever I went. I had escaped from the people who made me feel worthless. But they had left scars that I could never erase.

I turned to Leigh. 'I'll go and change.'

But he'd had enough. As I walked through to the bedroom, Leigh exploded at Eddie. 'How dare you?'

I had never heard such fury in his voice as he started to vent an outpouring of frustration at Eddie that had been building up for months. 'You have no right to speak to him like that, and Mikey, don't listen to this fool, you have never looked more handsome than you do tonight.'

He followed me into the bedroom and picked up his bag. 'Don't you dare change. Let's go.'

I took my courage from Leigh's support and nodded my agreement. As we headed towards the front door, Eddie shouted in a voice that shook the walls, 'I want you both out in a week.'

Leigh and I stared at each other in the open doorway. 'Fine!' Leigh shouted back, in his most upbeat tone, before closing the door.

That night we celebrated in style. I felt triumphant. I had set out to change my life, to prove to myself that I was capable of more than just partying, and with Leigh's help and the vote of confidence from Robert the head of drama, I had done it. I was on my way.

Leigh moved out of Eddie's flat the following week. But after days and days of apologies and tears from Eddie, I felt I couldn't leave him. It had suddenly dawned on me just how lonely the man was. He had no real friends: without the drug supply, no one really wanted to know him. And he was still very much in mourning for Matt, the lover he had lost.

Leigh told me I would be crazy to stay with Eddie any longer, but if I really wanted to and thought it right, then he wouldn't try to stop me. He also told me he expected me to join him in his new bedsit within a month, because Eddie was beyond help.

He was right. By that time, as well as a daily bottle of scotch, Eddie was taking copious amounts of cocaine, and within three days of Leigh's departure, Eddie had forgotten he'd begged me to stay and was cruelly taunting me because I wouldn't join his drug binges. I'd had enough. I thanked him for the good times and wished him well, and then I moved in with Leigh and we set up home together in a bedsit in the student area of town.

The bedsit was tiny, just one room, and it was an absolute hovel, with a matted carpet and grubby walls. But we didn't care. The two of us got on so well that sharing was easy. Our room had a bay window with a seat in it, and in the evenings we would sit at the window and smoke and catch up on what we'd been doing.

In September that year my college course started. By that time I had been in Manchester for two years and at nineteen I was the grandpa of the group, since I was three years older than most of them. But it didn't matter. I threw myself into college life and had a wonderful time. I spent hour after hour practising on the computers in the student library and consequently my reading and writing skills improved rapidly. I developed a taste for plays and literature and verse, soaking up the knowledge I had longed for. I made a group of friends who had never known the person I was before, either the Gypsy boy or the party animal, and we sat around in cafés talking about plays and studying texts.

It was only when I had to stand in front of everyone and perform that it all fell to pieces. But that, my tutor told me, would improve with time. Robert said that nerves were always a good thing to have before walking out onto a stage. It was not having them that would be worrying. I didn't think I was any good at acting. All I knew was that it was something that no full-blooded Gypsy I had ever heard of had done before me. It was a challenge, and it represented a possible way of life and a future that I had never even dreamed of. I desperately wanted to get better at acting and to move towards that future.

Leigh and I were both now in full-time education and working in the evenings. I had a bar job a few nights a week and studied the rest of the time, and it was the same for him, so often we wouldn't see each other until it got to wash day, when we'd go and sit outside our local launderette and smoke and sip coffee, as our clothes and bedding were being cleaned and dried for the week ahead.

The rest of the time we would leave notes for each other, gossiping about random dates we had or nights out with our new circles of friends. When we did manage to go out for an evening together it was always wonderful. But neither of us hammered the scene the way we used to. We would stop by in Canal Street for a visit sometimes, but that was really all it was for us now – somewhere to visit occasionally.

One night we decided to drop in at the Old Navy. I hadn't seen Harry for a long time, and thought it would be nice to catch up. The Old Navy was never seen as the best of the Canal Street bars and the more snobby gays looked down their noses at it, as the 'working man's pub' of the area. I hadn't been in for a very long time and it was good to take in the old décor, the dodgy trannies, the wonderfully tacky music and the punters with their tight Lycra T-shirts and multi-tone hair. It was fun, and watching it all, I missed my old Willy Wonka coat and my platform shoes.

It wasn't hard to spot Harry; I almost choked on my drink. There he was on stage in a huge blonde wig, full make-up and Jessica Rabbit dress, banging his tambourine to Cher's 'Believe'. His act had certainly come on since we had last met. When he noticed me at the end of the bar, he jumped from the stage and bounded towards me with his arms outspread. 'You've changed,' he said, with a smile.

'You have too,' I laughed.

He grabbed a drink and pulled up a stool.

'How are you Harry?' I grinned, offering him a cigarette.

'I've changed my name, by deed poll,' he said. 'I'm called CeCe now. CeCe Cemon.' And by the look on his face, he wasn't joking.

He assured me that it was nothing to do with wanting to have a sex change, or anything like that. They finally gave him a proper paid job in the bar and he decided to get rid of his former name as a kind of shedding of skin. He told me that none of his new friends knew his former name and he never intended them to. As far as he was concerned, he was born CeCe. And with that he struck a pose, very much like Edith Piaf, only with a paunch.

It was wonderful to catch up with him again, to reminisce about old times and to talk about our plans for the future. CeCe's dream was to be a successful drag queen, putting together his own comedy and impersonation act and doing the circuit. I told him that I had started college, which made him cry, so that his make-up streaked and smudged. He was so happy for me, and so genuine about it.

It seemed to me that night that Harry was truly long gone, and CeCe's new look and outlook had changed his life. People stopped to speak to him, to take pictures with him, to compliment him, and he was gracious and lovely with each one of them. I was proud of him. We swapped phone numbers and I left him performing a great mime act to Bonnie Tyler. The audience loved it, and he revelled in it. He waved at me from the stage and blew me a kiss as I slipped out.

That was the last time I ever saw him. I knew he would be there, living out his dreams, but I never went in again. He didn't need me as a constant reminder of his former self.

As I neared the end of my first year of college, Leigh told me that he was going to be moving again very soon to London, to start university and further his career as a writer. I had another year to go, but we planned that as soon as I finished, I would go down and join him. Talking about it, we grew more and more excited. In London we would find new lives and success. I had dreamed of living in London ever since I was a small boy and my parents, desperate to get baby Henry-Joe to sleep, would get me and Frankie out of bed late at night and pile the family into the car to drive us round the sights of the great city.

Now I would go to London, not as one of Fagin's pickpockets, which was all I could imagine as a little boy, but as a professional adult: an actor.

Leigh left, but we kept in constant touch and he told me how great it was living in the halls of residence at his university. I was so envious. The room we'd shared felt empty and soulless; it seemed as if he'd taken half the light from Manchester with him, and nothing was the same.

I kept busy with college: we had exams coming up and the final months were flying by. But I knew, deep down, that there was no way that I was ready to face the world as a professional actor yet. I loved the idea of it: the rehearsals, the readings, the putting a play together and discussing it at deeper levels. But I wasn't ready to get up on stage.

I approached my tutor, Rob, and came clean. I told him I wasn't ready to act, but I was desperate to keep learning. Rob told me that, quite apart from my own fears, if I really wanted to make it in the acting profession, I had to attend one of the country's top drama schools. He listed four of them, in London, but told me it would be incredibly hard to get into any of them, and suggested I have a back-up plan of a degree in Manchester.

I knew what he said about the back-up plan made sense, but I couldn't bring myself to do it. It seemed to me that every time I got the jitters about a plan, it fell apart. So I decided I would just go for a place at drama school in London, looking forward all the way and in complete denial of the fact that it might never come to pass. Tens of thousands of would-be students apply to get into these drama schools every year, and only a handful are accepted. So it was a long, long shot. Rob went through the prospectuses with me and talked me through the applications, explaining the questions and what they needed to know. But when I looked at my first completed application form I felt it looked pathetic. They would see I didn't even have basic schooling, I had never passed an exam and I had yet to complete the course I was on. Why on earth would they let me in?

Then Rob told me, confidentially, that I would receive a distinction for my college course, and that I could put it down on the form. It was the best mark anyone could receive and I was absolutely overwhelmed. For the first time, I started to dare to believe that perhaps I wasn't as bad at acting as I had always thought.

Rob showed me the place on the form that said 'any other comments'. 'That's where I want you to tell them about you,' he said. 'Not about your training, not about your knowledge of playwrights, not about your education. Just about you. What you are, where you're from, and how much you are absolutely ready for the opportunity to join these schools.'

So I did. I told them that I was a Gypsy, and about what I had done so far to get to where I was. I said that I wasn't a great actor, but I wanted to learn to be one. And I knew that I could, because I sensed that I was ready. I filled in all four applications and sent them off. After that, all I could do was wait.

19

Reunion

While I was waiting to hear from the drama schools, I wrote another letter to my mother. I had been writing to her regularly for the past two years, never saying much more than, 'I'm safe, I'm fine . . . and I love you.' But this time, I decided to tell her everything: what I was, what had happened and how I had been living my life since I left home. I wrote in the usual block capitals and phonetically so that she would be able to read the letter, just as I always had done. At the end of my letter I said that I loved and missed her more than I could ever put into words and I was desperate to see her again. I said I would understand if it was not possible for her to see me, but I hoped she would, and I asked her to meet me outside the Britannia hotel in Manchester Piccadilly. I gave her two dates and two times, just in case she was unable to make one of them.

I felt ready. I was doing well in college and about to move to London, with or without a place at drama school. And I had learned more in the past year and a half than I had in the rest of the time I had been away from home. I had started reading books, mostly starting at the halfway point, just so that it would be a bit less daunting, but even so, I was getting to grips with it. I was studying plays, picking up new words, descriptions and meanings all the time, and I had a vocabulary that I had never thought I would achieve. I sounded different too. Partly because of the accents and voices around me, but also because I had tried hard not to sound the way I did in the past. I didn't want just to be a more educated man, I also wanted to wash myself completely clean of the person I used to be. Not because I wasn't proud of where I came from, but because of my paranoid insecurities about the way Gypsies are usually treated in Gorgia society. I wanted to prove to myself that I could fit in and be just like anyone else. And being able to stand up in the class and read Shakespeare aloud proved to me that I could. But now I started to worry – what if my mother thought my lifestyle was a betrayal of our culture? As the day for our meeting drew closer, I became more and more nervous. As much as I longed to see my mother, could I actually handle this return to the past?

On the first of the two dates I had given my mother I sat for forty minutes waiting for her to turn up, chain-smoking, my eyes scouring the faces of everyone who passed. Was she going to come? It didn't seem like it. I could hardly bear the sick disappointment. Just as I got up to leave, I heard the sound of a car horn. I looked across the road and there she was, sitting in her little white van. As our eyes met, we both burst into tears. I ran over to the van and she opened the passenger door. As I leapt in, she took me in her arms and held me, squeezing me as tightly as she could.

'I knew all along,' she said. 'I always knew, and I don't care . . . you're my boy. You're my boy and I love you more than you'll ever know.' I sobbed into her chest as she rocked me. 'You did good, my boy. You did what you had to do. And you did what people never thought you could do.'

She cupped my face in her hands and raised it to hers. Her dark eyes swirled with tears and mascara. 'Look at me, now. I'm the proudest mother in the whole world. And you came back to me.'

She said she had been across the road all the time, unable to resist just watching me for a little while, as a grown-up. She wiped the tears from her face and leaned into the back of the van, piling things onto my lap: cards and gifts of clothing she had been buying me for the past three years and keeping under the bed.

We went for a walk along Canal Street. I thought she might be uncomfortable there, but she wasn't, she was smiling as she looked around, chuckling to herself at every turn. We went for dinner at one of the bars, where we had a burger and chips while we spoke about the family and how they all were.

So much had happened. Frankie had a little boy, Frank junior, so I was an uncle. Frankie's husband Wisdom had become more and more violent towards her, beating her up daily, even after she became pregnant, and keeping her prisoner on the camp his father owned. At night she would steal change from his pockets to go to a phone box and call our mother. One day she called and asked our Mother to come and get her. When our Mother arrived at the camp, Frankie was in a full-scale fist fight with her husband, having smashed all the crockery his mother had given them as a wedding present. Not only was he beating her, but his two sisters were also taking hits at her. Frankie was eight months pregnant and knew she had to escape for her baby's sake, so she leaped into the van and they were gone.

When my father saw what had happened to Frankie he went to the camp himself and beat the hell out of Frankie's husband and his father, before the police were called and my father was arrested. After that our family moved to many secret locations to avoid Wisdom finding her. Whenever he did, they would simply move on. No one ever understood why she chose him; I can only guess that love is blind.

After baby Frank was born, Frankie's husband continued to stalk her, while taking no interest at all in his son. He called the baby 'It' because he had our father's name. But when Wisdom failed to get Frankie back, he decided to hit her where it would hurt most, by demanding visitation rights and custody of their son. He thought it would force her to go back to him.

My father took the letters to a solicitor – one who was friendly to Gypsies – who told him bluntly that there was nothing he could do: Frankie's husband would definitely win visitation rights. 'There's only one way to deal with all this, Frank, and that's to do what you lot always do. Find your own way to get shot of him.'

A month later, when the court date came round, Wisdom didn't show. My family received no more letters and he never bothered her again. No one knows what happened to him or what made him leave for good. But soon afterwards, my father decided to move the family back to Warren Woods, the place we had lived for several years when I was little. They had settled back there, with Frankie and her Frank junior living in a trailer next to our parents.

As soon as me Mum told me this, warning bells sounded in my head. Warren Woods was close to Tory Manor, where Uncle Tory and his family lived, along with Old Noah – now widowed, as Granny Ivy had died some years before – and Uncle Joseph. Sitting in the busy bar, overjoyed that I was actually sharing lunch with me mum, my mood suddenly turned sour. I felt sick at the thought of Joseph going near either of my brothers. And now there was Frank junior to worry about too. I had to force myself to concentrate on what Mum was saying.

Throughout this time my mother was visiting Old Bettie and collecting my letters, and she would discuss them with Frankie and the boys. She knew that one day, when I was ready, I would find her again.

As we talked my mother rifled through her bag, pulled out a pack of twenty cigarettes and lit up. My jaw dropped. 'How long have you been smoking for?' I gasped. She pulled the cigarette from her lips and flicked it into the ashtray.

'Since before you were born,' she smiled.

I was so grateful for the distraction from thinking about Uncle Joseph. I couldn't believe my mother had her own secrets. I wasn't the only one! All my life I'd thought she didn't smoke. She'd managed to keep it a secret not only from us kids but from my father as well. As we talked, she told me that only her sisters, and her best friend, my father's sister Prissy, knew. It wasn't that my father refused to let her smoke. She said she just felt it didn't look nice to smoke in front of him, and she had never been able to bring herself to confess. 'He knows now,' she chuckled. 'He says he don't care, but he keeps calling me Dot Cotton.'

I suddenly remembered all the times I was sure I'd seen her with a fag, while she was cleaning, only to run into her trailer to see her chewing on a straw, or piece of paper. Then there were the long drives with Aunt Minnie when we were little. We always had a big picnic blanket in the back of our car, and every time we went for a spin there would be a moment when both women would suddenly start screaming out, 'The witches are coming!' They would make me and Frankie and Minnie's daughter Romaine hide under the picnic blanket as they choked back on their fags and screamed. I laughed as I realised it had just been an excuse for my mother to get her nicotine fix. 'Don't come out yet,' Aunt Minnie would cackle. 'OH MY GOD, they're right up against the window,' my mother would shout. They would play out whole scenes of child-stealing witches flying by the car windows, while they puffed on several cigarettes. 'Go away! NO, there's no children in here for you, Piss off!'

My mother told me she had let Frankie and the boys know that she had come up to see me today. 'They really want to see you, Mikey. I'd love to bring them to see you.' I was overjoyed. But I was also curious about what my father would think of the whole idea. 'He'd love to see you too, Mikey,' my mother explained. 'He stopped chasing you a good while back and he won't hurt you now. He loves you, you know.'

Then she told me that a few months earlier my father had been diagnosed with throat cancer and told that he had only months to live. She and my father had been about to tell everyone and start preparing for the end when Uncle Jaybus, Aunt Minnie's brilliant and hilarious husband, pulled him to one side and suggested he go private and get another opinion before he gave in. Luckily, my father took the advice; he was told that the cancer could be treated and they started him on chemotherapy right away.

'He's over the worst now,' my mother said. 'He's doing well, his hair's growing back and he's eating again.' She could see the tears in my eyes and she smiled. 'Don't worry, Mikey, he's got plenty of years left in him yet.'

I asked if she was going to talk to him about today when she got back. 'Of course I am,' she laughed. 'And I'm gonna get him to bring us up to Manchester Airport, so we can all come and see you . . . would that be all right?'

'It'll be more than all right,' I grinned. 'I can't wait to see them. Do you really think they'll all come – even Dad?'

'He'll come. He wants to see you, Mikey. He'll never say he's sorry, but he does love you, you know.'

'I love him too, Mum. And I love you – so much. I'm never going to lose you again.'

There was a hint of a tear in her eye, as she batted my comment away. 'You just try it, Mikey,' she laughed.

For the next couple of hours we smoked and drank coffee. It was my mother who brought up the one subject we hadn't broached: my sexuality.

'Mikey, I don't care about what you are, I really don't,' she said. 'But if your father finds out you're gay he'll not be able to deal with it. He's not from this time, Mikey. He'll only blame me and everyone else for it and he'll kill the lot of us. So promise me, for all our sakes, that you'll never tell your brothers and sisters.'

She told me that she would take my secret to the grave with her, and she hoped that, for her sake and the sake of the kids, I would do the same. I felt very sad about it, but I didn't want to put pressure on her, so I nodded my agreement.

Eventually we took a long stroll back to the van. Before she left, she threw her arms around me. 'I'm never gonna lose you again,' she said. I held her as tight as I could. 'You never will, Mum. I love you.'

She got into the van and wound down the window. 'I love you more than you'll ever know, Mikey. See you soon, my boy.' I stood on the pavement and watched as her little van disappeared out of sight. At that moment I felt happier than I had ever felt before. I had my mother back – and what's more we would stay in touch and see each other again. How many times had I dreamed of this, never believing it would happen? I walked home lost in thought, reliving the few hours and going over everything she'd said.

A week later, I took the bus down to Manchester Airport. The clothes that my mother had bought for me were all eight sizes too big, but I wanted to wear them anyhow, even though their bright colours made me feel incredibly conspicuous.

My family had always loved airports, even though none of us had ever been on a plane. I walked along the moving walkways, through the tunnel to the lobby of the hotel next to the airport, where my mother had said they would be. As I approached the end of the tunnel, I could see a lone figure standing at the vast window looking out at the aircraft on the runway. It was Henry-Joe. Only now he was no longer the little boy I once knew. The last time I saw him I could lift him above my head, but at thirteen he was almost as tall as me.

As I watched him he turned his head. A great smile spread across his face, and turned into a flood of tears. He ran towards me with his arms outstretched, then threw them around me and lifted me from the floor. He dropped me to my feet and I threw my arms around him too. The tears streamed down my face as I took a step back to look at him. 'I've grown a bit, haven't I?' he laughed, wiping his cheeks. With his arm around my shoulder, we walked together towards the hotel lobby. There, sitting around a table, were my mother, my father, Frankie, Jimmy, Minnie and a toddler I had never seen before – Frank junior.

Frankie leaped up when she saw me and came running across the lobby, tears streaming down her face. 'You're still the same,' she cried, throwing her arms around me. 'Still exactly the same.'

If I was, then she was not. When I'd last seen her, Frankie was completely under her husband's influence, drinking heavily and taking drugs. She had been overweight, with black shadows under her eyes and a permanent snarl on her face. Now all of that had been washed away and she glowed, her skin clear, her long black hair tied into a ponytail.

She turned around and held her hand out to her son. 'Frank, come and meet your uncle Mikey,' she said.

He came forward, shy and fascinated, and I stooped to hold my hand out to him. 'Hello, Frank,' I said. He was adorable, with dark curly hair and Frankie's large, dark eyes.

Jimmy was close behind, with Minnie at his heels. Jimmy was ten, and although he wasn't as tall as Henry-Joe, he was broad and solid and I could see he was going to be a big man. As for Minnie, she was almost six, with hair down to her waist and the same green eyes as mine. I hugged them both.

As I held them, there was a tap on my shoulder. 'How you doin', mush?' my father said, smiling.

I smiled back at him. 'I'm OK, Dad. It's lovely to see you.'

They ushered me to the table, where it was clear from the empty glasses and packets of crisps and chocolate that they had all been sitting there for some time. We sat talking for several hours. Anxious to avoid the subject of why I left, and what had happened to me since, we turned to stories of the past and reminisced over tales of Frankie and me at school, the jobs I did with my father, the places we stayed, and the people we knew.

The boys couldn't stop chuckling every time I opened my mouth. 'You're a proper Gorgia now, my boy,' my father said with a smile. My mother and sister chipped in, saying it was a good thing that I'd adapted to my new world, but I knew there was an underlying insult there. Even so, despite my anxieties, I felt calm. I realised there and then that my father's power over me was so much less than it had been. That felt good.

I asked my brothers what they had been up to. 'Oh, they've been off every weekend with Joseph, Mikey,' said my mother. 'He comes up every Friday and takes 'em to all kinds of places. He's been spoiling Jimmy rotten, he has.'

I smiled politely, but her words were like a punch to my stomach. I looked at Henry-Joe, who looked back knowingly. He clearly hadn't forgotten my warning, but I couldn't ask him anything here.

Eventually my father stood up. He was ready to head home. I wished I could go back with them, to see Warren Woods once more. They were living on the same plot my father had created out of a sea of mud when I was just six. But this wasn't the time to talk about going back. Things were still too new, too raw. And besides, I needed to talk to Henry-Joe.

I walked with them down to the car. My father was once again doing well – though I had no idea what he was up to this time – and they had a Toyota Land Cruiser, huge and silver, with sheepskin rugs inside and a pair of ivory boxing gloves hanging from the rear mirror.

My mother asked if they could drop me back to where I lived. I was glad of an excuse to spend a bit more time with them, so I climbed into the back. As I gave directions through Manchester city centre, my father jumped in with a question that suddenly silenced the whole family. 'Did you ever see that Caleb feller again, Mikey?' he asked.

I was totally unprepared for this, but somehow I kept my wits about me. 'I haven't seen him since I lived up on the camp,' I said with a laugh.

'So you didn't run off with him, then?'

'No,' I said, with as much conviction as I could muster.

Sensing danger, my mother butted in. 'Shut up, Frank, why ever you talking 'bout him for?'

My father didn't reply, falling into deep thought at the wheel. I wondered what he was thinking about and how much he really knew. Did he know I'd been with Caleb in the months after I left? Did he know that we'd split up under the pressure? Had he seen Caleb since then – they'd both been back in Newark, so it was more than possible. I longed to ask, but I knew that to go there would only provoke my father to anger.

We pulled up to a stop at the end of my street.

'Can we see your flat?' Frankie asked.

Still ruffled from the effort of lying about Caleb, and dealing with all the emotions that came with thinking about him, I couldn't think fast enough to come up with a reason to refuse, although I was already going over in my head all the things inside it that would give me away as a big old homosexual.

As the family climbed up the stairs to the bedsit, I hoped my platforms were well hidden under the bed. They piled in and I instantly felt ashamed of my room. The carpets were matted, the bed was a mattress on the floor, and I had a great big poster on the wall of Miss Piggy, in a mock perfume advert with the words 'No Escape' written across the bottom of it.

'It's nice, ain't it,' said Frankie politely.

'Yeah, it's good for one person,' my mother said, rubbing her hand on my back.

My father was looking at a picture that had completely slipped my mind, of me, Leigh, Eddie and, sitting on Eddie's lap, Eartha – Canal Street's most tragic transsexual. All

woman in mind and heart, but with the physical make-up of
John Candy.

'Whoever is this?' my father said, peering at the photograph.
I grabbed the picture, exclaiming that it was an old boss of
mine and his wife. 'Well, she dicks like a mush (looks like a
man),' he said with a deadpan expression on his face.

Catching on that my father was on the prowl for signs of deceit,
my mother announced that they should all be getting off, just as
Jimmy yelled, 'Hey. Look at me!' before trotting around the room
in my Herman Munster platforms. Horrified, I attempted a laugh,
as my mother announced that I had only used those kinds of shoes
for the catwalk modelling I'd been doing. This attempt to be
helpful only made things worse. For a moment no one said
anything. Neither of us were doing a very good job of trying to
hide what I was. I only hoped my father's powers of denial were
sufficient to blot out the obvious, and that he wouldn't give
my mother a hard time after they left.

Thankfully the family trooped out, following my
mother's lead, and before I went after them I managed
to scribble my number on a piece of paper for Henry-Joe.
I wanted to be able to speak to him privately. I caught
up with him at the bottom of the stairs and put it in his
hand. 'Call me, will you?' He nodded and put his arm
around me as we walked out of the front door.

I kissed Frankie and little Frank goodbye and hugged
my brothers and little sister as they piled into the car.

'Nice to see you, Mikey,' my father boomed as he
climbed in.

My mother held out her hand to me and kissed me
on the cheek. 'Maybe next time you can come and see
us at Warren Woods.'

Just the idea of seeing it again thrilled me. 'I'd like that very much.'

My father started the engine, revving it to full volume. Frankie wound the window down. 'Good luck moving down to London, you old tramp.'

My mother placed her hands on my chest and spoke softly. 'Call me soon, all right?'

'All right,' I whispered. And with that, she hoisted herself gracefully into the passenger side and pulled the door closed.

I stood and waved until they were completely out of sight.

After they had gone I went back into my room and sat on the bed with a beer. I felt as though I'd been put through a wringer. Seeing them all at once, after so long, was both wonderful and weird. There was so much to say, and so much that couldn't be said. Emotions welled up in me – joy, sadness, frustration, hope. Would this be the start of a new, better relationship with my family?

I thought about my father's reference to Caleb. I wished that at least I knew how Caleb was, and if he had recovered from all he went through. I missed him so much. There were times when I thought I always would. For a while I was lost in sadness, but I forced the thoughts away. It had been a good day, I'd seen my family again and that meant so much.

I thought about my brothers and sisters. They'd all changed, and I'd missed it. Then there was the visit to my room. Had my father twigged that I was gay? He was a canny old fox, and didn't miss a lot and the clues were everywhere. I hoped he hadn't put them together, and that if he had, he hadn't taken it out on my mother.

Worried, I phoned her the next day, hoping to catch her when he was out at work. He was, and we were able to talk. I asked her if there had been any trouble after they left.

'He was fine,' she said. 'All he said was that you had some funny friends and you'd taken on Gorgia ways. He ain't thrilled about that, but he was pleased to see you.'

Perhaps the old man was mellowing, at last.

20

London

Over the following weeks I spoke to my mother almost every day, but I never got the call from Henry-Joe. I could only hope that everything was all right. And I soon had other things on my mind, because the Guildhall School of Drama invited me for an audition. To say that I was excited would be an understatement. When I sent off my applications I had told myself there was no Plan B, but at the bottom of my heart I had never really believed I would even get an audition. Now I had to prepare for the biggest challenge of my life.

I couldn't wait to see Leigh, who had invited me to stay with him while I was in London. The evening I arrived, he was at work, in a dingy bar in King's Cross. I found it on the corner of a street littered in rubbish, the exterior of the building painted in hot pink and silver, but with no name on the outside, just a house number.

Leigh had warned me that it was 'sports kit' night, so I arrived wearing tracksuit trousers and a hoodie. Leigh was in full Liverpool football club kit, pouring a pint of Stella for a man dressed as Martina Navratilova. He gave me a wink as he served her her drink. Then he climbed over the bar and into my arms, collecting a few whistles and lewd comments on the way. 'Welcome home, Mister,' he said.

He sat on the stool next to mine and lit up a cigarette as the manager, a man who looked as if he had been living on the gay circuit for forty years too long, appeared wearing a pair of boxing shorts and a head guard and poured me a pint of Guinness.

Leigh tapped me on the leg. 'So, you nervous about your audition?'

Of course I was. I was up against hundreds of others for a place in this school. I had been told to prepare two classical monologues, two modern monologues and a song. I had worked hard on them with Rob, but now that I was on my own, all I could remember was my Romeo speech and a verse and the chorus of Annie Lennox's 'Little Bird'.

'Good choice,' Leigh laughed when I told him that was my song. But my heart sank at the fresh realisation that I felt too unprepared and had a first-round audition at three o'clock the next day. By midnight I had sunk several pints of Guinness, two tequila shots and was singing Annie Lennox on the karaoke machine.

The following morning I sat in a coffee shop around the corner from the Guildhall, going over and over my speeches and monologues, while downing as much water as I could to wash away my hangover. I had gone back to Leigh's halls of residence the night before, where we sat up practically till sunrise, as he listened to me trying to slur out my material.

I had no real idea what to expect from the audition. While I had, of course, auditioned to get onto the course in Manchester, this was the big time. I felt out of my league. I was dressed in loose clothing and carrying my audition speeches, in case I needed help remembering my lines once I was in there. The auditions were being held in a small rehearsal room, just off from the student bar, where each of the auditionees was given a number and asked to sit and prepare until we were called. I sat around a large table with twelve others and three former students from the school who had been asked to help out.

My nerves weren't helped by the company of the others waiting with me. There was one girl squatting in a corner of the room, dressed in period costume and making strange vocal warm-up noises to herself. Another woman had a bag full of props that looked like they came from the nineteenth century, and several of the girls seemed to be relying on layers of make-up and low-cut tops. There were only two other men. One of them was wearing an off-the-shoulder sweater and leg warmers and was heavily into whatever he had playing on his earphones; the other looked as if he was about to throw up.

I kept quiet, giving the odd nervous smile and answering questions politely. We waited for what seemed an eternity, until a tall man in beige with tiny spectacles opened the door and asked that we all gather in the rehearsal room for a warm-up. My legs turned to jelly as I walked down the steps into the room. It was long and narrow with tiny spotlights that shone down on the glossy wooden floor, which felt as slippery as ice beneath my bare feet. At the very end of the room was a desk, behind which sat a man with a thick brown beard and glasses, and a woman with a long grey ponytail, wearing a pink and black unitard.

As we each found a space, the woman stepped out

from behind the desk and put us all through several stretches, jogs around the room and yoga-type stances, before having us all sit cross-legged on the floor. She explained that one by one we would be called in and told us not to be nervous – they were simply looking for people who were ready to be there. I wiped the toxic sweat from my head, trying as hard as I could to listen through my hangover.

We were sent back into the waiting room, where I watched silently as, one by one, the auditionees were called. Many emerged furious with themselves or in tears and I began to worry about what was happening to them in there. I felt I was edging closer and closer to a snake pit and my mind went blank. I couldn't remember any of my speeches and I felt as if someone had thrown a bucket of water under each of my arms.

Then the man in beige came for me. 'Mikey Walsh?' he said, holding a clipboard to his chest.

I got up from the table. 'I'm really nervous,' I said, hoping he might say something that would give me some comfort. He said nothing at all. I was just another of the thousands to him.

I walked through the door and towards the desk at the end of the room. As I approached, the bearded man held out a flat palm. 'Just there will do, if you please Mikey.'

I dropped my bag to one side and stood as tall as I could, hoping it would fool them into thinking that I might actually have a clue about what I was doing.

The man looked down at my application form. 'Ah, the famous Romeo speech,' he said. 'I'd like to hear that one if you don't mind.'

I took a deep breath and looked over at my bag. I was too embarrassed to get the speech out of it, so I just glared for a few seconds, hoping that I might discover I had X-ray vision. I thought of my chances of getting in here, which were minimal, and of the pitiful attempt I had made at being graceful in the movement session, and decided I had nothing to lose. I took several deep breaths, chose a single spot on the wall as my balcony, and just did it.

In what seemed like moments, it was over. I had no idea if I had been any good, because I was given no indication. All I knew was that I didn't mess up my lines and for several moments, at least, I believed what I was saying. Though Juliet wasn't what I was seeing when I was staring at that spot on the wall. I was addressing my words to my future, the one chance I had of doing something that no travelling man before me had done.

My modern speech was next. I had found a great piece from a Christopher Hampton play called *Total Eclipse*. The speech was from the character of Arthur Rimbaud, a teenage poet genius, who was borderline crazy. I did the whole thing directly at them, sitting on a chair. I just kept thinking of what my tutor Rob had said: 'Just speak the lines as if you were right there at a table with them, over a couple of pints and a box of cigarettes.'

They didn't stop me during either speech, and didn't ask for either of my other speeches, or my song, which I was so relieved about, because if they had, I'd have had to confess that the lyrics had escaped my mind.

After it was over, they invited me to come and sit at the desk with them and I saw that they had been reading my application. 'A Gypsy, Mikey?' asked the woman in the unitard.

I smiled and wiped the sweat from around my eyes. 'Yup.'

They asked if I could tell them more about it. I gave them a quick rundown of where I had come from and how I had got to where I was today.

'Fascinating,' they kept repeating. And every time they said it, I knew that, just maybe, I might be remembered and in with a chance.

I told them how much it would mean to me to go to their drama school, and how much I wanted to learn. To move to London to study with them was my dream. They rewarded me for this information with brief, impersonal smiles, and scribbled notes on the paper in front of them.

After our chat I went back into the waiting room to await my fate. The worst was over. And all I could think of was just how much I really did want to get into this place. I'd pretty much chewed my fingers to the bone by the time the last audition of our group was over and the man in beige returned with his clipboard. He adjusted his spectacles and looked down at the board, then in a flat voice he said, 'Thank you all very much for coming. As you know, there is not room for everyone this year and if you don't make it through this time, you can always try again next year.'

The whole group sat up poker straight, desperate with suspense as he droned on. 'If I call your name, then you will be invited back for a final audition next week.'

Several girls clasped at each other as he scrolled down his list.

'OK . . . Mikey Walsh.'

I nearly passed out.

'The rest of you, thank you very much for attending today.'

He asked me to follow him into another room to be briefed on the next round of auditions. I leapt to my feet as quickly as I could for fear that the girl with the full set of props was about to smash my head in with a mock Victorian tea set.

I walked out of the building twenty minutes later with 'Bitter Sweet Symphony' by The Verve blaring through my earphones and called Rob to tell him that I would be staying in London for the final rounds. He was euphoric. 'I knew you would do it son! I bloody KNEW IT,' he yelled.

Leigh called me right afterwards and when I told him the news, said calmly, 'I told you, you would.' He said he'd come and meet me as soon as he'd finished lectures. In the meantime, I had London all to myself for a couple of hours. And there was only one place I wanted to go: St Paul's Cathedral.

During our family's late-night drives through London I would sit in the back of the car, clutching Skeletor, my favourite action figure, and dream. I somehow knew, even at the age of six or seven, that one day, just like my hero Oliver Twist, I would live here. London would be my home. *Oliver!*, *Mary Poppins* and *Bedknobs and Broomsticks* were movies that my sister and I had watched over and over again when we were children. Just the sight of the wonderful backdrop of London in each of those films made me fall in love with it instantly.

I longed to leap into a chalk painting and ride a carousel horse in Hyde Park, to see smoke bellow from the chimney tops and to be in a place where suits of armour came to life, the streets were filled with bopping 'bobbies' and old ladies sold breadcrumbs for tuppence a bag.

There had only been one occasion when we went to London during daylight hours – the day our mother promised to take us to St Paul's Cathedral to see the bird woman and feed the pigeons. Our father parked the car as our mother clipped me and Frankie to our 'Huskie harnesses' to stop us running off. Mine was bright red and Frankie's a frothy pink. Our mother used these all the time when she took us to our local supermarket or into town for shopping. With one leash in each hand, we'd pull along in front of her like reindeer attached to a sleigh.

Our father took hold of Frankie's leash while our mother took hold of mine. Frankie and I spent the whole of our walk towards St Paul's looking right up into the sky. I remember that the clouds hung grey and thick that day, and pigeons swooped over our heads, weaving in and out of the buildings that seemed to stretch right up into the clouds. In the build-up to our arrival before the great cathedral, our mother was going over and over scenes from *Mary Poppins* that Frankie and I already knew word for word.

Every now and then, our father would shout out, 'Did you see him?', hinting to us that he had just seen one of Fagin's boys picking someone's pocket and running off into some dark corner or narrow street.

Eventually our parents came to a halt. 'There she is,'

said my father. Frankie and I looked up to see the most magnificent building we had ever laid eyes on. Standing within a great square, upon a stone pedestal, with its wide steps, was the building we had seen so many times in the movies. An enormous cake, with pillars upon pillars and windows upon windows and a door as big and cavernous as a dragon's mouth. I gawped in such amazement it froze me to the spot and my mother had to give me a good tug on the lead to get me moving again. We crossed over the road, through the square and the crowds and climbed up the wide steps. This close, the building was so huge, we could no longer see the actual shape of it.

Suddenly, our mother yelled, 'There she is, there she is'.

She grabbed hold of both of us, leaning down and pointing. There, at the end of her finger, was a figure in brown rags and a straw hat, carrying several bags that our mother said were full to the brim with breadcrumbs. We stared in amazement, watching the figure struggle slowly up the steps.

'She's got a beard now,' said Frankie, sounding disgusted.

'No she hasn't,' said our father. 'That's just her hair over her face.'

I couldn't help but notice that not only was it most definitely a beard, but the bird woman was also wearing a pair of trousers with a rope around them, a Jessica Rabbit T-shirt and swearing at the top of her voice.

As the figure disappeared into the distance, our mother pulled out a half bag of bread from her bag, sharing it out between the two of us, slice by slice. I sat next to Frankie on the steps, throwing out little bits of bread I'd mashed between my fingers as the birds swooped and cooed all around us.

I looked out across the sea of grey and pink pigeons pecking at the crumbs and told my mother and father this would be a day I would remember for the rest of my life. And in my head, I promised myself that when I was older, I would return and do it again.

Now, thirteen years later, here I was. I came out of St Paul's station with the memory as clear in my head as if it were yesterday. I walked around the corner to the cathedral . . . and paused. Something wasn't right. Obviously this was St Paul's – all the signs proved that. But it wasn't the place I remembered. I walked around in a daze. Where had everything gone? Had I dreamed the crowds and the open space, or created some fantasy in my mind? I felt saddened that I had come back to recreate the sense of wonder and mystery that I had as a child. Now the memory was ruined and for a moment I wished I'd never grown up.

There was nothing to be done but turn to the future and concentrate all my energy on getting what I now wanted more than anything in the world: a place at the Guildhall School of Music and Drama. That night Leigh and I drank toast after toast to our success so far – here he was in London, and with any luck I'd soon be joining him.

Over the following days I worked hard to make sure I knew all my speeches and went over and over my Annie

Lennox song. The next audition process took two days, and in that time I seemed to repeat my speeches and the song several times over. It was exhausting, but somehow my confidence was high. Looking back, I think I was fuelled by pure longing to make it.

Eventually I was told I had made it to the final one hundred applicants. We were sent into different rooms in small groups and after a long wait in which my group sat looking at one another and sweating with anxiety, two of the audition panel came in and told us that we had all won a place, and they were looking forward to seeing us in September. The relief was indescribable. I felt ecstatic. We all hugged one another and there were plenty of tears. I certainly cried my fair share. I could hardly believe it. Against all the odds, I, Mikey Walsh, Gypsy boy, was going to one of the most prestigious drama schools in the world.

When I got back to Manchester the first person I told was my mother. I phoned when I knew my father would be out at work and told her I'd made it into one of the best drama schools in the world.

'Well,' she said, and there was a long pause, followed by plenty of sniffing. 'You've done good, my boy,' she said at last. 'Who'd have believed it, eh, you managing something like that. I always thought you had it in you to do something special. And I was right.'

'Thanks, Mum,' I said. 'Will you come and see me in London?'

'I will,' she said. 'We can go and feed the birds.'

21

Drama School

A few weeks later I said a sad goodbye to Manchester, leaving behind the memories and the friends I had made there.

Excited as I was about the move, and my new life, it was sad to say goodbye. There were my old friends from Canal Street, my new friends from the college and of course, Rob, the teacher who had believed in me and given me a chance to make up for years of lost education. I would miss them all.

I arrived in London two weeks before the start of my course. I had missed out on getting into the halls of residence, so I moved into a house-share in Mile End that I found through an ad.

I wanted to get to know the city, so I unpacked and then got the tube into central London to see the sights, get myself lost and wander round my new home without my leash. On my way down to Big Ben, I stumbled upon Trafalgar Square. And as I stood there it hit me. This was the place we had visited all those years ago, looking for the bird lady! Our mother had fooled us into thinking that the National Gallery was St Paul's Cathedral because to her it looked more beautiful. And she was right. With its great columns and imposing steps, it couldn't have looked more graceful. I went and sat on the steps and

smiled at the pigeons, wishing I had a bag of breadcrumbs. Then I walked over to Nelson's Column and
looked up at the lions. I remembered watching those
lions from the back of the car, and thinking that one of
them could swallow me whole. Now I climbed up one
of the plinths and sat myself down right between the
paws of a great iron lion and surveyed the city.

The next day I got the bus right over Waterloo Bridge.
It was the most incredible view of the river and the
buildings either side of it as it curved away. So many
wonderful landmarks right there, from the window at
the top of a bus. Throughout the three years I was at
the Guildhall, whenever I got the time, I would get on
a bus and go over that bridge.

Once term started, drama school ate up just about
every bit of free time I had. The only person from outside
the Guildhall who I ever saw was Leigh. It was around
this time that Leigh started to say I should consider
writing a book about my life story. I laughed it off, but
the idea lodged somewhere in the back of my mind. We
would meet for a weekly coffee and go over everything
we had been doing. Leigh's creative writing course was
going well, but he was moving from one bad relationship
to another. He always fell for men who were horrible to
him and I hated that. He was so deserving of a person
who could be wonderful to him, and yet he seemed
doomed always to find the one person who could not
be more cruel.

I, on the other hand, was in no place to find love,
whatsoever. I felt as though I was going through ten

hours a day of therapy. Each day at college was filled with movement classes, period dance, poetry, and a whole mess of exercises that would generally test our inner psyche, little by little. We were never told if what we were doing was good, bad, right, or wrong, and so, whether we had made a breakthrough or not, we were generally the last people to know about it. The only comfort we got was from our fellow classmates.

I was never a confident person, and I certainly never thought much of myself as an actor. Not even now that I was in one of the best-known drama schools in the world. But I loved the discussions, the delving into classical text, the imagery of Greek tragedy and witnessing the incredible talent of the people in my year. It was amazing to watch as they lit up and came alive through the exercises and speeches we were all given to work on in front of the group.

As for me, I spent the first term humiliating myself constantly through my complete lack of confidence. Time and time again I was forced to look at the awful complex that made me feel I could never fit in anywhere, and it was incredibly draining. But I kept on going, and did what I was asked. Whether I was spending thirty minutes being a sloth in a zoo, pretending I had been sitting on a raft on the ocean alone for three days, belting out a text that made no sense to me, or just having to parade around a room in jazz shoes and a pair of leggings, I threw myself in with all I could give.

They say drama school breaks you down and builds you back up again. This is not true. You break down all by yourself. And it's up to you, and you alone, to face your fears and embarrassment and just get on with it. Then, you either drop out – as several of our group did – go crazy or, with luck, find that one day you break through those barriers that are holding you back and it all starts to come together.

The trick, I discovered, was not to care about what people thought of your talent, or how you looked up there, because caring would always hold you back. Watching my fellow classmates slowly fall apart and build themselves up again, I learned that to be able to be ugly on stage was the most attractive thing an actor could do, and the best lesson you could ever learn.

One day, fairly early in the first term, the drama teacher told us he was introducing a session each week called 'biography', in which the students would take it in turns to tell the rest of the group their life story, taking as long as they liked. As each person spoke, the rest of us would watch them being as real and as open as any human being can be, as they dragged themselves through their own past. We were also told that how much or how little we chose to open up would give away a lot about us as individuals.

Of course, being as paranoid as I was, this made me feel that if I didn't break down and writhe in pain over my past, confessing my sins along the way, then I would not be truly honest to myself or to the school, and that would make me a rubbish actor. I wasn't the only one; a number of people in our group seemed equally horrified and totally unprepared to reveal so much of themselves to twenty-odd people who barely knew them.

After the discussion, I caught up with the drama teacher

as he made his way outside for a cigarette. I felt I had been so bad at every single part of the course so far, I just had to do something brave to wipe my blackened slate clean and prove to them – and myself – that I had a right to be there. 'I'll go first if you like,' I said. He asked if I was sure I wanted to. I told him I was.

A week later the group met again. We moved our chairs into one big circle, before the drama teacher announced that I had agreed to go first. I sat as calmly as I could and the whole group looked towards me with such support, I couldn't have been more grateful. I had no idea what I was going to say or how long it would last. I just needed an opening. And so I started from the very first fact.

'I am a Gypsy.'

An hour and a half later I had poured out my whole life story. And it was the most liberating experience I had ever had. For the previous few years I had tried hard to leave my past behind and live in the moment, so to reclaim it, in front of an audience, felt wonderful. The other students were interested and appreciative and I felt totally accepted.

That night I went through my old journals, thinking that I might finally be able to take Leigh's advice and make a start on turning my story into a book. I did start to write, but I was constantly trying to be clever, or witty – whatever it took to avoid writing about what I really felt. I just couldn't put my feelings into the right words and I gave up, much to Leigh's annoyance.

The course was in any case taking up almost all of my time and I was glad of it. I had been having a miserable time at the house-share in Mile End. It was not a healthy place to live. I didn't speak the language my housemates spoke – to this day I have no idea what language it was – and I felt very alone there.

Then I found that I wasn't the only English speaker in my house after all. I came home late one afternoon to an empty house, threw my bags down in my room and went through to the kitchen. I flicked on the kettle and sat down at the dining table, looking through my lines for yet another speech that I didn't understand.

As the kettle boiled, a voice as clear and strong as if it came from someone sitting right opposite me asked 'Are you having tea or coffee?' I was about to say 'tea' when I remembered I was alone. I looked up from my paper to a thick smell of violet filling the room. Leaving the kettle to click itself off, I walked back to my room. I wasn't superstitious and didn't believe in ghosts, so I just put it all down to stress. But as time passed, the house began to play tricks on me that I could never understand. I was pushed over, locked in my room, and wherever I went, and whatever I did, I felt an ugly presence there, as if I was being watched. And if the housemates and the 'ghost' weren't bad enough, I arrived home one night to find my room had been picked clean by burglars.

It was time to move out.

Luckily for me Jake, a friend from drama school, offered me a room in the house his father had bought him in East London. Grateful for the offer, I moved in, along with another guy from our course. It was a nice house, clean and comfortable, and Jake, Danny – another Guildhall student – and I became good friends.

Jake was a very funny, sweet-natured guy, who liked to pin up cleaning rotas and organise housemate meals. We didn't tend to go out together, because we had different circles of friends, but we'd sit around the kitchen sharing a bottle of wine and gossiping.

I ploughed on with all my classes and got to the end of my first year, but I struggled to find any confidence as an actor. I couldn't shed my self-consciousness or the feeling that I was a sham. My tutors told me it would come with time. I hoped they were right, but I was far from certain.

22

Home

One night after I finished college, my phone went. It was Henry-Joe. A year after I gave him my number, he had finally called.

I asked if he was all right, and he started to cry. He said that he had seen something and he didn't know what to do about it, so he'd called me. He told me that Uncle Joseph had been coming to stay with them every weekend, taking him and Jimmy out to the cinema, bowling, and to all kinds of other places, along with their friends. They had been on the way back from Alton Towers late one afternoon, with a friend at the wheel, when Henry-Joe, who was in the passenger seat, glanced into the rear-view mirror. Jimmy was fast asleep, leaning on Joseph's shoulder. Then Henry-Joe saw something that sent a shiver through him. Joseph was stroking Jimmy's leg and sniffing his hair as he slept.

'I don't know what to do, Mikey,' he said through his tears. He was scared to speak out. And if he did, he was scared to death that he might be wrong, and that he would get into trouble for making an accusation against his uncle.

I told him not to worry, I would sort things out.

That night I left a message at the drama school to say that my father was unwell and I had to go home to be with him. It was less than a week to the Christmas holidays, so I was just taking a little more time off than the others.

I called my mother and asked if I could come to see them. She jumped for joy at the idea. 'I'll ask your dad,' she said. 'But he's in a good mood these days; I'm sure he'll love to see you.'

An hour later she called back to say that they couldn't wait to see me. I boarded a train and Frankie picked me up from the nearest station. She was looking better than ever and as we drove she excitedly asked questions about my life in London.

The family was no longer living at Warren Woods. A few months earlier my father had taken the decision to buy some land and, for the first time, a real house, in West Sussex. Frankie was living on her own plot in a trailer outside, and my father had already arranged for my brothers to set up in trailers there too, once they got married. With Henry-Joe now fourteen and Jimmy twelve, it wouldn't be long. It was what a lot of travelling people were doing. With the tension between the Irish travellers and the Gypsies escalating, the culture had become too rough and many Gypsies wanted out of it. The fights, the arguments and the ongoing battles between the various travellers was growing beyond a joke and was putting a knife through the guts of our once great culture. So my mother and father, like so many others, were leaving the road to find a place they could use as a permanent base. The children would still be free to travel to the regular Gypsy camps and fairs around the country in the summer, then come the cold months they could come back to the security of home. But, as my father was quick to point out when I saw him, moving into a house did not mean that you were no longer a Gypsy. That is something that, like skin colour, you can never erase.

When I arrived I walked into the kitchen where the whole family had gathered to greet me. The house was still a bombsite, since my mother had insisted on gutting the whole place before adding her 'Marie Antoinette meets Elizabeth Taylor' decorating touches throughout. But despite its unfinished state, all the family photos were up, and I looked at pictures that I hadn't seen in years.

My mother had told me over the phone that Uncle Joseph would be there too and wanted to see me, so I had prepared myself for meeting him once again. It was many years since I had last set eyes on him. Now in his early forties, he was a little greyer and a little wider than before and he was wearing what appeared to be leder-hosen, leather sandals and a pair of socks with 'Harrods' stitched all over them in multi-colours.

He greeted me enthusiastically and my stomach turned over. I forced a smile from over Henry-Joe and Jimmy's shoulders as I hugged them.

I needed to talk to Joseph, but not until I got him alone. After a quick tour of the house, and a look through the boxing trophies the boys had earned over the last few years, we made our way back downstairs to where my mother was making coffee.

My father was polite, but quiet; he seemed to be deep in thought. He sat and stared, smoking heavily and looking me up and down, as if he were about to say something. It was as if no time had passed: I found myself feeling just as I had all those years before when I was at the mercy of his fury. I realised that, as usual, he was a powder keg waiting to explode and it would only be a matter of time before he let out the anger he felt towards me. If I thought he had mellowed after our reunion in Manchester Airport, I was discovering that I had been very wrong. He was as bull-headed and angry as he had always been.

My mother had obviously made it clear to everyone that all that mattered was that I was home now. So I guessed that the safest option would be to play along and be guided through easy-topic conversations that were steered by my mother.

I was still intent on getting Joseph alone, when he beat me to it by asking me to go with him for a drive to the shops. I downed the rest of my coffee, placed the cup on the kitchen table and rose to my feet. He smiled. 'You've got tall, ain't you?' he said, before leaning in and giving me a hug.

I allowed him to hug me. I even hugged him back. I needed Joseph to trust me so that I could engineer a set-up in which he would betray himself. This thought had been forming in my mind all through the train journey.

His latest car was a best of the best Mercedes, with every extra a car could possibly need. All paid for, I had no doubt, with my grandfather's money. Since Granny Ivy's death, Joseph, along with Tory, was looking after Old Noah, now elderly and unwell and beyond managing his own affairs. Noah had made a lot of money, and I didn't doubt that his eldest and youngest sons were happy to help him spend it. My father played no part in all of this. Tory and Joseph had always been close, while my father, the middle one, had always been on the outside. He never said much about it, but I always believed it was to do with his jealousy of Tory, who was the favoured son. Unable to compete, my father went his own way, determined to do well and to impress his father through his own sons. And because of this, his fury with me was fuelled not just by his own disappointment in me, but by his father's disappointment in both of us.

As we drove around the back roads, Joseph asked me where I had gone, all those years ago, and why. I told him the truth. About Caleb, about our secret relationship, and that I was now happily living my life as a gay man, though only my mother knew, and that, as she had made me swear never to tell my father or my brothers, I wasn't about to make this visit a 'coming out' party. It wasn't easy to open up to Joseph, but I had decided I must, so that he would believe there was a real connection between us.

As we drove and talked as adults, Joseph was sincere, sweet, understanding and vulnerable. He put his hand on mine. 'I'm so glad you came back, Mikey. I came to look for you, you know? I knew you'd have gone to Manchester, I could feel it.' He was quiet for a moment. 'I've got something to say to you,' he said.

I wondered whether he was going to talk about what he did to me as a child. Would he admit it? Would he acknowledge that it had been wrong?

'I think I'm gay too,' he whispered.

I waited, but there was no more. 'I'm glad you told me,' I said.

He said that I was the first person he had ever told and that he had been scared to death at the thought of ever saying it. But now that the words were out, he knew it was true.

'What do I do?' he whimpered. 'What will my lot do if I ever came out with it? I'm stuck, I just don't know what to do with myself.' He began to pour out the feelings that had haunted him for years. He said he dreamed of leaving everything behind and starting again, but couldn't bring himself to do it. He spoke of nights when he had drunk beyond his fill and thought of ending it all.

As I listened to his agony, I thought about how much I had loved and hated him over the years. What he did to me left me with such an unhappy, turbulent relationship with sex that I had never been able to feel comfortable, and always ended up hating myself afterwards, every single time I had done it. I had lost relationships over it, and I didn't know whether I would ever find a way to feel good about sex.

Apart from Caleb, I had never spoken to anyone about him, not even my closest friends. I had decided that I could only rid myself of him by totally blanking him out. But of course that didn't work. I couldn't blot out the memories, or the parts of me that reminded me of him. Our voices were so similar, so was the way we moved, and people had constantly commented on how much I looked like him. There had been times when I couldn't bear to look at myself for fear of feeling him near me again. I could never understand how this ever happened, why any adult could be attracted to a child. And I tried, I really tried, in the hope that it would help me to let all the pain go, and move on with my life. But I couldn't . . . I just couldn't.

Yet despite everything he had done and the lifelong emotional scars he had inflicted on me, as I sat and watched him pouring his heart out over the steering wheel, with tears streaming down his face, I pitied him. And I knew, right there and then, that I had finally outgrown him.

I gave him my phone number and said that he could call me to talk about it any time, and that I would be there for him if he wanted to come out. I was lying to him, setting him up, to get him away from my brothers for good. I still wasn't sure how I would do it, but I knew the first step was to get Joseph to trust me and open up to me.

When Joseph and I got back from the shops, we all ate a Sunday dinner that my mother had prepared. I had missed her terrible cooking so much; every mouthful of the near-black pile on my plate burst onto my taste buds like the greatest thing I had ever tasted.

That night I sat up in bed with Henry-Joe and we went through every suspicion that he had. He cried with fear and asked me how I knew he wasn't just imagining it. I reassured him that he wasn't imagining it at all and told him that he was not to worry and that I was going to do all I could to fix it. I didn't tell him what Joseph had done to me. It didn't feel right, or necessary, to burden him with that.

After he fell asleep I lay in my bed, looking up at the ceiling. I knew Henry-Joe wasn't imagining it because, apart from everything I knew to be true about my own past, I had witnessed first-hand the way Joseph had been with my youngest brother. He constantly hugged him and kissed him on the cheeks and mouth at any opportunity, right in front of the family. But how were they to know? Such a hideous suspicion wouldn't enter the minds of people who are part of a society that believes so strongly in the spirit of family and tradition and old-fashioned ways. To my family, Joseph was a good man – a good son, brother and uncle. Even if they had asked more questions about Joseph, they wouldn't have reached the right conclusion because they believed that men who abused children – just like gay men – simply didn't exist in the Gypsy community. Even my mother, who knew that I was gay and accepted it, was very set in her ways and had never questioned bigger issues within our race.

But I had seen the way Joseph said goodbye to Jimmy earlier that evening, and now, thinking about it again, my blood ran cold. When he left, Joseph had asked Jimmy to walk him out to his car. I ran upstairs and turned off the lights in the boys' room and watched the two of them by Joseph's car in the dark.

Jimmy could not stop hugging him. It was clear that Joseph had found a favourite in him. He held Jimmy tight for a few seconds and then crumpled what looked like two twenty-pound notes into his hand before placing a finger over his lips. Then he held him again before leaning back and looking into my brother's face. When I saw the way Joseph looked at Jimmy, I knew I wouldn't be able to rest until I had destroyed him. It was a look I knew well, a look of lust that sent a shot of poison down into my guts. Then he kissed my brother on the lips. I counted the seconds – one, two, three. I couldn't be sure if anything was already happening, but knowing what a strong character Jimmy was, I hoped that Joseph might have been more cautious and held back. But without a doubt he was grooming Jimmy; testing the water to see how far he could go, and softening him up with money and favouritism.

I watched as my brother stood, waving, as Joseph reversed out of the driveway. When he came back inside I asked him to come upstairs. Then I asked him about Joseph and how close they were, trying my very best to bite my tongue and not just blurt out the question I was desperate to ask. Jimmy spoke very fondly of his uncle, and went on to excuse him for his strange behaviour. It seemed even my twelve-year-old brother had an excuse for why Joseph, who was generally seen as a good catch, was, and always had been, without a lover, a girlfriend or a wife, even now in his early forties. He had sacrificed his youth to take care of his own father in his old age. That was the story everyone stuck to. I had heard it so many times already. If there were others who asked more questions, and spread rumours that he was gay, then our family didn't know it, or didn't want to know it. The truth, of course, was something infinitely more shocking. If my family were in denial about me being gay, how much more in denial were they about the horror of child abuse that was staring them in the face?

The next day I headed back to London. But I knew what I had to do. And I would be back the following weekend, ready for his next visit.

23

It Comes Out

I spent the next five days walking what felt like the entirety of London, planning, plotting and going over and over in my head what I could do to stop Joseph. I knew that my father would never believe me if I simply accused him. He had to know for himself that his brother was after his youngest son.

During that week I had countless phone calls from Joseph. At first they seemed harmless enough, with general chit-chat and enquiries about how I was getting on. Then one day, while I was sitting on a bus, I got a call from an anonymous number. I picked up the phone and said hello, and after a few seconds of silence, he began to speak. I knew it was him; I could tell by his breathing and his tone. I had been waiting for something like this. He was putting on a strange accent and breathing heavily as if he were about to climax. 'I want you to fuck me,' he said. 'I want you to fuck me hard.'

My stomach churned, but I forced myself to let out a laugh and say, 'Well, next time we meet, maybe I will.' The sex talk went on for another minute or two, before he hung up. Five minutes later he phoned again and, in his normal voice, asked how I was and if I'd had a good morning.

I didn't mention a thing about the earlier call. I knew

he'd called to see if I had guessed it was him. It hadn't been difficult – his voice was unmistakable and he was lousy at doing impressions. And besides, I had heard his heavy-breathing sex talk many times in the past. It stuck in my mind like a foul residue that was impossible to wash away.

Joseph's calls just confirmed what I already knew: whatever it took, I would have to let my parents know what Joseph really was. I was well aware that this might mean my father disowning me again. He would probably hate me for showing him the truth. I felt desperately sad about it. I was just getting my family back – would I now have to lose them again?

I knew I didn't have a choice. I hadn't been there for my brothers in the past few years. I hadn't been there to protect them from my father's obsession with fighting, or his violent temper. But I could protect them now, and I knew that I would rather die than let Joseph do to Jimmy or Henry-Joe what he had done to me.

The night before I went to see them again, I met Leigh and some of his friends for a drink. I hadn't told Leigh about what was happening – I couldn't bring myself to tell anyone. He knew that I was seeing my family again, but nothing more.

When my phone went, towards midnight, I saw that it was Joseph and got up to take the call outside. Joseph was crying as he told me he was driving along the motorway and was going to end it all. As he sobbed loudly into the phone I could hear the gears grinding and the engine revving. He said that his life meant nothing, and that he didn't know what to do with himself any more. 'This is it, Mikey,' he said. 'I can't take any more of it.'

I tried to calm him as he told me he had just been with a rent boy, but the whole thing just felt so sickening and wrong. He kept repeating that he hated himself.

I felt torn. Why was I even trying to stop this man from ending his life? If he died, no one would ever have to know what he had done, and my family would be spared the shame of it. There had always been a part of me that felt I would never be free of him until he was gone, and for a moment that freedom seemed tempting. But I knew that if I let him go through with it, I'd never forgive myself. There was still time for him to change and right his wrongs. And I would rather live with the fact that I had been performing sexual acts for this man since I was seven years old, than know that I stood back and did nothing as he took his own life. Not to mention the lives of others, as he was on the motorway.

I pleaded with him to pull over, just to calm himself down and talk with me about everything properly. He dropped the phone on the seat as he made his way into a service station, shouting out every few seconds to see if I was still there.

Once he had parked and picked up the phone again I asked what he needed to do to make things better.

'I want you back,' he wailed, sniffing and sobbing. 'I want us to be together. I can make you so happy, Mikey, I swear I can; you'll never want for anything. I love you.' He went on to say that he wanted to get us a flat, somewhere no one knew about, so that we could be together.

I was reeling from all this but I could sense my

opportunity to trap him. I summoned all my acting skills and gritted my teeth. 'Would you like to have a proper talk about our future when I come up at the weekend?' I asked him.

'You'll forget about it, I know you will,' he wept. I assured him that I wouldn't. I made him promise me that he would stay exactly where he was in the car and have a sleep before driving any further.

'Promise me you'll think about my offer then?' he countered.

'I'll definitely think about it, Joseph.'

When I arrived at the station the next day, Joseph was there to meet me. He was planning to stay the weekend at my parents' house, as usual. I held him in my arms as he cried and said how sorry he was, and I told him I loved him and I was glad that he was safe. In a way, I really was, but not for the reasons he hoped.

My mother had made a vast banquet of sandwiches, sausage rolls and crisps. We all gathered in the lounge and we sang, danced, laughed and spoke about childhood memories. As the night went on I kept a close eye on Joseph and Jimmy, making sure that neither one were out of my sight for a second. Henry-Joe was keeping watch too. Every time Joseph pulled Jimmy onto his lap and planted kisses on his face, we shared a look of disgust. None of the rest of the family could see it. Without a suspicion that anything was wrong, they simply failed to see the obvious.

The following day I went to the shops with Joseph and Jimmy. While we were out, my mother came across Henry-Joe, deep in thought. He told me later that when she asked what was wrong, he simply couldn't keep it in any longer. He asked her to go with him to Frankie's trailer, so that our father wouldn't hear what he had to say. Frankie was already in the trailer with little Frank. As Frankie and our mother listened, Henry-Joe sat down on the bunk and came out with the whole story of what he had seen, how he had told me and asked for my help, and what we had both seen Joseph doing to Jimmy.

At first my mother scoffed, but as Henry-Joe spoke about Joseph holding Jimmy on his lap and kissing him on the mouth, coming down every single weekend and lavishing him with attention and constantly finding ways to be alone with him, she looked increasingly worried.

The first I knew of all this was when we got back from the shops and my mother asked Henry-Joe to grab Jimmy and get him to help clean out the dog kennels. I could tell from her tone that something had happened. Then she asked me to come to Frankie's trailer. We left Joseph, looking slightly worried, sitting in the living room, and headed for the trailer. Inside, the blinds were still drawn and the bed was still out and unmade, in typical Frankie fashion. The atmosphere was tense. My mother told me what Henry-Joe had said, then she asked me if it was true.

'Yes,' I said. 'Believe me, he's not safe around the boys. We have to stop him.'

I felt relief welling up inside, grateful that it was all coming out, but at the same time I knew my father might react badly and refuse to believe it. I didn't say that Joseph had abused me, because I knew that if my father heard that he would be convinced that the whole thing

was invented and that I was just trying to hurt Joseph.
I had tried to tell him once, when I was seven years old,
and he had beaten me viciously for being a liar. My only
hope of getting my father to believe his brother was
grooming my brother was to prove that his son was in
danger.

My mother began to cry. 'I can't believe it,' she said,
lighting a cigarette and wringing her hands. 'I want that
fucking pervert out of my house.'

'I've been trying to think of a way to tell me Dad,' I
said.

'He won't believe you, you know that don't you?' said
Frankie.

My mother jumped to her feet. 'I'm going in there to
keep that pig away from my boys. When he goes tonight,
we'll tell your father. All of us. If he don't believe us,
then he can fuck off too.'

After she had gone I sat with Frankie in the trailer,
stunned by the turn events had taken. It had been a long
time coming. We were both upset.

'I've missed you,' she said. 'I haven't had a chance
to see you alone, and to say that. But I mean it, Mikey.
I love you so much. This life has torn me to pieces.'
She began to cry. 'I've been made to feel like a whore
since I've been back here, for marrying that man, yet
that pervert has been welcomed in this house.' She wiped
the tears from her eyes. 'That family – the Walshes –
they always behaved as if they were royalty, better than
everybody else. No one was ever allowed to question
anything, or say anything. But I saw it, you know . . .
I saw the way he was with Jimmy. I didn't *want* to see

it, I didn't *want* to believe it. That made me blind. I'll help you. I'm right with you. I love you. I've missed you so much.'

We threw our arms around each other and sobbed away years of being apart. Then we sat and smoked a cigarette together. I felt so sad for her. Divorced with a little boy before she had left her teens, and now stuck here. The irony was that she had been so desperate to escape our father's rigid control that she had picked the first man who came along and promised her freedom, and it had led her straight back home again. Only now she was 'damaged goods' and she believed that no Gypsy man would ever marry her.

When I went back to the house, Joseph was still sitting in the living room. He shot me a look full of questions. I ignored it. My mother asked me to take Henry-Joe and Jimmy for a walk. As we wandered the back streets of the town, Joseph called several times and left messages on my phone, saying that he was going soon and was wondering where we were. I didn't answer.

When we got back, my father, mother and Frankie were sitting on the patio chairs at the front of the house, while Minnie and little Frank played with a pile of sticks and pebbles nearby. There was no sign of Joseph. When my father spotted me walking up the drive he marched over and punched me as hard as he could in the guts, demanding that I tell everyone that I had put stories into the boys' heads and that it was all a bunch of lies.

Apparently, after Joseph had left, my mother and Frankie had been unable to contain themselves and had told my father – who, as I had known he would, blamed

me. As he punched and hit me, Frankie, my mother and
Henry-Joe tugged at him, pleading for him to listen and
insisting it was all true. My mother told him he needed
to hear what Henry-Joe and I had to say, and eventually,
panting from the exertion, he sat down again.

It had been a while since I'd taken one of my father's
beatings, and in truth I'd had many worse. This time I
barely felt the blows. I just wanted this life of lies to be
over, with everything out in the open so that my family
wouldn't be in danger any more. Henry-Joe and I went
through the whole story, beginning with the moment he
had seen Joseph sniffing Jimmy's hair in the car. I was
so tempted to remind my father that I had told him about
Joseph all those years ago. Had he forgotten? I wanted
to speak out, but the words stuck in my throat. I couldn't
have borne it if my father had accused me of lying once
again.

As Henry-Joe spoke about his worries, Jimmy's face
fell and my father looked like thunder. Henry-Joe said
other friends had begun to notice, and to gossip, and he
hadn't known what to do. But as he spoke, it was clear
that my father was not going to hear any of what we
were saying. Instead he flew into a rage and began to
throw accusations at me: what a disgrace I was to his
family, how he would never trust me as far as he could
throw me, how he had looked upon me as a child and
known I'd be the one to ruin his life, how he couldn't
stand the sight of me, that I had never done him right
and that he truly believed I did it all to spite him.

He began hitting me again and I didn't even attempt
to raise my hands or block him. I knew the truth was

out now, and soon enough he would have to face it. He only stopped when Frankie, Henry-Joe and Jimmy all jumped on him together.

My mother grabbed the phone. 'Call him,' she said to me. 'Take your dad in there and call Joseph.'

My father gave her a cold stare.

'You sit and listen to it,' she said. My father walked back into the house. 'It's because you know he's right, Frank,' she shouted after him. 'You know he's telling the truth.'

My father came back out, grabbed the phone from her hand and headed towards Frankie's trailer. Telling the boys to wait with Minnie and little Frank, my mother followed him, with me and Frankie behind her. My sister gave me a wet tea towel to mop up the blood that was running from my mouth, and my father handed me the phone. He heaved and coughed as he lit a cigarette and leaned forward on his knees, his head down.

After dabbing away the blood on my face, I picked up the phone and dialled Joseph's number. My stomach was in a tight knot and I was finding it hard to breathe. Things were going to come out that my father would find even harder than what he had already heard.

As the phone began to ring I pressed the loudspeaker button.

'Hello, mush,' Joseph answered, thinking it was my father.

I cleared my throat. 'Hello, Uncle Joe, it's me.'

His voice rose. 'Ah, hello beautiful, where did you go?'

I told him we had got sidetracked, looking for a video

to bring home. He asked what time I was going back to London and if I would be down next weekend and whether I fancied doing something, just the two of us, on the Saturday night. I said that would be nice.

I paused and looked up at my mother and father, who were both leaning forward, cigarettes hanging from their mouths.

'What's up?' Joseph asked, a slight trace of anxiety – or was it hope? – in his voice.

'I'm just going to come out and say this, Joseph.'

'What?' he giggled.

I took a deep breath. I had no idea what I was going to say until I said it. It was the only thing I could possibly say. 'Stay away from my brother.'

Joseph replied, 'Are you jealous?'

I swallowed hard. I was burning with shame and fury at having to go through this sham with Joseph, but it was a price worth paying for my brothers' safety.

'Yes,' I said. 'I am jealous. And if you carry on fooling with him, I will never see you or speak to you again.'

He began to cry and assure me that he had only been flirting with Jimmy and he was sorry. 'I love you, Mikey,' he cried. 'I've loved you since you were a little boy.'

My father's face was grey. He was finally beginning to comprehend, from one short phone conversation, not only that his son was gay, but also that his brother had been abusing him for years. I pushed on. 'I'm still thinking about what you said, you know, about us going off together.'

Excited, Joseph talked about the life we could have together. 'I won't go near Jimmy again,' he promised. As he continued to say how much he loved me I told him I would see him the following week, and said goodbye.

I put down the phone, glanced at my father's frozen features and then got up and left the trailer. Frankie came with me. As we went down the steps I could hear my mother repeating my father's name, trying to get him to respond. When he finally emerged, a few minutes later, he ordered me to pack my bags, get out and never come back.

My mother came up to the bedroom as I packed, and cried as she put her arms around me. 'Things will get better, my boy,' she said. 'I promise you.' But as I piled my stuff into my bag I could only feel great relief. It was finally out. And whether I was ever to come home again or not, I knew that I had done what I had to do.

In fact, I went back to my parents' far sooner than I had expected. Not long after I got home to East London, totally exhausted by everything that had happened, my mother called. She asked if I would come back for Christmas, which was only days away. 'Your father's just in shock, Mikey,' she said. 'He'll get over it.'

I was nervous about returning but I knew that there was still so much work to be done before I could really hope that our family was safe from Joseph. No matter how much I wanted to believe that things would all be fine now that Henry-Joe and I had confessed our fears, and now that Joseph had condemned himself out of his own mouth, I knew that secrets like this don't get cleared up that easily. Wearily, I agreed to go back for Christmas. Somehow, I didn't think it was going to be all that festive.

Two days later I was back on the train. When I got to the house my father took me aside and told me that what he had heard was not to be spoken of until my grandfather had passed away. At this point Old Noah was very ill and my father didn't want him to hear what the son who had been looking after him all these years had been doing.

The family would make excuses so that Joseph would not be able to come and stay, and the boys had been ordered not to answer the phone to him or to say a word about anything. He told me that our cousin David, Aunt Sadie's oldest boy, and Henry-Joe's best friend, had come to stay that night and we were to mention nothing of it while he was here. My father was determined not to let it come out until our grandfather was gone, and the rest of us just had to accept it.

At least steps were being taken to keep Joseph away from Jimmy and the other boys, and that was the most important thing. But how long would it be before Joseph could be shown up for what he was?

That evening my mother made her usual heaps of sandwiches and everyone drank and sang and talked into the night. The room that Joseph usually used at weekends was spare, so my mother told me to sleep in there. But around three in the morning I was woken by someone hitting me hard over the head. I leaped out of bed to find Jimmy, wild-eyed and crazed, swinging at me with the end of the vacuum cleaner pipe, and shouting that I was a pervert.

My first thought was that he had obviously not responded well to the alcohol the boys had clearly been sneaking into their bedroom. I shouted at Jimmy to stop and he threw down the vacuum cleaner pipe and leaped on me, punching and kicking me with all his strength. My father and mother came running in, and without asking a single question, my father joined in the attack on me.

Frankie, who was still in the house, came running upstairs screaming loudly as my mother leaped onto my father's back to prise him off me. Henry-Joe and David, still in a more or less comatose state from the amount of alcohol they had drunk, just stood at the door in complete shock as my father and Jimmy continued to pound into me. Then my father grabbed me by the hair, dragged me downstairs and threw me out of the front door into the street.

I had no idea what had gone on. I was in total shock. What had I done? What had just happened? In pyjama bottoms and vest, with no shoes and in the pouring rain, I walked a mile to the local police station. I just couldn't think what else to do. By the time I got there I was soaked through and freezing cold. An officer came out to the reception area and I explained that my wallet and my clothes were all back at the house I had just been thrown out of, and without them I couldn't get back to London.

The policeman said that all they could do was come back to the house with me and make sure I got my stuff. I decided that going back there with a police escort would have made my father hate me even more, so I declined the offer and walked barefoot another mile to the station. The next train was due in half an hour, just after 5 a.m., and I decided I would get on and hope to sit in the toilet to avoid paying the fare.

I sat in the waiting room, bruised, bitterly cold, shivering violently and still baffled. All I could think was, why did Jimmy go crazy? And why, without even questioning my brother's violent outburst, did my father join in? Did he really blame me for everything that had happened? I had dared to hope, when I saw that Joseph had been asked not to come for Christmas and when my father and I talked about keeping things quiet until Old Noah had died, that on some level, at least, my father had accepted that what I said was true and could see that I was just doing my best to protect the family. Apparently I had been wrong.

Ten minutes later my father's car pulled up in front of the station. He wound down the window and demanded that I get in, because my mother wanted to see me. At that point, I pretty much burst.

I stamped, I screamed and I spat. 'Why did you do this? I've done absolutely nothing but love you and try to do what was right and you throw me out into the street!'

As I continued to scream, Henry-Joe, Jimmy and David climbed out of the back of the car and dragged me inside. Jimmy and my father sat silent in the front as I kept shouting, 'Answer me, answer me!'

By the time we got back to the house I had calmed down enough to have a conversation. But I could see I wasn't going to get any answers from my father. I went up to my mother's room. She was comforting Frankie, who had hurt her arm when my father had shoved her from the stairs as she tried to stop him throwing me out.

'Go and get changed out of those wet things and get yourself a blanket,' she told me. 'Then I need to talk to you about Jimmy.'

It seemed that my father, in his attempt to train a hardened fighter, had bred a famously feared man. At twelve Jimmy was already big and very strong, and when the mist appeared before his eyes, no one could stop him. Even my father knew that there was a problem with Jimmy, but the only thing he'd done to try to help him control his 'violent feelings' was to take him to a church to be blessed.

I could see that the realisation that he had been groomed by Joseph had upset Jimmy terribly and, as he brooded on it, he must have become more and more angry. Not only that, but my father had made things worse by telling him that I was no better than Joseph, because I was gay. Somehow, perhaps because of the phone conversation, he had linked us in his mind. I felt sick at the thought. Jimmy had asked Henry-Joe if it were true, and Henry-Joe had said, 'I don't know and I don't care.' But questions had continued to ferment in Jimmy's mind as he drank alcohol all night, and the attack on me was the result.

'But why did me Dad join in?' I asked.

'I don't know,' my mother said. 'Since he found out about Joseph, he's not in his right mind either. I'm sorry, Mikey.'

I gathered my things together, kissed Frankie, Minnie, little Frank, and Henry-Joe goodbye and my mother drove me to the station. My father and Jimmy were nowhere to be seen.

As I sat on the train back to London, I thought about Jimmy. He was a beautiful soul, vulnerable, funny and compassionate. But this other side of him, the paranoid side, was dangerous and frightening. How had that happened? Was it really my father's brutal training regime that snapped something inside Jimmy? Or was it caused by Joseph's poisonous attentions? Was this sleeping dragon always there? I had no way of knowing, but I felt fearful for him. One day he would get himself into terrible trouble.

I decided, on that freezing cold morning of Christmas Eve, that I would not go back to the family home again. I had faced enough violence in my life, and with Jimmy's unpredictability and my father's anger, I would not be safe. Now that other adults knew what was going on, and some of them at least believed me, I would have to rely on them: my mother and sister, to be vigilant about Uncle Joseph.

That evening I went to see Leigh at his bar and told him the tale.

He was mortified. 'Why on earth are you going back into all this, Mikey?' he asked.

I shrugged and told him I'd just wanted to give it a try, for old times' sake.

'Well, do me a favour and don't go trying again, please.' He poured me a large vodka and Coke, and then told me I was invited to spend Christmas with him and his family.

I assured him that I had already planned to hang out with people from college. It was a rotten lie, but I was never one to want to spend Christmas with other people's families and so I chose to spend Christmas alone.

On Christmas Day I sat and nursed my bruises, while watching all those childhood movies that made me love London. And as the night drew in, I walked the city streets, watching the lights, like stars, along the river.

I felt calm. I had done what I could. My father couldn't bear to look at me for it and Jimmy hated himself for not seeing it. But at least they knew now. And knowing that Jimmy would now be safe was the best present I could ask for.

24

Death of My Grandfather

I was relieved to put Christmas behind me, and, with a sense of relief that at least my brothers were safe, I started the New Year determined to throw myself into my course.

Late one evening when I was coming out of a rehearsal, about three weeks into the New Year, I got a call from my mother telling me that my grandfather was in hospital. She said that he had not long left and that he had asked to see me. After what had happened with my father and brother, I was terrified. But I had to go.

For almost as long as I could remember, my grandfather and I had such a distant relationship. He was a regal and well-respected man in the Gypsy community. But just like my father, my grandfather had always seen me as a failed Walsh man. Ever since the day I first got into the ring at seven years old and humiliated myself by getting beaten by a twelve-year-old Irish boy, he hadn't looked at me or talked to me in the same way. As far as he was concerned, from that point on I was one of the girls.

I always felt so ashamed of myself in his presence. The talks and jokes we had shared before that night had vanished, and all I had left were distant stares and sideways glances. He was always polite, and always said hello, but our relationship had disappeared. So when my mother said that he wanted to see me, it filled me with hope. I wanted so very much to tell him how much I had always loved him, and how sorry I was that I had disappointed him.

I asked my mother if my father would be OK with me coming.

'He's got no choice, Mikey. I'm sending your uncle Alfie and cousin Sid to come and pick you up and bring you here.' She asked how long it would take me to get to Knightsbridge, so that they could meet me there.

I rushed home and packed an overnight bag, then jumped onto the tube. An hour later, I was in the back of Uncle Alfie's car. Alfie was my mother's older brother, and I hadn't seen his son Sid since he was a little boy, when I used to play with him on their plot at Warren Woods. Now he was grown up, and he seemed like a lovely guy. We reminisced about his sisters Olive and Twizzel, and all the stuff that we used to get up to as children at the camp. Both Alfie and Sid were wonderful, and they promised they would stand by me and make sure that nothing happened to me while I was there. They knew that my father's older brother and his sons, not to mention a dozen other Gypsy men who would be present, were more than capable of turning on me for leaving our people and way of life. It was almost five years since I ran away, but to them that would make no difference. My mother's family had always been kind and understanding towards me, and Alfie's warmth on that car journey meant a great deal.

When we arrived at the Royal Berkshire hospital there was a huge crowd of old and new faces gathered outside the main doors. Gypsies from far and wide had come to pay their respects to a great elder of our race. As we walked across the car park, Alfie and Sid on either side of me, some gave me a polite nod and others turned their backs. But all that I wanted was to get into that hospital and see my grandfather.

Inside I was met by Uncle Joseph.

Old Noah had died, minutes earlier.

Joseph asked if I wanted to go and see him, and I nodded. He walked me into the ward, where he pointed to a bed, curtained off in the corner. 'I'll be outside,' he whispered. Through the glass doors I saw him sit on a bench in the corridor, his head in his hands. He still had no idea that my parents had listened to our phone call. I felt terrible for betraying him. Ever since that awful day I had tried to avoid his calls, without alerting him to the truth of what had happened. Looking at him now I thought that he must have noticed the change in behaviour from his closest family, the excuses made so he couldn't stay in their trailer, like he had done so many times before. But I wasn't here to see Joseph. I was here to pay my last respects to Old Noah, a true patriarch.

I walked down the ward and pulled back the curtain. The man in the bed was nothing like the big, strong fighting man I had known. He looked ancient and very frail. His face was badly bruised from a fall, and he was painfully thin. His left arm was in a sling that hung in the air and the scar from the heart bypass he'd had a decade earlier stuck out like a roll of pink pennies along the centre of his chest. After such a traumatic operation, and such a heroic life, it was a mere splinter, trapped under his fingernail, that finally did for him, poisoning his bloodstream and causing septicaemia. His eyelids were closed. I would never look into those steely blue eyes again.

The king was dead.

I sat down beside the bed and held his heavy hand in mine. And with nothing to say, I sang my childhood party piece, Dean Martin's 'Bumming Around'.

He'd always loved that song. When I was three or four he used to pay me to sing it to him. I will never know why he wanted to see me, or what he would have said. But I would like to think that his last words to me would have been kind.

When I got outside, the hospital car park was a city of shiny vans and four by four vehicles, and the small army of travelling people had swelled by several dozen more. I saw my mother waving wildly to catch my attention and made my way over to where she was standing with Frankie, Henry-Joe, Minnie and her whole family, who had turned up to be there for my father and to pay their respects to Granddad Noah. Granny Bettie, Aunt Minnie, Uncle Jaybus, Aunt Sadie, Uncle Matthew, Uncle Alfie and Sid were all there and I felt overwhelmed at seeing them all. As they welcomed me, wringing my hand and thumping me on the back, it felt as though I had never left.

My father, Jimmy and Uncle Tory were on the other side of the car park, with my father's family and their closest fans. I hesitated, unsure whether to go over. As I stood talking to my mother's relatives, I heard a voice behind me say, 'Hello, Mikey.' I turned to see my Aunt

Prissy, now looking considerably older, and in a wheelchair due to the crippling arthritis she had suffered for many years. She was my father's twin sister and had been my mother's best friend since they were little girls. It was sad to see her looking like an old lady – once she had been one of the most beautiful women I had ever seen. As I leaned down and put my arms around her she whispered, 'You 'aven't changed a bit, my babe.' Then, turning to my mother, she said, 'He ain't changed a bit, av' 'e, Bettie?'

'Just as ugly as he always was,' laughed Uncle Jaybus, giving us all a much-needed chuckle. He was a great bulky comedian of a man who would say something at just the right moment that would make you fall in love with him instantly. Aunt Minnie, Granny Bettie, Aunt Sadie and my mother passed out sandwiches and packets of crisps as we joked, reminisced and shared stories about my grandfather.

Before we got into our cars, I walked over to Uncle Alfie and thanked him for keeping an eye on me. 'Ah, don't be silly, mush,' he laughed. 'It's been lovely to see you again, Mikey.'

We left my father and Jimmy at the hospital, still greeting and thanking the hordes of people who continued to arrive. As my mother drove to Granny Bettie's house where we were going to stay, I couldn't stop talking about how wonderful it was to have seen my aunts and uncles again. I was in the back with Henry-Joe and little Frank, while Frankie sat in the passenger seat and blew smoke from the open window. She teased my mother that they'd be living off ham and chicken sandwiches for the next two months because old Hagatha Christie (her new nickname for my mother) and her sisters had gone overboard as usual.

As we ploughed along the motorway my mother told stories of her family, wonderfully hilarious tales, weaving our grandfather into them as much as she could, always in the fondest and most loving way. Henry-Joe and I munched our way through several sandwiches as we joined in.

I stayed at my grandmother's for two weeks, while the 'sitting up' was going on back at Tory Manor. It meant missing drama school, but it was important to me to be as much a part of this hugely important family occasion as I could, even if most of the time I was consigned to the fringes of it. Just as with Granny Ivy, Old Noah was displayed in his coffin in his trailer while Gypsies and travellers from far and wide came to pay their last respects and share stories with my father and his family. This process is called the sitting up: the family sit beside the coffin in shifts, twenty-four hours a day, greeting visitors and providing endless cups of coffee and plates of biscuits and sandwiches, until the day of the funeral. Because of this my father and Joseph, along with the rest of Old Noah's close relatives, were staying at Tory Manor, while my mother and the rest of us stayed with Granny Bettie, who lived about half an hour away. My mother thought it best that I stay out of the way, so while she and my brothers and sisters went over to help out each day, I spent most of my time having chats with Granny Bettie, helping her with house chores and making her endless cups of tea. She was now my last living grandparent and it was lovely to be able to spend this time with her. She told me that since I had gone, the number of cousins in the family had quadrupled. Granny Bettie was now a grandmother and great-grandmother to more than fifty children – and that number was growing by the day. She never missed a birthday and adored every single one of them, insisting I look at the stacks of photos she had kept of each of them.

The day of the funeral finally arrived. Gypsy funerals are, if anything, even bigger than weddings. Everyone who has ever met the deceased, no matter how briefly, turns up to wish them a grand farewell, and there are often five hundred people or more following the coffin.

My grandfather had requested that his grandsons carry his coffin. This gesture touched me deeply but my father and Uncle Tory, who walked directly behind the coffin with Joseph, were not happy for me to take part, much to the dismay and fury of Aunt Prissy.

'If he can't carry that coffin, then he will push me along right behind it,' she said. And I did.

We passed through the crowds to filthy looks and whispered jibes. Never had I been more conscious of the fact that the influence of the outside world I now lived in had changed me dramatically. I looked like a Gorgia. And I was made to feel like one. I tightened my grip on the wheelchair handles, lowering my head. Then Aunt Prissy leaned back and looked me in the eyes.

'You've done better than any of these misfits, my boy. Not a one of them could ever do what you have done.

You should be proud. Don't give them that kind of satisfaction. You have more right to be here than any of 'em.'

She raised a hand over her shoulder, curling her fingers around mine. 'Fuck 'em . . . fuck the lot of 'em.'

My father never spoke a word to me during the entire two weeks. Although I hadn't seen him for most of the time, while I was at Bettie's, I had been in the same room with him; I had even stood right next to him beside my grandfather's grave. But we shared not a single glance. I had planted a bomb and my father could not forgive me for it.

After the funeral I kissed my mother goodbye and headed back to London. But as I'd known they would, things were about to come to a head. I learned later that before Old Noah died, my father had told Aunt Prissy about the phone call to Joseph. She said that she had always suspected Joseph was gay, but never had an inkling about his sinister interest in children. She took my father's advice and agreed that she would say nothing until the funeral was over.

What neither my father nor Aunt Prissy knew was that their two brothers, Tory and Joseph, had long been planning to cut them out of any part of Old Noah's estate. It turned out that the two brothers had been siphoning off Old Noah's wealth for years, leaving him with nothing but a few pounds. Far from caring for his father, Joseph had been systematically stealing from him. He had been keeping the old man locked away and treating him like a child, while taking control of everything he had.

Nobody knew any of this until some time after Old Noah's funeral, when the family sat down to sort out his business and money matters, and the theft came to light.

As my mother reported it to me, my father and Aunt Prissy went to Tory Manor to have it out with the other two. Not because they wanted the money, but because they were furious at the disrespect and callousness their brothers had shown for their father. In the row that ensued, my father told Joseph he had heard the phone call and knew what he was. Joseph, hotly denying everything, pushed my father to the ground. At which point Jimmy, who had gone along, punched Joseph in the teeth, knocking out four of them. My father's training had paid off handsomely.

Apparently Old Noah knew that his sons had been stealing from him. Before he died he had asked to see my mother alone. 'I've been a fool, Bettie,' he said. 'You have always done the right thing. And I know that you and my Prissy have been best friends since you was babies. Me and Ivy, God rest her soul, had three big strong boys, but our only girl was born with illness in her bones. But you've looked after her, you have. I'm so happy to know that you've had each other.'

Then he held out his hands, still adorned with gold rings and bracelets, to her. 'Take these things and give them to my Prissy. As soon as I go, those boys of mine will pull them from my fingers and my girl will end up with nothing.'

My mother had done as he said, wiping his tears as she prised the rings gently from his withered hands. He had given her his wallet too, with a wad of fifty-pound notes and a picture of Granny Ivy inside it.

My mother passed the wallet and the jewellery to Prissy, who was deeply grateful. It was all she had from her father. My father ended up with nothing.

As for Joseph, word soon spread through the Gypsy community and there were rumours that he had interfered with several other boys. Rather than go to the police – something few Gypsies would ever do – the men made Joseph's life a nightmare. He was beaten up, reviled and isolated. He moved away, to another town, but they hunted him down and beat him up again.

When I got back to London after my grandfather's funeral, I fell apart. Knowing that I had been rejected by my father yet again hit me hard. I had tried to do the right thing, and it had rebounded on me. In one sense, of course, it had been a success – Joseph's crimes were out in the open and children would be protected. I took huge comfort from that; but at the same time, I felt I was being punished for revealing the family's secret. I was more hated by and isolated from my people than ever. And though my mother and I talked occasionally on the phone, I knew I would never be welcome in my father's home.

Once again I found myself pining for Caleb. I'd sit up in bed at night thinking of him, going over and over what I had with him and what I had lost. A love that was powerful enough to crack my heart into little pieces. His last words to me had been true. I was yet to find anyone who had showed me a fraction of the love that he had for me. I began to believe that I was unlovable and unworthy of ever feeling real love again.

I struggled on with my course, doing my best to keep going. I knew that having to turn up each day and do the work was helping me hang onto my sanity. I had to get through it. I had to prove to myself that all I had done and been through was worth it. But actually my happiness and sanity were hanging by a thread. I was vulnerable to the tiniest knock.

One evening I was walking home when an estate car with six Irish travellers pulled up alongside me. They asked if I wanted to buy a video camera. I politely said, 'No ta, mush.' I wanted them to hear that I knew the lingo that Gypsies and travellers understand, in the hope that they might just leave me alone and move on to someone else. But before I knew it, the two men from the back of the car had got out and grabbed me, demanding that I get in the car with them. Unable to get free, I knew the best thing I could do was stay calm and go. If these were people still looking for their reward, then they were a couple of years too late. But, as I soon found out, this was nothing to do with who I was, or my past.

They demanded that I take them to a cashpoint and give them everything I had, or they would kill me. I tried to explain that I was a Gypsy myself, using the lingo as much as I could, though I was very rusty and must have sounded ridiculous. They drove me to a supermarket in Hackney where three of them got out and walked me over to the cashpoint outside the main doors. I put in my cash card and drew out all I had – three hundred pounds. Then they drove off, leaving me standing there, bewildered by the way things just seemed to keep coming at me.

When I got back home I walked up to the bathroom. I stood and stared at myself in the mirror. A mist of rage and sadness came over me. Then I drew back my fist and punched it as hard as I could, sending shards of glass exploding all over the room. I went into my bedroom, smashed the mirror off the door of my wardrobe, and tore everything I could get my hands on to pieces. Everything seemed pointless. Everything I owned was rubbish. Everything I had become and accumulated over all these years was nothing. The pain hadn't stopped, and I couldn't help but feel that I had somehow cursed myself to this rotten fate.

My housemate Jake appeared, alarmed by the noise. He sat with me on the bed as I wept so hard into my pillow I couldn't speak. Then he put his arms around me and pulled me into him. 'It's going to be OK,' he said, kissing my cheek. He rose to his feet and left the room, returning moments later with a warm wet cloth and a handful of plasters. He nursed my hands, which were bleeding profusely. And then, together, we picked up and cleared away the shattered glass.

25

Normality?

I threw myself into my life in London, knowing that for now, there was no hope of getting closer to my family. Leigh was a huge source of support, as always. He continued to push me to write as well as pursue my acting. In fact, writing was a component of the course, and I loved it. The whole course was a rollercoaster of highs and lows. There were lessons in which we would get to write and discuss poetry and prose, and to me this was worth its weight in gold. I cherished every moment, sucking in the thrill of being able to portray an emotion by comparing images to feelings. But I still didn't think I was an actor, and that made me feel like a sham.

One evening I found myself walking along Oxford Street, going over and over some lines for a classical speech I was supposed to perform the next day. I went into a record shop to buy a CD, and as I left I saw someone looking at me, and recognised a well-known writer who was a hero of mine. I did a double take and went back into the shop to check, but he had gone.

Half an hour later I was waiting for a bus and there he was, looking at me again. This time we got talking. I told him I loved the books he wrote and he smiled and asked me about myself. Then he invited me for a coffee. As I told him a little of my story, he said I should consider writing a book. I told him I had been trying for years, but was a bit crap at writing.

'I'll help you if you like,' he replied. My stomach did a somersault.

It turned out that he was writing a book himself, the first of a series of what turned out to be very successful novels.

From that evening he befriended me; he became my mentor and I was his muse. He came to see me in a second-year production, read my journals, took me to the theatre and dinner, read wonderful literature to me and took me for long walks. We talked for hours, and he encouraged me and made me feel he believed in me. He was gay, but we were never lovers, simply friends.

This friendship meant a great deal to me, but it ended abruptly when a man I had never met came to see me and told me he was the famous man's partner. I hadn't known there was a partner. He told me that the famous man had no plans to help me with my writing and was only using me as the basis for a character that lacked depth in his book. He gave me back my journals and said I would never see the famous man again.

I felt so sad and hurt. Had I been used, or had he really been my friend?

When the book came out, I went into a shop and flicked through the pages. It wasn't hard to find my character. It was all there – the way I looked, the way I spoke, the way I walked and smoked a cigarette. It was like a photograph in words. The story was about the writer's feelings towards me. It was, in some ways, a beautiful form of flattery.

The book went on to be a bestseller and it made me very sad to know that I could no longer talk to my former friend, just to thank him and let him know how much his interest and encouragement had meant to me. He had urged me to write at a time when I felt so unsure of myself, and very down after all that had happened with my family, and I will always be grateful.

In our third and final year we spent three weeks in Italy, working with directors, students and teachers from famous drama schools all over Europe. I chose to take part in a 'work in progress' of Kurt Weill and Bertolt Brecht's *The Threepenny Opera*. And during those three weeks I felt, for the first time, that I really got to shine.

I was part of a group of people who were coming together for the first time, none of us knowing each other. No one knew about the lack of talent I perceived in myself, or the mistakes I had made in my past. In that beautiful mountain town, rehearsing in an ancient church, I came into my own. I felt free and happy.

We rehearsed all day long and at the end of each day we met up for dinner with the rest of the students from the other groups. I spent many an evening taking myself for long walks through the little town, climbing right to the highest part of it and standing on the old brick wall that had been built around the lookout point. On a clear evening, the mountains would peek out through the clouds and the world below was a patchwork quilt of summer colours. I'd stand for hours and think of my life, of my past and where I was going. And then I let it all go. What better place to leave it all? As a warm breeze splashed over my face, my heart soared. I felt more at peace than I ever had before; it was as if the wind had taken every piece of rubbish I was carrying – all the pain and hurt – and cast it away. I promised myself that I would remember that feeling for the rest of my life.

After weeks of rehearsals and run after run of every standard that Weill and Brecht ever wrote, my group gave a concert in the church, to the people of the town. Our director told us that he wouldn't give us a list of songs to perform, he would simply introduce us one by one, in whatever order he chose, and each of us would perform a song that meant something to us personally. As the audience settled in the pews, we stood in the wings, waiting to be called.

'Mikey Walsh.' He had called me first.

I walked out and faced the crowd, swallowing hard and clenching my sweaty palms as the pianist took his seat. But as soon as he began to play the first few bars, I knew I would be all right. My tutors were there and my fellow classmates, plus a whole mass of people I could only hope knew the song and would be willing to cheer me on if I croaked. I sang 'Every Time We Say Goodbye', the great classic by Cole Porter, and when I got to the end the audience applauded and whooped.

On our final day in Italy the group came together for a speech from the director. He was Spanish and had a translator who had followed him around like a shadow for the whole three weeks. We sat around him and I noticed that he kept gesturing towards me as he spoke. Then the translator repeated what he said. He had been thanking me personally. As the translator went on, my eyes filled. He said that he had chosen me to go first on the night of the concert because he knew that everyone else would have to try to keep up the kind of standard he believed I gave and always had given, ever since I came here.

I was truly honoured. It was the perfect end to my time out there. Of course, when I arrived back at college the doubts were ready to grab me again. But at least for that time, I felt truly worthy of my place in the school.

There were plays in the third year that I had parts in, which I was OK at playing. But by that point, though I was hating myself for thinking it, I knew I could not go on with a career on the stage. It never made me happy, it never contented me, I never felt as if I had done anything right, and it generally tore me to pieces just to get up on a stage and act. I think in the end that I just didn't have the confidence. Every audition felt like being put through the wringer, it was just too hard to lay myself open to judgement and criticism over and over again. I kept telling myself that I could do it – I even got picked up by an agent when we put on our classical showcase at the end of the final term. But the thought of a career that involved risking rejection over and over again was simply making me miserable, and in the end it was a relief to take the decision to walk away. So my acting career ended before I had even graduated. I left the agent and put my three hundred pounds' worth of acting photos to good use by cutting and pasting them onto the front of my CV, which got me a job in a local gay bar. I started the day after my final term ended.

I had no idea what I wanted to do with my future. All I knew was that I wanted to stay in London and have a steady job. I came out of the 'I'm not an actor' closet to my friends from drama school pretty much as soon as we all left, and it felt like a great relief just to say it. They didn't judge, they were still my friends, and I blessed them for that.

I would sit in my room when my housemates were out and hate myself for being in my twenties with no career hopes of any kind and absolutely no idea what I could possibly be good at. All that training and therapy and getting to know myself, and yet all I wanted to do when I got out was to find love and a person to complete me.

But life doesn't work like that, of course, and relationships were still very hard for me. Unfortunately, my desperation was always pretty obvious, resulting in a string of men dumping me for being too full on with them from the start. But I persevered. And I broke my heart over and over again. I certainly hadn't learned to be able to hold myself back. I could never play the games. I longed for someone honest, who wasn't afraid to just come out and say what they felt. Whether people say it or not, they still go through the emotions like everyone else . . . so why not let someone know if you care? If I fell for someone, I would just tell them. If they liked me back, then wonderful. If not, my heart would have broken anyway, whether I'd told them or not.

Sadly, this belief in transparency isn't considered the most attractive of traits. I had many short-lived and intense relationships. Well, flings, if I'm honest. They all walked away, and I don't blame them. I was an open wound. There was so much going on in my head, and my story was enough to put the chills up anyone who was just looking for a bit of fun. My background was a mood killer, every time. No matter how cheerful I was, my lovers found it very hard to look beyond the crap. But then again, I was that guy who would fall in love with you, just for being kind to him. I know, scary, right? But true. And I am still that guy.

While I was limping from one failed romance to another, Leigh, who had been a rock throughout the time when I was making the agonising decision not to pursue acting, was in trouble himself. He was in a relationship with a man twice his age, who had terminal cancer and who wouldn't let him out of the house for fear that Leigh might realise that there was a world outside those four walls, and leave him. Many of Leigh's friends had become so sick of his possessive boyfriend and so frustrated that they ended up turning their backs on him.

I would go over every week to their flat and suck up to Gareth as much as I possibly could because it was the only way I could keep Leigh in my life. Of course, while Gareth was in the loo, or popping out to the shop, we would bitch about him like a couple of old fishwives. Leigh had loved Gareth at the start, but now he was trapped less by love than by his guilt and his inability to walk away. I tried to make him see this, but Gareth had been chipping away at Leigh's self-confidence for the past year, making it virtually impossible to help Leigh believe he could be anything more than Gareth's adoring partner.

I bought a laptop with the idea that it would spur me on to finally write my book. It didn't. I spent many nights just sitting staring at it, then wanting to hurl it across the room into a wall.

A few months after I finished drama school and went to work in the bar, I had a call from my mother to say that Joseph had died. He'd had a heart attack. He was alone at home, and no one found him until the next day, when his brother Tory called round.

Joseph's last months had not been happy. My mother told me that the hounding and the beatings continued, and he had little contact with anyone other than his eldest brother.

The news of his death was a shock. I had hoped I would feel liberated, but I didn't. The memories of what he did would always be there. I just felt very sad – for him, for me, and for our whole family. For Joseph there was no big funeral, just a quiet cremation, witnessed by his eldest brother.

My mother and I would talk from time to time on the phone, but whenever I called, she would talk around the real issues and I would do the same. We both found it hard, especially over the phone, to talk about how we really felt.

She told me that my brothers were growing up, and they were working with my father, growing masses of marijuana out in the large steel sheds my father had put up at the back of their home. I was not surprised to hear that my father's latest incarnation was as a drug baron, if only a minor one. And not only that, but he was dragging my brothers into this sordid business. My father had always earned his money dicing with the wrong side of the law, but this was by far the most dangerous and immoral thing he had ever done. No doubt he justified it by saying that the weed was for Gorgias, but I worried that he and the boys would end up in prison if a sniff of what he was up to got out.

And the enterprise was flourishing: my father had always been lucky as the devil himself at coming up with money-making schemes. His problem was that he was greedy and careless and always lost it all as quickly as he made it.

One weekend, while my father was away, I went up to stay. It was the first time since my grandfather's funeral, almost two years earlier, since I had been back. My mother had phoned and asked me to go, promising me that my father need never know. I was desperate to see her, and my brothers and sisters, so I packed a bag and got on a train, hoping that I wouldn't get there to find that my father had suddenly decided not to go away after all.

The last time I'd seen the house it had still been a shell, in need of a great deal of work and restoration, so I was amazed to see that it had been transformed. My father had gone all-out with the place, even having the family initials bricked into the grand gateway.

Frankie ran out to meet me and greeted me with a bear hug so tight that I could barely breathe. 'It's so good to see you, Mikey,' she whispered in my ear. The boys and Minnie were close behind her. I had worried that things might be difficult with Jimmy, who was now fourteen and taller than me, but without my father there to sway him, he seemed happy to see me. Henry-Joe was sixteen, but he danced up and down with delight like a six-year-old. As for Minnie, she was the prettiest nine-year-old Gypsy girl I'd ever seen, with waist-length dark hair and green eyes, like mine.

My mother stood at the door, smiling. Her flaming hair still tumbled around her shoulders, and she was wearing an apron covered in flour. She had told me over the phone that she had started a cake-baking business. Cakes were the one thing she was good at cooking, because they gave her free rein with her wonderful, off the wall creativity, and she loved devising all kinds of new designs for them. She'd also bought a whole mass of different breeds of chickens that ran freely about the farm, chased by little Frank, who was now a sturdy and talkative four-year-old.

The whole family, it seemed, were set on going into business. Frankie had decided that she was going to start breeding bull terriers. She had two puppies named Pooper and Mr Turd who followed her and little Frank wherever they went. My sister hadn't registered the fact that she had bought them as a brother and sister from the same litter, and was still expecting them to be able to produce prize-winning puppies.

Over the next couple of days we had an idyllic time. I wrestled with my brothers out in the paddock, took my sister's bull terriers for long walks and then got smashed and danced to eighties songs with them all evening. It was the happiest time I'd had with them since I was a little boy, singing karaoke with Mum and Frankie.

My father's absence changed everything. The wall of tension he carried with him was gone, and we were able to be at ease together.

The only thing I was sad to hear about was that Gypsy life was changing even for those, like my brothers, who had stayed within the community. They had stopped going to any Gypsy events, and it seemed that they weren't the only ones who had backed off. Appleby, Stowe and Cambridge, the biggest Gypsy events in the calendar, had now been taken over by a different traveller culture, and the Irish travellers and the Romanies were never good at keeping peace with one another. Times had changed since I was small, when these events were an integral part of our year.

My father had ordered the boys to stop going after the two of them were set on by a bunch of Irish travellers intent on a fight. Henry-Joe and Jimmy were holding their own, until knives were drawn. By the time they got away, Henry-Joe had several slashes down his back and Jimmy had been caught by someone's blade, right down his face, from hairline to lip.

I had hoped that this visit would be a new beginning with my family and that one day we could all be close enough to see each other more often. But I knew this was only ever going to happen when my father was away. I knew he was never going to feel at ease with me around. He had made that perfectly clear. And his attitude infected everyone else, causing tension everywhere. There was so much to be said that never was.

By this point I was in my mid-twenties. I had moved out of the shared house a few months after we graduated, and I now lived alone in a little bedsit in East London. I worked in a bar and I was single and terrible at being so. I had no idea where I was going or what I was doing with my life. One night, while I was working behind the bar, a man who had spent the whole night sitting by the beer taps, spouting nonsense and drinking pint after pint until he could no longer stand, lost patience with my inability to follow his drunken ramblings and called me an 'uptight, middle-class twit'.

The moment he said it, I thought, 'There you go.' I had successfully achieved my goal, to become just like everyone else, and it wasn't that special after all.

26

An End and a Beginning

One day, about six months after my visit, my mother phoned to say that my father wanted me to come and talk to him. She asked me to go home for the weekend. I hadn't spoken to him since the Christmas before Old Noah's death, when he decided to punish me for revealing the truth about our family. I had no idea what he wanted to say, and my mother gave no hint.

Leigh came to visit me at the bar, and at the end of my shift we went for a drink and I told him that my father wanted to see me. He had recently made the split from Gareth, and I was incredibly happy about it. He'd finally found the courage to walk away and had moved into a flat-share with a couple of friends. I felt I'd got the old Leigh back, he was his sweet, funny self again and I was looking forward to spending a lot more time with him.

I told him about my father's request. Hard as it was for me to tell anyone, Leigh was my closest friend and I owed him the truth. Without it, nothing else in my story really made sense. Now we sat, nursing our favourite White Russians, going over every possible scenario, good and bad, and discussing at length whether or not I should go and have it out with him. But deep down, I knew I had to. I loved my father so very much, and at that point in my life I understood him more than I ever had before. I had thought about everything that happened, going over and over it in my mind, and was now able to see it from my father's perspective. He was a Gypsy from the old school, and so much of what had gone on was strange and unnerving for him. It shook his world. I wanted, so badly, to find a way for us to be able to forget everything and start again, and I just hoped that he wanted the same.

That evening Leigh and I got a little drunk, and when 'Nessun Dorma' came on over the speakers we laughed out loud, because Leigh had always said that he wanted it to be his funeral song. He wanted to be raised out of his coffin as it played, then on the high note at the end, he said he'd like his body to explode and shower the whole church with glitter.

At the end of the evening, still laughing, we said goodbye to each other and went our separate ways. I went home to pack and the next day I caught the train to see my family. It was good to see them all, but with my father there, things were far more muted than on my previous visit. And despite asking me to come, my father was still finding it hard to speak to me, beyond a polite, 'Hello, Mikey.' He kept his distance. Whatever he had wanted to say, he wasn't rushing to come out with it.

On the second morning he walked into the kitchen and sat down as I was eating a bowl of cereal. He lit a cigarette and we sat in complete silence. The only noise in the room was the sound of the smoke going in and out of his lungs and me chewing on my cornflakes.

Then my phone rang. It was my manager at work.

'Do you know someone called Leigh?' he asked. Leigh's mother had remembered where I worked and got someone to call the bar. My manager didn't know much, just that something had happened. Leigh was in hospital.

I was gripped by total panic. If Leigh's mother had called for me, then this was bad. I had to get to him as fast as I could. I had to see him.

Five minutes later, my father was driving me as fast as he could to the station. 'Don't you worry, Mikey, you'll get to him in no time,' he said.

As we pulled up to the entrance to the station he passed my bag over to me. 'Take care of yourself. Give us a call and let us know how he is.'

I grabbed the bag from his hand and dropped down from the front of the lorry. My father put his hand around my wrist as I lowered myself out. 'I love you,' he muttered, as I looked up into his yellow eyes.

I burst into tears. 'I love you too, Dad.'

I slammed shut the lorry door and ran down to the platform to jump on the next train back to London and get to the hospital to see Leigh. I sat on the train in a blur of emotions. My father had finally told me he loved me. It meant so much to me. But all I could think about was Leigh. 'Wait for me, please wait,' I whispered over and over again.

When I ran into the hospital I saw his mother's face. And I knew.

Leigh was in a coma. He couldn't speak or move. I held his hand and whispered that I loved him.

Leigh had been out with friends in a nightclub. Someone, out of malice or stupidity or both, had spiked his drink with a massive dose of liquid Ecstasy. He was found in a coma in a friend's flat. He had been unconscious for three or four hours before anyone even thought of calling an ambulance. We still don't know exactly what happened to him. And what I do know, I can't bring myself to even think about.

As I watched him lying in his hospital bed, I remembered how he used to say he wanted his death to be like that scene at the end of *Beaches*. 'You can hug me and tell me how jealous of me you've always been. Then you can give a big speech at my funeral and make everybody cry,' he laughed.

So I hugged him. And told him how jealous of him I'd always been. And then he died.

Losing Leigh was more than losing a friend. He was my family; he was my little brother; he was my soulmate. He knew me better than anyone else in the world, and I knew him. And loved him. I can't express just how much I adored him. How happy I was to see him every time we met and how I took for granted that he would always be there. He could bring me back down to earth in a sentence, and he had a smile that shattered the darkest of my moods.

He was also the king of not practising his own good advice. When he finally escaped a horrible relationship to start making a life for himself, he would dive right into another just as bad. He always lost out.

He gave so much, and all he ever wanted was for someone to love him back. And my God, he deserved it. Because despite the absolute heartbreak that he suffered, he never lost his optimism or his belief in the good things in the world.

There was never physical attraction between Leigh and I. In fact, we used to joke that if we were a couple it would be a recipe for an even worse disaster than anything we'd had so far. But over drinks one night, and a good blast at every failed relationship we'd ever had, we made a pact that if we were still single once we hit thirty, we would walk down the aisle together.

Married or not, we planned on growing old together. Living in a nice little flat, eating Jammy Dodgers and watching Bette Midler movies until our eyes hurt. We had watched her films together so many times while coming down from drugs or hung over from big nights out. We could quote *Beaches*, *The First Wives' Club* and *Big Business,* word perfect.

His death bulldozed the life out of me. I don't think I will ever recover from losing Leigh. It's been five years now and I still catch myself mimicking his traits. When I dance, sometimes I find myself moving just the way he did, and in that moment, he lives in me.

If it weren't for Leigh, I'd never have put pen to paper. It was grief that finally got me writing. Over the months after he died I slowly isolated myself from my world and my friends and, very gradually, my book began to take shape. I put my heart and soul into it. I knew that if putting my story down on paper didn't affect me, then it wouldn't affect anyone, because I wouldn't have been truly honest.

Many of the people I once saw regularly disappeared from my life for good. Not because of anything that had gone wrong, but just because it had become very awkward for people to know what to say to me, in my grief. And so those who couldn't find the words walked away. And once they had left it so long that calling me would be difficult, they never contacted me again.

Leigh's death was covered in the local free gay magazines, without his name being mentioned. He was just another statistic. Just another careless clubber who hammered the scene a little bit too hard. Oddly enough, in one magazine his story was headlined in fine print on the cover, right next to a piece on none other than Bette Midler.

There was a court case that did not turn in Leigh's favour simply because he had at some point in his life taken a club drug before. I felt very bitter about that for quite some time.

Leigh's death left me utterly bereft. It was the darkest time of my life. I had thought we would always be there for one another, and suddenly he was gone. I spent the time up to his funeral with his family, all of us trying to come to terms with what had happened, and at the funeral I gave a eulogy I hoped would make him proud.

Going back to work afterwards was incredibly hard. But in all of the unhappiness and grief, there was one good thing. Dillon was the replacement barman who was brought in when I was off, and when I got back to the bar they kept Dillon on. He was Australian, busy seeing the world, bright, funny and full of life. We fell in love, and Dillon gave me a reason to keep going in the bleak months after I lost Leigh. He decided to stay in England and we soon moved into a little flat together. We loved each other so very much. We revelled in simple domesticity – just being together, cooking, shopping, cleaning the bath, taking out the rubbish. For the first time in my life I wasn't alone.

It was a long time before I could revisit what had happened with my father. He had told me he loved me – something I had never believed I would hear from him – and it meant the world to me. After Leigh died I rang home to tell them what had happened. But I didn't visit again for a long time. I preferred to remember that moment of warmth from my father, rather than to risk going back to the silence and anger that had preceded it. So I called, from time to time, and spoke to my mother, but it was many months before I saw any of them.

It was Leigh who got me started writing, but it was Dillon who helped me to finish my first book. He was so wonderfully supportive through the whole journey of writing it. It's funny how things turn out though. The day after *Gypsy Boy* got picked up by a publisher, the bar we worked in was shut down.

Once I finished the book I decided that what I wanted to do was to work with children. I got a job as a teaching assistant in a school for children with special needs. As the children learned, I learned, soaking up geography, history, biology – all the things I missed first time around. I was brought up to hate schools, yet here I was working in one, and loving it. I loved the kids, the classrooms, the teachers. I had found the place I wanted to be, for the time being, anyway.

After two years together I asked Dillon to marry me, and he said yes. Henry-Joe beat me to it though – he married Layla, a girl he had known since he was ten. I watched them dance at their wedding and then he came to be best man at mine. It was always my dream to get married in ruby slippers: I walked down the aisle in a pair of red-sequinned Converse sneakers that made my feet ache, but also made me ridiculously happy. And Frankie was there, dancing down the street in a huge yellow dress. For my parents to come would have been a step too far, but my mother made the wedding cake. Three tiers high, swathed in white chocolate and at the top a huge white chocolate skull, covered in flowers and pearls.

27

Today

New Year's Day 2011. One a.m.

The air is still and damp and the streets are surprisingly empty as I walk home from a party. I never stay too long at parties these days. I am a great lover of my own company once the sentiment of the season kicks in. I pull my scarf up over my chin as I skip through songs on my iPod that remind me of the last year.

What a year it has been. *Gypsy Boy* has, to all our surprise, become a bestseller. When it got to the top of the charts I had to keep checking, to make sure it was really my book that people were buying. It led me to all kinds of unexpected realms. I got to meet my heroes, people I had come to admire as I watched them on TV. And I received so many messages, letters and emails from readers who were supportive and generous about my story.

Many of them said, 'I'm glad you found your happy ending.' Unfortunately, I can't help but feel that I have somehow betrayed them now. For I am no longer where I was in life when I wrote it. The book brought me so many good and wonderful things, but it also brought a painful backlash and I spent much of 2010 being afraid, insecure, angry, and so very lonely. There were those who felt the book was an attack on my people. Others who tried to kill my story by making me out to be some kind of vindictive nutcase. Then there were the literary types who insisted that I wasn't even a real person and was just some creation of a publisher.

The pressure became unbearable. I closed off from Dillon, spending day after day sitting alone with my thoughts. Caleb had been unaware of what being with me could do to him, and it was the same for Dillon. He hadn't known how hard it would be, being with me. I couldn't let the ghosts go. Everything I had been through was suddenly right there again. Which was both funny and sad, because I wrote the book in order to finally let it all go. Feeling deeply wounded by the detractors, all I could do was talk about and think about and revisit the events of the past, over and over again.

The life I had lived was not typical of every Gypsy child. I knew that, but it was my life. I never wanted to leave home. I had to, for my sake and for the sake of my family. My culture, like so many, was not open to change. I was a gay man and a full-blooded Gypsy and I fought so terribly hard to live as both. You can't change what's in your blood. God knows I tried to. And I am happy that I was able to finally accept myself for what I am.

The book was a testament to everything I had been through and battled with and learned and I worked hard to get it noticed. Writing it and just having it in print wasn't enough: I wanted it to be a success. It was out there a good year before the UK media suddenly went crazy over my culture, though still, sadly, getting most of it horribly wrong.

As I struggled with my post-publication angst, Dillon

said I needed to see a psychiatrist. I told him that all I needed was him but maybe, in hindsight, he was right. At the time I felt it would be a waste of time. I had been before, many times, without discovering anything new that could help me. I have analysed myself over and over again; I have done ever since I was a little boy. I know my traits. I know why I do the things I do. And all in all, despite my demons, I get along very well. But there are some things, deep down, that you can never really shake off.

I had taken myself to such depths, places I had never been before – my darkest thoughts. But while happy ever after is a wonderful thought, it isn't real. Dillon was not meant to be a Londoner – he missed the sunshine of Australia. And I couldn't blame him for wanting to go back there.

As the aftermath from the book took hold, our relationship began to crumble and fall apart. Every day there was another call, another online post, another threat from a faceless person. I was told that if I didn't make a public announcement admitting that I was mentally unstable, someone in my family was going to get hurt. It was too much to bear. Dillon decided to go home. Our dream was over.

As I walk the streets of London in the early hours of New Year's Day, I think of Dillon and what he would be doing right now, all the way out there in Australia. I miss him. I miss his family. I miss our happier times.

And I miss Leigh. Dreadfully. He was a wonderful writer, better than I could ever be. The short stories he read out to me were inspiring; I couldn't believe that someone could have so much talent. He would have been so happy for me, when my book came out. Happy and proud. Leigh, more than anyone, knew how hard I fought to try to be someone other than who I was. He knew how I lay in bed at night, praying that I wouldn't be gay, and wishing that I could beat the next boy who came to my door and make my father proud of me, just once.

People ask me if I need an apology from my father. The answer to that is no. Because I know that he was doing all he could to help me survive in our culture. After the book came out, he was there for me when the threats began. And for that, I can never thank him enough.

Having survived cancer, he had two heart attacks, one after the other, soon after the book was published. He was in prison at the time; he been sent down just days before my book came out. He had closed down his weed-growing business when the police started sniffing around, and had gone back to laying drives and fixing roofs for gullible punters. He was the same old trickster he had always been and he had already been warned about his shoddy work. He'd even made it on to a *Watchdog*-type programe for it. All in all he managed to get more primetime screen time than I, as an actor with three years of acting training, could possibly have dreamed of. When he was charged he assumed that he would get off again. He got quite a nasty shock when the judge gave him a two-year sentence.

It crushed me to know that they had finally put him away. He was in his early fifties, but you would never think it to look at him. He looked old and grey.

When I got the news of his second heart attack, I called my mother to see how he was. I was not for a second expecting to hear his voice, but my Mother was visiting him in the prison hospital when I rang.

'Hello, my boy,' he rasped.

'Hello, Dad.'

'I want to tell you something,' he said. 'You're more of a fighting man than any of 'em. And I am proud of you. I am proud to say that you are my boy . . . I love you. Don't you ever forget that, will you?'

I sobbed into the receiver. 'I love you too, Dad. So very much.'

My mother took the phone back from him, and in her most casual tone said, 'So . . . what you having for tea tonight?'

I was afraid that had been my final conversation with him. Perhaps he thought it was too. But the old man pulled through a major heart operation and within a couple of weeks he was out of hospital and back into prison to wait for his appeal.

Since his release last year, we have rarely spoken. But I called home over Christmas and he pulled the phone from my mother. 'How ya doin', boy?' he laughed. There was no need for me to talk to him about what I am, or how I live my life. It wouldn't change anything anyhow. We just spoke about the weather, the family and him living with a police tag as me mum's prisoner. 'You have a Merry Christmas, my boy, and remember, I loves you all the world. I'm proud of you.'

What better Christmas present could I have got than that?

There are still a few New Year's revellers out and about on the streets. A man the size of a shed runs over to me from the opposite side of the road, grabs me by my shoulders and kisses me on the forehead. 'Happy New Year, beautiful man,' he shouts, before running to catch up with the rest of his gang. I can't help but laugh at how absolutely absurd and magical this city can be.

Sometimes the simplest gestures of kindness can change a person's life for ever.

My father telling me he loved me.

The man who walked over and hugged me after I gave a talk about my first book.

The teacher who never let me stop believing that I could be anything I wanted to be.

As I start another year, I'm right back to where I started fifteen years ago: living alone in a great big city, with no idea what to do next with my life.

I can just hear the scarecrow asking, 'What did you learn, Dorothy?'

Well, what I learned is this: I spent all those years trying to seek something extraordinary. Only to find that extraordinary was my whole life.

Today, to be ordinary is my extraordinary . . . my dream come true.

I am thirty years old, I live by myself in London, I have wonderful friends and I work in a special needs school as a teaching assistant and get weekends off. I drink too much coffee. I watch re-runs of *The Golden Girls* far too much. I get lonely. I'm still smoking cheap cigarettes. I'm rubbish at the dating game. I get lost in my own thoughts. I hate getting older. I hope that one day I can go to the town where *The Goonies* was filmed.

I am a Gypsy. I am a gay man. I am a nightmare of insecurities.

As fireworks pop in the distance and I walk down the steps to my little basement flat, the gnomes on either side of my door look up and smile. They glow bright green and glisten in the damp. Aside from the two-kilo chocolate skull and my ruby Converse All-Stars, these decorations are all I have left from my wedding day, two years ago.

I open the door to my little flat, walk in and pull on my tracksuit bottoms and thick socks. I turn on the heating, boil the kettle, and smoke a cigarette out of the back door. My flat is full of eighties toys; he-man figures, and two huge framed posters of *The Goonies* and *Return to Oz*. Dillon, who was so minimalist, would die to see what I have done to it now. But I love it.

I have my own front door. How incredible is that?